ORT, THE SECOND WORLD WAR AND THE REHABILITATION OF HOLOCAUST SURVIVORS

> Dedicated to the memory of Minnie Wingate,
> a tireless supporter who devoted so much love and effort
> to ORT during her lifetime.
> A founder of British Women's ORT and International
> Women's ORT, her invaluable contribution enabled
> others to rebuild their lives.

This publication was made possible through the financial support of the Claims Conference.

We wish to acknowledge the involvement of Royal Holloway, University of London, where Dr Kavanaugh held a Research Fellowship in the History Department while working on the project.

World ORT
Educating for Life

ORT,
The Second World War and the Rehabilitation of Holocaust Survivors

SARAH KAVANAUGH
Royal Holloway, University of London

VALLENTINE MITCHELL
LONDON • PORTLAND, OR

First published in 2008 by Vallentine Mitchell

Suite 314, Premier House,	920 NE 58th Avenue, Suite 300
112-114 Station Road,	Portland, Oregon,
Edgware, Middlesex HA8 7BJ	97213-3786

www.vmbooks.com

Copyright © 2008 Sarah Kavanaugh

British Library Cataloguing in Publication Data
A catalogue record has been applied for

ISBN 978 0 85303 806 1 (cloth)

Library of Congress Cataloging-in-Publication Data
A catalog record has been applied for

All rights reserved. No part of this publication may be reproduced, stored in or introduced into a retrieval system or transmitted in any form or by any means, electronic, mechanical, photocopying, recording or otherwise, without the prior written permission of the publisher of this book.

Printed by Biddles Ltd., King's Lynn, Norfolk

Contents

Foreword by David Cesarani	vii
Foreword by Robert Singer	xi
Acknowledgements	xii
Introduction: ORT and Displaced Persons, Historiography and Methodology	xiii
1 ORT and the Pre-War Years	1
2 ORT's Work during the Second World War and Life in the Ghettos	23
3 The Liberation of the Concentration Camps and the Arrival of the ORT Missions, 1945–46	57
4 Life in the DP Camps: ORT and the Mature Period of Work, 1946–48	86
5 The End of the DP Camps, Israel and Emigration	115
Conclusion	132
Bibliography	135
Index	150

Foreword

These days we are so familiar with the concept of humanitarian intervention and disaster relief that it is easy to forget that once upon a time they did not exist. The Jewish Diaspora was actually a pioneer in the field of overseas aid, albeit focussed on co-religionists in need. ORT started life in the 1880s as a Russian institution but by the 1920s it had became one of the arms by which Jews in stable, prosperous and free countries were able to send assistance to Jewish populations in crisis. This story has been told several times in celebratory brochures and specially commissioned volumes, but such has been the scope and extent of ORT's operations that none were able to comprehend every phase and zone of its activities in detail. Inevitably, the earlier histories tended to pay most attention to the founders and the formative years. For others the period dominated by the Nazi persecution of the Jews and the genocide waged against them in Europe by the Germans was too recent to chronicle objectively and, in any case, there was a dearth of published and available documents on which to base a narrative. Thanks to the archivists of World ORT the latter deficiency has been remedied; and sufficient time has now passed to allow ORT's work during the tragic and tumultuous decades between 1930 and 1950 to be scrutinised with a scholarly eye.

Dr Sarah Kavanaugh has approached this task with all the right skills and sensitivities. Her doctoral research, conducted at Southampton University, led to an important study of the cultural leadership of the Jews in the Terezin/Theresienstadt ghetto and the place of culture in the lives of the inmates. For this research she used published memoirs, documents, unpublished testimony and also oral history. The latter was crucial: it was the only way to enter the inner life of the camp population and to assess the impact that cultural activities had on their lives in such terrible, traumatic circumstances. Sarah showed immense sensitivity in handling the written material and throughout her extensive contact with survivors. She dealt with agonising questions about the conduct of the Jewish leadership, their relations with the Nazi camp authorities, and the function of culture as an opiate or a distraction. Some of these painful issues would recur in her research into the work of ORT and her exposure to them fitted her perfectly for the task.

In this book she chronicles the reaction of ORT to the persecution of the Jews in Germany and Austria and the role it played in alleviating the consequent refugee crisis. The vocational training that ORT gave to Jewish youth in these countries made it possible for hundreds to qualify for emigration to places of safety in Palestine and elsewhere. When the ORT school in Berlin was evacuated to Leeds, England on the eve of the Second World War, over 100 pupils and teachers travelled with it. Thanks to the joint efforts of Werner Simon in Germany and Col. J.H. Levy in England, they were saved. Sarah's moving account of the liquidation of the Berlin school in June 1943 graphically illustrates the fate from which the lucky few were rescued by ORT.

The ORT schools and workshops in the ghettos of Poland, notably in Warsaw and Kovno, also helped to save lives. A place in an ORT school was the ticket to better rations and a work permit that could stand between a Jew and deportation to the death camps. But ORT gave something even to those who were not destined to survive. For as long as they were allowed to live it gave them a sense of purpose, activity and dignity. Some of the most heart-wrenching passages in this study recount how Joseph Jashunsky, the director of ORT in the Warsaw ghetto, fought to keep his workshops and training programmes open. One survivor, Rachel Gourman, recalls how he would arrive at the school 'with broken glasses, his face covered with blood' but determined to continue for the sake of those in his charge. In the Kovno ghetto the ORT school was allowed to function when many other institutions had closed down, offering much more than mere training for the workshops that offered a chance of life to those deemed workers by the Germans. It became the base for a range of educational and cultural activities, growing into the 'spiritual centre of the ghetto'.

Tragically, only a tiny proportion of those who passed through the ORT training schemes or workshops survived. Many of them ended up in the Displaced Persons camps in Germany, Austria and Italy. There they found themselves alongside young Jews who had been deprived of any education for years on end and older people whose skills had atrophied and whose self-confidence had been battered out of them. The ORT mission to Germany in 1945 brought much needed relief and comfort to thousands of demoralised and physically weakened Jews. It faced huge challenges, not least the scepticism and outright hostility of some British officials in the Control Commission. ORT activists saw that there was a desperate need to get the DPs into some form of education and training as part of their rehabilitation, not least to disperse the (wholly false) image that they were lazy scroungers. Yet everywhere, in the more congenial US Zone of Occupation as well as under British control, they faced shortages of food, equipment and raw materials.

The story of how ORT set up a network of programmes in the camps and in every locality where DPs were to be found is a stirring one. Eventually ORT was running 700 courses and over 22,600 Jews were enrolled in them. It is estimated that as many as 80,000 Jews passed through ORT-sponsored centres or training projects between 1945 and 1950. This training was vital to restoring their self-esteem and reviving habits of work and self-discipline. It was also essential to facilitate their emigration to Palestine, later Israel, and other destinations. In this way ORT helped tens of thousands of Jews to begin new lives far from the killing fields in Europe. These Jews, in turn, contributed massively to the development of Israel after 1948 and to the economies of the many countries to which they moved.

This is an untold story of humanitarian relief on a large scale that has never been fully told or properly appreciated. Thanks to Sarah Kavanaugh's narrative, a gap in modern Jewish history and the history of international intervention has now been filled. Perhaps more important still, Sarah's sensitive use of life stories has recaptured the experience of ordinary Jewish men and woman whose lives were saved and transformed for the better by the men and women of ORT. This book is a monument to their achievement and a memorial to the fortitude of Jews who surmounted persecution and genocide and, with the help of ORT, went on to rebuild their lives.

DAVID CESARANI
Research Professor of History,
Royal Holloway, University of London

Foreword

ORT, The Second World War and the Rehabilitation of Holocaust Survivors is the moving and inspirational account of one of the most significant episodes of ORT's history – the story of how ORT's training programmes in the Displaced Persons (DP) camps of post-war Europe gave life and hope to those who had survived the Holocaust. We are indebted to the Conference on Jewish Material Claims Against Germany (The Claims Conference) and to the family of the late Minnie Wingate, through the Harold Hyam Wingate Foundation, for funding the research and making this publication possible.

The story begins well before the war, when ORT established itself as the premier provider of vocational training for Jewish communities in Eastern Europe. The experience gained during that period and the outstanding personalities who carried out the work of the organisation provided the impetus that enabled ORT to carry out its life saving work during the war and after it. The publication of this book is a tribute to these selfless individuals – many of whom tragically did not survive the Holocaust. It is also a tribute to those who had the vision to record their experiences and those who devotedly preserved the evidence to ensure that this important story can be told.

The majority of the research material used by Dr Kavanaugh in the preparation of this book is drawn from the World ORT Archive, a collection of reports, correspondence, photographs and other materials that document our organisation's remarkable history. The painstaking work to catalogue this historical collection was begun in 1999 and is ongoing. As this work progresses, and outcomes such as the present volume are made possible, we increasingly realise how important it is to preserve the record so that future generations can learn from the past and be inspired by it.

On behalf of World ORT, I would like to express my appreciation to all those involved in the production of this book, and especially to Professor David Cesarani (Royal Holloway, University of London) who freely gave of his time, his enormous knowledge and his expertise, and for supervising the research and assisting Dr Sarah Kavanaugh with writing sections of the text, and to Dr Kavanaugh who executed the work so professionally.

ROBERT SINGER
Director General, World ORT

Acknowledgements

This book would have been impossible without the help of many individuals and institutions. In particular I would like to thank all those who took part in interviews - their testimonies are an invaluable source of information and, together with interviews from various archives, form an important part of this book.

A special thanks must go to Rachel Bracha, the World ORT archivist, whose extensive knowledge of the archive proved invaluable. Every effort has been made to obtain permission for the use of the photographs in this volume. However, while it was not always possible locate the copyright holders, we would welcome contact from any concerned in order to rectify the omission.

I would also like to thank Judah Harstein at World ORT for his constant support, and Angela Cutler for her artistic input. I am also grateful to all the staff at the Wiener library in London for their help and advice.

In particular, I would like to thank Professor David Cesarani from Royal Holloway, University of London for supervising this project. He was been unfailingly generous with his time and expertise.

Finally, I would like to thank my husband Kit for his love and encouragement and my daughters Mary and Rose.

SK

Introduction: ORT and Displaced Persons, Historiography and Methodology

One of the most remarkable efforts of reconstruction is the movement known as ORT.[1]

On 1 October 1945, Jacob Oleiski launched the first ORT (Obshestvo Remeslennogo i zemledelcheskogo Truda sredi evreev v Rossii, The Society for Trades and Agriculture among the Jews in Russia) school inside the Landsberg Displaced Persons (DP) camp. At the opening Oleiski claimed:

> We must give camp residents a purpose; we must reorganize their daily lives and introduce them to every possible kind and aspect of work. They must have the feeling that everywhere there are things to do. This is the only way we can prevent our fellow sufferers from letting their minds atrophy and become even more demoralised.[2]

These strongly held beliefs of Oleiski's had been formed during his many years involvement with ORT. Oleiski had been prominent in ORT in Lithuania during the 1930s and had played a crucial role in the ORT school and workshops inside the Kovno Ghetto during the war. Oleiski was dedicated to the founding principles and ideologies behind ORT, believing that it was only through dedication to education and a positive attitude towards the future that survivors could rebuild their lives and begin again.[3] He claimed:

> Whenever I spend time in training workshops or visit vocational classes and look into the eyes of former concentration camp inmates, my faith grows stronger and stronger ... Indeed it is only through productive, creative work that we can lessen our anger at having lost so many years.[4]

This first ORT school which was established inside the Landsberg DP camp laid the groundwork for future ORT schools in the American and British zones of occupation. Although subsequent ORT schools were run along similar lines as the one in Landsberg, the mission and ideology of the World ORT Union changed during the post-war years as issues surrounding emigration and the creation of the state of Israel moved centre stage. Angelika Königseder and Juliane Wetzel claim that in the immediate post-war period when the World ORT Union resumed its work, 'Its first priority was to provide training for Jewish DPs adequate to qualify them for employment in their new homeland'.[5] Königseder and Wetzel stress the point that although the organisation remained dedicated to education, 'ORT began to shift some of its emphasis to teaching the Hebrew language, general Jewish history, and Palestinian Jewish History'.[6] This change reflected a more general move towards preparation for the new life in Israel.

The primary aim of this book is to highlight the role played by World ORT Union inside the DP camps and to assess its contribution to the rehabilitation of Holocaust survivors. World ORT Union's work in the DP camps will be examined not only in isolation, in terms of how it benefited those who took part in courses, but also against its own history and record of rehabilitation and training. Through this exploration of the post-war role played by World ORT Union, this book hopes to expand the existing body of work on the history of DPs in general and on World ORT Union in particular.

The history of the Second World War, the Holocaust and even the liberation of the concentration camps have been extensively covered by historians while, in comparison, there is a lack of material on the history of the DP camps. More specifically, the work of the World ORT Union inside the DP camps remains virtually undocumented.

There are only two existing works on the history of World ORT Union: Jack Rader's, *By the Skill of Their Hands* which was published in 1970 for the 90th anniversary of ORT and Leon Shapiro's *The History of ORT: A Jewish Movement for Social Change* published in 1980.

Rader's work is a fairly comprehensive study of the history of ORT from 1880 to 1960.[7] However, even though Rader's work contains sections on the Second World War and its aftermath, World ORT Union's work in the DP camps is only superficially addressed. Rader focuses primarily on the number of DPs who took ORT courses and where these courses took place. He fails to illustrate this history with personal narratives and testimonies with a corresponding risk that the voices of those who took the courses become lost.

Shapiro's *The History of ORT: A Jewish Movement for Social Change* broadened the work of Rader, bringing more depth and clarity to the history of ORT.[8] However, as with Radar's work, Shapiro's study is a sweeping history of the organisation which, due to its breadth, is unable to focus on the DP era in any great detail.

Although there is a growing body of scholarship being published on the history of the DP camps and the plight of the DPs in the aftermath of the Second World War, there is still much to be written in this field. Important work on the history of the DPs has been produced by Mark Wyman and Angelika Königseder and Juliana Wetzel. Wyman's *DPs Europe's Displaced Persons, 1945-1951,* is a wide-ranging look at the lives of the displaced at the end of the war while Königseder and Wetzel concentrate solely on the Jewish experience.[9]

Wyman's general study of the DPs at the end of the Second World War includes a separate chapter on the fate of the Jewish DPs pointing to their unique experience.[10] Wyman highlights the specifics of their situation, initially discussing their desire to leave Europe which, he claims, had in their eyes become, 'The graveyard of their people, its major monuments not the Eiffel Tower and Saint Peter's but the Nazi death camps where humans were turned into objects and plundered for their labor, gold fillings, hair.'[11]

Angelika Königseder and Juliane Wetzel's *Waiting for Hope – Jewish Displaced Persons in Post-World War II Germany* is perhaps the most relevant work to this study as it focuses specifically on the lives of the Jewish DPs, both inside and outside the DP camps.[12] Königseder and Wetzel identify the key issues faced by the Jewish DPs and concentrate on the questions that plagued the survivors in the immediate post-war period:

> How were they to go on with their lives? Would they, like some non-Jewish DPs, be forcibly repatriated and sent back to countries that were no longer home to them? What was the fastest way for them to obtain information about their families? Where would they live and where would they get food and clothing in the midst of the chaos, inside a country destroyed by war?[13]

In addition to the more general works on the lives of the DPs, research on the British and US policies towards the DPs has been carried out by Joanne Reilly, Leonard Dinnerstein and Hagit Lavsky.[14] Dinnerstein focuses on the US zone of occupation and its policy towards the DPs, whereas the work of Reilly and Lavsky is centred in the British Zone.[15]

Ben Shephard's *After Daybreak – The Liberation of Belsen, 1945* is an important new work on the immediate post-war period, the liberation of the Belsen concentration camp and the surviving Jews in the British zone of occupation.[16] However, none of these works pay extensive attention to the work of World ORT Union with Holocaust survivors in the DP camps from 1945 to 1950.

While spanning ORT's history from its origins in Russia in 1880 to its arrival in the new state of Israel in 1948, this book focuses primarily on ORT's role inside the DP camps from 1945 to 1948. It traces how the organisation grew, changing from a philanthropic Russian Jewish charity to a worldwide educational and vocational programme. This book follows the history of the World ORT Union (WOU) and its work in Europe during the 1920s and 1930s highlighting the history of the Berlin ORT school on the eve of the Second World War.

Through an analysis of World ORT Union's work during the Second World War and its administrative set-up between 1939 and 1945 this book examines the work carried out by ORT workers inside the ghettos of Eastern Europe during the Holocaust, highlighting the Warsaw and Kovno workshops. The analysis of the work carried out inside these ghettos assesses the importance of the ORT schools and examines what ORT's contribution meant to those who benefited from it.

The concept of 'Rescue Through Work' and how ORT participated in work programmes in the ghettos is also discussed. By asking what it meant to have a place on an ORT course inside the Warsaw or Kovno Ghetto we get a clearer idea of life in the ghettos and how ORT tried to ease the day to day situation for those imprisoned there. Other issues raised include whether a place on an ORT course inside a ghetto meant extra rations, better housing or even exemption from the transports and could and did ORT save the lives of those it taught and employed in its workshops.

Having examined the wartime work of ORT the narrative moves to a discussion of the liberation of the concentration camps, the post-war Allied zones of occupation and the establishment of the DP camps. This account covers the British and American policies towards the DPs, how they viewed and administered the Jewish survivors in addition to the survivors' internal political organisations. Central to this discussion are two case studies: Landsberg DP camp in the US zone of occupation and Belsen DP camp in the British zone of occupation.

After the introduction to the DP camps and ORT's arrival and set-up within them, the mature period of ORT's work inside the camps between the years 1946-48 is discussed. The two case studies of Landsberg and Belsen are examined here in further detail in the light of the day to day problems faced by the DPs: the lack of adequate housing, poor sanitation and inadequate food in addition to the continuing psychological traumas they were up against – the loss of family and loved ones and in some cases the continuous search for missing relatives.

Woven into this analysis of ORT's work in the DP camps is the continuous discussion of the ways in which the World ORT Union attempted to, and succeeded in, improving the lives of the DPs while inside the camps and in arming them for their future.

The creation of the state of Israel, the closure of the DP camps and the subsequent emigration and resettlement of the DPs are the final chapter to this story. The creation of Israel marked a turning point in the lives of many of the Holocaust survivors who went through the ORT schools inside the DP camps in Austria, Germany and Italy.

Throughout this study issues surrounding the transitory nature of the lives of the DPs and the idea of the DPs being liberated, but not free, will also be considered. The differences between the US and British policies towards the DPs and World ORT Union's work in the DP camps as a continuation of the 'Rescue through Work' policy that existed in the ghettos during the war are also points for scrutiny. During the Holocaust the policy of 'Rescue through Work' was a means of physical survival, but in the DP camps it can be seen as a method of psychological survival and an important key to rehabilitation. When discussing 'Rescue through Work' in the DP camps, it is important to ask, how did keeping busy in the DP camps and being trained by ORT help to revive feelings of self-worth and purpose in the survivors?

In its exploration of the role played by the World ORT Union in the aftermath of the Second World War this book seeks to combine survivor memoirs, letters, diaries and oral histories with more traditional archival sources such as official government and institutional documents.

The existing DP diaries, memoirs and oral histories are vital to an in-depth appreciation of the conditions inside the DP camps. The details contained in oral and written testimonies provide information that cannot be found through examining official government, army or institutional documents because these fail to explain how the camps were experienced by the DPs themselves. By concentrating exclusively on more official reports produced by the US and British authorities, World ORT Union and other relief organisations, there is a danger that the voices of the majority of Jewish DPs become lost.

It is important that the DPs' experiences are heard and incorporated into the history of the DP camps. Zelda Fuksman who took ORT classes inside the DP camp in Stuttgart claims that the courses offered by ORT 'revived my lost childhood and provided me with an appreciation and value of the self'.[17] It was not only Fuksman who felt this way and who recorded her feelings on the work of ORT. Elly Gotz claims that ORT has 'given untold humans a solid, permanent base of joy in life. I know it did it for me.'[18]

Hundreds of ORT graduates have expressed their gratitude towards World ORT Union for the help it gave them in forging new lives after the Holocaust. It is only by including these testimonies that we gain a more complete history of the period.

When using first-hand accounts it is necessary to address complex linguistic and methodological issues: the language the text was written in, the language of publication, when and where the text was constructed and for whom it was written or recorded. The question of how the testimony is used is also crucial. The historian has to ask whether it is being used to establish facts or to ascertain a view point on a certain aspect of DP life; whether it is being used to back up more traditional primary sources or as a primary source in its own right. When focusing on a survivor testimony or a diary we need to ask whether the completed text is representative of what the author wanted to write or whether there is a gap between what the author wanted to write and what is actually written.

Several differences exist between memoirs and diaries. For example, the memoirist knows how his or her story is going to end and can therefore either consciously or unconsciously order events, dialogue and meaning accordingly. Diarists on the other hand are not aware of what is going to happen to them and can only imagine what is to come. Anyone using these sources therefore has to consider whether diaries are perceived as being more truthful and more immediate because they are written as events unfold. The two genres have different agendas. Diaries are recorded at the time by individuals, often in secret as an act of resistance, sometimes to be used as 'evidence' at a later date. Memoirs however are written long after events took place and rely on memory. They can be used to memorialise, to bear witness, or to influence contemporary people and events.

Despite the often problematic nature of survivor sources, the use of memoirs and other forms of survivor testimony is important not only in relation to this study of the World ORT Union, but also to scholarship on the DP camps in general. The everyday experiences of those in the DP camps must be explored if this period of history is to be understood and use of testimonies can assist in this task.

NOTES

1. Wiener Library, London, UK (hereafter WL) Bulletin, 'Reconstruction – the Work of ORT', Vol.3, No.2 (March 1949), p.13.
2. Jacob Oleiski in Angelika Königseder and Juliane Wetzel, *Waiting for Hope – Jewish Displaced Persons in Post-World War II Germany* (Illinois: Northwestern University Press, 2001), p.110.
3. See Chap. 1 of this work for the origins of ORT.
4. Oleiski in Königseder and Wetzel, *Waiting for Hope*, p.110.
5. Königseder and Wetzel, *Waiting for Hope*, p.111.
6. Ibid.
7. Jack Rader, *By the Skill of their Hands* (Geneva: World ORT Union, 1970).
8. Leon Shapiro, *The History of ORT – A Jewish Movement for Social Change* (New York: Schocken Books, 1980).
9. Mark Wyman, *DPs: Europe's Displaced Persons, 1945-1951* (Ithaca and London: Cornell University Press, 1989) and Königseder and Wetzel, *Waiting for Hope*.
10. Wyman, *DPs: Europe's Displaced Persons, 1945-1951*, Chap. 6, 'Jews of the Surviving Remnant', pp.131-55.
11. Ibid., p.132.
12. Königseder and Wetzel, *Waiting for Hope*. For the chapter on Belsen see pp.167-210.
13. Ibid., p.12.
14. See ibid.; Hagit Lavsky, *New Beginnings. Holocaust Survivors in Bergen Belsen and the British Zone in Germany, 1945-1950* (Detroit: Wayne State University Press, 2002); Joanne Reilly, *Belsen, the Liberation of a Concentration Camp* (London: Routledge, 1998); and J. Reilly, D. Cesarani, T. Kushner and C. Richmond (eds), *Belsen in History and Memory* (London: Frank Cass, 1997).
15. Leonard Dinnerstein, 'The United States and the Displaced Persons'. Taken from: *She'erit Hapletah, 1944-1948 Rehabilitation and Political Struggle. Proceedings of the Sixth Yad Vashem International Conference* (Jerusalem: Yad Vashem, 1985), pp.347-64. Lavsky, *New Beginnings*; Reilly, *Belsen*, pp.50-77, 78-117 and 145-84.
16. Ben Shephard, *After Daybreak – The Liberation of Belsen, 1945* (London: Jonathan Cape, 2005).
17. Zelda Fuksman interview with Sarah Kavanaugh, 27 January 2006.
18. Elly Gotz, 'My Story of how ORT influenced my life', email to Sarah Kavanaugh, 19 March 2007.

ORT and the Pre-War Years

Have you had a good view of the ORT school? Must not one be proud indeed of this wonderful creation of the ORT, of the enthusiasm of pupils and teachers? I know of no better Jewish Trade School in Germany.[1]

ORT was started by a small group of prominent Jews in Russia in 1880 who called a meeting in St. Petersburg to discuss the condition of Russian Jewry. They were concerned about the living and working conditions of Jews in the Pale of Settlement.[2] Those who called the meeting included Baron Horace de Gunzburg, Samuel Poliakov, Nikolai Bakst and Dr L. Katzenelsohn. At this meeting they formed 'Obshestvo Remeslennogo i zemledelcheskogo Truda sredi evreev v Rossii' (ORT) 'The Society for the Promotion of Trades and Agriculture Among the Jews in Russia'. According to Solomon F. Bloom,

> From its leadership and ideology it was clear that originally ORT was a movement 'from above'. To begin with, it had a philanthropic character, tinged with a political aim. It began its work by helping individual artisans to find better jobs and individual farmers to obtain cheaper credit. It sent children to industrial and other schools ... It helped to establish several vocational schools and industrial branches in 60 Jewish schools, from 1880 to 1905, the year which is a milestone in so many things Russian.[3]

It was not long before ORT expanded so that instead of helping Russian Jews on an individual level, it began to address the situation on a corporate level: 'Instead of trying to save an artisan here and a truck gardener there, it turned to help cooperatives of workers obtain cheaper credit for the purchase of raw materials.'[4]

By 1909 ORT had established courses in Wilno and Petrograd; in 1911 it had set up a system of loans to market gardeners in Kovno and by 1913 ORT was working in at least twenty towns and cities across Russia.

The First World War was to change the direction of ORT's work. Bloom explains:

> The need behind the Russian front was no longer to improve handicrafts, study markets or establish cooperatives. Men and women must be given an opportunity to earn a livelihood, no matter at what or how. Thousands of dislocated people found themselves in strange places, idle and hungry. The slogan became 'Relief Through Work'.[5]

In order to combat these problems, ORT had to create work for the homeless and unemployed. In response to this situation ORT opened offices and registered 60,000 people for work in a total of seventy-two different towns and cities. This shows that ORT was no longer simply addressing the physical needs of the unemployed or the unskilled but also attending to the psychological needs of those left 'dislocated' and 'idle'. It was these same two components, the physical and psychological, that would become the focus of attention inside the DP camps after the Second World War.

It was the First World War which also prompted the expansion of ORT out of the Pale of Settlement and beyond the Russian border. The strains of war made it clear that Russian Jewry was not able to help itself to the extent that it needed: there were simply not enough wealthy Russian Jews to take care of the masses of poor. It was this situation that pushed ORT towards becoming a worldwide educational and vocational charity. Bloom concludes that unable to help themselves, Russian Jews 'decided to call on the West and the Americans to help'.[6] William Graetz adds:

> Active ORT work in Germany lasted scarcely more than two decades. The period when the ORT developed from a model *Eastern* Jewish self-help organisation into an all-Jewish movement embracing the whole of Jewry dated only from the end of the First World War, when distress became ever more widespread, so that

the burden of the ORT's construction work in the East could no longer be borne by the Eastern Jews alone.[7]

In 1919, two ORT workers set out from Russia on a fundraising mission. These two ORT delegates were Dr David Lvovitch, an engineer, and Leon Bramson, a prominent Jewish leader and long-standing ORT member. They visited Germany, France and England in addition to all the countries bordering Russia.

Initially ORT existed in order to fund its work in Russia, but in 1919 when Russian ORT was taken over by the Soviet government, the global parent ceased to have contact with it and formed a separate organisation.

In August 1921, the first ORT conference was held in Berlin. The conference was attended by delegates from Russia, Poland, Lithuania, England, Latvia, Germany and France. Those present voted to establish an ORT Union. Lvovitch explains the election process which took place after this first conference: 'A central elective council was formed. Eighteen councillors are chosen by the annual conference and these choose five additional members of the council. These twenty-three men select a central committee of five members, which is the executive body of the International ORT Union.'[8]

After this initial conference and the formation of the World ORT Union, ORT spread its work further afield. Bramson visited America and discussed ORT with the Jewish Joint Distribution Committee and American Relief Organisation. This meeting resulted in the American Jewish Congress pledging their support to World ORT Union. According to Lvovitch, 'Expressions of sympathetic interest were soon followed by promises and accomplishment of concrete help'.[9]

During the early 1920s there was an internal World ORT Union debate about what direction their work should take. Was their future to be in agriculture or artisanship? They needed to decide where they were going to locate their resources and centre their expertise. In the end they made the move towards artisanship as there were other organisations that dealt with agriculture. Lvovitch explains:

> The ORT ... turned slowly to the promotion of artisanship as its main activity ... Agriculture, it believes must still be encouraged. But that phase of Jewish reconstruction work had ceased to monopolise the field, so far, at least, as ORT is concerned.[10]

He adds that,

> Vocational work is closely allied to artisanship and industry. The trade schools prepare boys and girls for various crafts and industries, and adult courses help to improve and modernise the methods of the artisans and shop workers.[11]

It was during the late 1920s and the early 1930s that the role of World ORT Union in Western Europe began to change. In 1921 the Central Administration moved its headquarters to Berlin. In July 1923, the second World ORT Union conference took place in Danzig and a Central Executive was elected with Dr Bramson as chairman. By this time ORT was growing into a worldwide organisation.

By 1925 it had expanded its appeal and had started to play an important role within the German Jewish community. A meeting took place in Berlin in 1925 which proved crucial in the expansion of World ORT Union. Rabbi Leo Baeck presided as chairman at the Berlin meeting at which, according to Graetz, 'the work of ORT was presented to the German Jews not as a charitable activity on behalf of Eastern Jews but as the vital condition for the "solution of the Jewish question" in general'.[12] This was not only a crucial turning point for World ORT Union in western Europe but more specifically for German Jewry. As World ORT Union was above political affiliation, its mission was to represent the whole of German Jewry. Graetz further stresses the point when he adds, 'with the appearance of the ORT in Germany, the *whole* of German Jewry was for the first time given the possibility of doing practical work for a common Jewish cause in company and on an equal footing with their Eastern brethren'.[13]

In 1926 two important members of German Jewry were elected to the Central Administration of the World ORT Union. These were Justizrat Brodnitz, chairman of the *Centralverein deutscher Staatsbürger jüdischer Glaubens* (The Central Association of German Citizens of Jewish Faith) and Kurt Blumenfeld, head of the Zionist movement in Germany.[14]

The third World ORT Union conference was held in Berlin during the summer of 1926. This witnessed the further expansion of German ORT. During 1926 Bramson spent time fund-raising in South Africa and in 1927 he travelled through Europe raising World ORT Union's profile.

Following the move of the ORT Central Administration to Berlin, the committee in charge of ORT organisations in Germany was renamed, 'ORT Society, German Section, Limited'. William Graetz was appointed chairman and Professor Frankfurt became vice-chairman.

Once it was established in Germany, World ORT Union had to start broadcasting its message because the majority of German Jews neither knew the extent of the work ORT had already carried out in Eastern Europe nor what World ORT Union could offer them in the way of education and training. It was decided that if they were to inform German Jewry as a whole about their work they had to find a way to bridge the divide between the assimilationists and the Zionists. They had to craft their propaganda so it would appeal to both factions if it was to be effective. When searching for prominent German Jews to act in its Central Administration, World ORT Union sought members from across the political spectrum. This was important not only in terms of promoting harmony but also in staying true to their founding principals of being above party affiliation. However, when it came to forging links with prominent Zionists, there was some difficulty as many of the Zionists had serious reservations about ORT's work. This was primarily because they could only see the benefit of training Jews for immigration to Palestine and not for the rest of the world. However, as Graetz explains, the Zionists, 'finally became convinced of the value and necessity of training farmers and craftsmen as a contribution toward promoting the health of the Jewish body politic, the moral and social strengthening of which is the prerequisite for all constructive work'.[15]

World ORT Union and ORT Germany's propaganda launch was successful and, within a short period of time, several prominent German Jews were supporting and assisting ORT with their work. These included the renowned rabbi, Dr Leo Baeck. The political neutrality of the World ORT Union was familiar to Rabbi Baeck who was also prominent in the *Centralverein*.

World ORT Union was embraced not only by prominent Jews, but also by the mass of ordinary working Jews in Germany. According to Graetz:

> German Jews showed an immediate understanding of the constructive principles underlying the ORT programme – 'Help through work', ... and of the slogans 'Back to the land' and 'back to the workshop', the application of which has always been regarded by Jewry as a sacred precept.[16]

In order to set World ORT Union's work during the 1930s in the correct political and historical context, it is necessary to give a brief account of the rise of Nazism and the Third Reich. It is necessary to define the specific political, social and cultural atmosphere in which ORT Germany was working and to explore the difficulties it faced. The erosion of Jewish life and education in Germany and elsewhere across Europe and the proclamation of anti-Jewish laws which affected Jews on a daily basis is central to this exploration.

The Weimar Republic witnessed a continuation of the strong links between German Jewry and liberalism established in the nineteenth century, with three quarters of German Jews identifying themselves as socially and politically liberal. The most prominent political party to hold Jewish allegiance was the Social Democratic Party (*Sozialdemokratische Partei Deutschlands*).[17] Yet the influence of German liberalism in the Weimar Republic did not prevent a proliferation of political parties. Other prominent parties included *Deutsche Demokratische Partei* (German Democratic Party), *Deutsche Volkspartei* (Conservative People's Party), *Zentrum* (Roman Catholic Centre Party), *Bayerische Volkspartei* (Bavarian People's Party), the National Socialist German Workers' Party, and a selection of other far right and smaller parties.

Antisemitism flourished in the Weimar Republic. It was located in various political groups and parties, the most prominent being the German Völkisch League for Defence and Defiance (*Deutsche Völkischer schutz fur Trutz und Bund*), and it was part of the core ideology of the National Socialist German Workers' Party (NSDAP), run by Adolf Hitler.[18]

Jewish experiences of German antisemitism varied greatly although all Jews were aware of its pervasive nature. Middle-class families living in Berlin experienced antisemitism differently from those in small towns running businesses who were susceptible to antisemitic boycotts, while newly arrived families from the east in turn experienced different forms of discrimination to either.

The NSDAP, founded in 1919, remained a marginal party until 1928.[19] As its support increased, it stirred up racial hatred and encouraged the spread of virulent antisemitism. It enjoyed an electoral breakthrough during the years 1929-31 due to the economic crisis. In a series of elections during 1932, the Nazis gained support and Hitler was appointed Chancellor by President Hindenburg on 30 January 1933. After his appointment as chancellor Hitler began laying the foundations of the Nazi state.

Hitler's elevation to power immediately changed the situation for Germany's Jews.[20] Families who had identified themselves as German, whose mother tongue was German and who had fought for Germany in the First World War, became targets of National Socialist aggression. Jewish children who faced discrimination in school as well as in the streets were forced to recognise the 'differences' between themselves and the wider communities in which they lived. Löre Löwenthal from Hagen in Germany remembers, 'I had a lot of friends. The question of Jewish or not never came up.'[21] Almost overnight, however: 'We were singled out and made to feel not like everyone else.'[22]

On 27 February 1933, the Reichstag Fire gave Hitler the opportunity of suspending civil rights thus launching the Nazi state. This resulted in the SS being given increased power and political opponents became subject to intimidation, persecution and later incarceration. The Civil Service Law of April 1933 saw the elimination of Jews from public service while trade unions were abolished by the Nazis. With the passing of the Enabling Law on 23 March 1933 the Reichstag transferred legislative power to Hitler, and the Nazi party became Germany's sole political party. When Hindenburg died in August 1934, Hitler declared himself Führer in addition to Chancellor.

In February and March 1933, violence towards Germany's Jews escalated. During March the first concentration camps were erected at Dachau and Oranienburg.[23] On 17 March 1933, Victor Klemperer wrote, 'It is shocking how day after day naked acts of violence, breaches of the law, barbaric opinions appear quite undisguised as official decree.'[24] Klemperer followed the progression of anti-Jewish laws and wrote on 20 March, 'Every new government decree, announcement etc. is more shameful than the previous one.'[25]

Between 1 and 3 April the Nazis organised a boycott of Jewish shops and, on the 7 April, the compulsory retirement of Jewish civil servants was ordered under the Law for the Restoration of a Professional Civil Service.[26] In April 1933 the Nazis also restricted the number of Jewish students allowed to attend schools and universities. Further anti-Jewish legislation was passed during 1933 including the law on the Repeal of Citizenship which resulted in the majority of newly arrived *Ostjuden* becoming stateless.[27]

Throughout the summer of 1935, acts of violence against Jewish shops and businesses increased, and restrictions on civil liberties and legal infringements reached a pinnacle on 15 September 1935, with the introduction of the Nuremberg Laws.[28] These forbade sexual relations and marriage between Aryans and non-Aryans.

In *The War Against the Jews 1933-45*, Lucy Dawidowicz explains how, as early as 1934-35 ORT, together with other Jewish institutions, was being monitored by the Nazis because it was seen as a political threat.

> About a year later an ambitious research programme got under way, with the gathering of data about prominent Jews in Germany and abroad. The Jewish press was monitored. Studies were prepared about ORT, a worldwide Jewish organisation promoting vocational education and training, and the Agudat Israel, a worldwide organisation of Orthodox Jews.[29]

In March 1938, Hitler achieved his most daring and aggressive pre-war move, annexing Austria and securing the Anschluss.[30] From 1938 onwards, the Nazis unleashed their antisemitic terror on the newly incorporated areas of the enlarged German Reich. For Ernst Kolben from Vienna, the changes were immediate and devastating. 'I felt very bad. It was frightening. It bothered me. Everyone pointed and I couldn't sit on a bench. I was only 13 years old.'[31] Acts of violence continued across the Reich, and on 9 June synagogues in Munich were destroyed. On the 23 July, the Jews of the Reich were issued with separate identity cards, and on 17 August, Jews were forced to take the names of 'Sara' and 'Israel'. Attacks on Jews were facilitated by the identification process that had begun in 1933 and continued throughout 1938. On 5 October Jewish passports were stamped with a red 'J'. Cut off from the non-Jewish population and targeted for persecution, the Jews of Germany turned to their leaders for guidance. In 1933, the *Reichsvertretung der Juden in Deutschland* (The National Representation of the Jews in Germany) was established as an umbrella organisation to unite the various Jewish communities across the German Länder both in terms of politics and religion.[32] Avraham Barkai states, 'The vilified and persecuted Jewish minority was permitted that which was expressly forbidden to all others: it alone was allowed to maintain its existing institutions of democratic representation.'[33] Why was it that German Jews were permitted to maintain their *Gemeinden* up until 1938? Barkai argues that the Nazis saw these organisations as a convenient butt for propaganda and antisemitism. Perhaps the Nazis also believed that the divided and heterogeneous nature of German Jewry would work against them, and that their internal struggles for unity would ultimately fail.

The *Reichsvertretung's* first declaration stressed the importance of unity to the Jewish community stating, 'When it comes to all the great and decisive tasks, there can be only *one* representative body ... Only then will we be able to struggle for every right, every job, every inch of space in which to exist.'[34] The community leaders decided that Rabbi Leo Baeck should take overall command of the *Reichsvertretung,* and in 1933 he became the figurehead of German Jewry.[35] Otto Hirsch was appointed executive director and he nominated Siegfried Moses as his deputy. The committee consisted of nine men, of which three were committed Zionists, three liberal Jews and three were chosen to represent the orthodox. This remained the case until 1939 when the *Reichsvertretung* was transformed into the *Reichsvereinigung* – a compulsory Gestapo organisation for all those defined as Jewish by 'race' under the Nuremberg Laws.

Baeck and Hirsch fought tirelessly for the rights of the community, at grass roots by establishing welfare projects, and at a higher level by petitioning the regime on behalf of their communities. On 22 September 1935, in response to the Nuremberg Laws, they sent a signed declaration to Adolf Hitler. They demanded that he 'create a plane on which tolerable relations will be possible between the German and the Jewish peoples ... The precondition for such relations is the hope that ... the Jews and their communities in Germany will be left with a basis for moral and economic survival'.[36]

Against this backdrop of anti-Jewish legislation and mounting antisemitism, World ORT Union and ORT Germany continued their work. Soon after Hitler's accession to power in January 1933, a deal was made between German ORT and Lithuanian ORT regarding the emigration of German Jewish Youth into Lithuania. During 1933 and 1934 groups travelled to Lithuania to carry out training, in order to evade restrictions placed on Jewish education and training and the mass of anti-Jewish legislation that was being passed by the Nazi Party. The German-Jewish youths travelled to Liepaja, in Latvia and Kovno, in Lithuania where they were enrolled on ORT courses. In March 1934, 150 German Jewish boys arrived in Kovno, half of which stayed and joined the Kovno ORT and the other half travelled to ORT in Ongarina and Klinova.

By 1934 many German-Jewish refugees had arrived in France and according to Norah Scharf, 'The vocational courses of the ORT were the first place to which the German-Jewish young refugees could apply for learning a trade and thus securing for themselves a chance of earning a living in their new home.'[37] In 1934 there were three courses and seventy-five students; by 1935 this had increased to ten courses and 306 students and to thirteen courses and 380 students by 1936.

In 1937 the Fourth World ORT Union Conference took place in Paris. During the meeting several important decisions were made regarding the future of ORT in Europe. All the delegates at the conference agreed that education and aid were the principal issues for the future of World ORT Union and it was decided that if ORT programmes were going to be of maximum service, more effort had to be put into finding and training instructors and teachers. In addition to educational and vocational training, emphasis was also placed on social aid. It was seen as vital to, 'enable poor children in villages, where vocational training is not available, to attend ORT centres in neighbouring towns ... It should therefore, appeal to philanthropic organisations and assist national ORT organisations in local collections of social and aid funds'.[38]

During the summer of 1938, Dr Bramson headed the World ORT Union delegation at the Evian Conference on Refugees. The conference took place at the spa town of Evian-les-Bains between 6 and 15 July 1938. In response to growing international pressure, the United States had called the conference in an attempt to discuss the crisis facing German and Austrian Jews and their possible emigration. Thirty-two countries were present at the conference to which, instead of sending a high ranking governmental official, President Roosevelt sent Myron C. Taylor, a businessman and personal friend. Although most of the countries present spoke eloquently about the plight of the refugees, very few offered any satisfactory change to their immigration quotas.

World ORT Union submitted a memo to the conference entitled, 'The Problem of Vocational Adaptation of the Refugees'.[39] This document had been produced in Paris by the ORT Union on 2 July 1938 and was divided into 4 sections: 1. 'The Nature of the Problem'; 2. 'The Work of ORT in the Field of Vocational Training of Migrants'; 3. 'The Training of German and Austrian Emigrants; 4. 'Our Suggestions'. The memo opens by stating that, 'The centre of gravity of the migration problem of German and Austrian Jewry lies in the economic domain. The problem can be fundamentally solved by a liberal admission of these migrants into various countries in Western Europe and overseas.'[40] While claiming that the problem could be solved by the admission of the migrants, World ORT Union did concede that, 'the problem confronting the Governments represented at the Evian Conference and the concerned Jewish organisations is of singular difficulty'.[41]

Section two of the memo which covered World ORT Union's work in the field of vocational training stressed the importance of their work:

> Everyone who saw himself forced to emigrate asked himself: was he sufficiently prepared to find work in the given conditions? Did he possess adequate technical knowledge and skill to establish himself securely in a new homeland? Tens of thousands of the first refugees from Germany learned from their own experience how difficult it is to become settled in new countries without proper preparation.[42]

The final section of the memo which contained World ORT Union's suggestions for tackling the refugee crisis reads:

> The right of entry to the immigrants in the individual countries must also ensure them the right to work in their special profession [and] it is desirable that the countries of immigration should grant the aforesaid qualified immigrants the right to import free of duty the machinery and utensils which they need for their own enterprises and employment.[43]

Following the Munich Agreement on 29 September 1938, one third of Bohemia and Moravia was placed within the borders of the German Reich. The Munich Agreement guaranteed the downfall of Czechoslovakia and sealed the fate of the Sudeten Jews as thousands were expelled from their homes.[44] As a result of this expulsion, hundreds of Sudeten Jews fled to Lithuania. In response, ORT Lithuania opened a refugee training programme in Mariampol. When the situation was made worse for the Czech Jews in 1939, many more fled to Lithuania and once again the Lithuanian ORT met the challenge. They enlarged their programmes in order to incorporate the refugees and organised training farms where families could live and work.

Lithuania had the largest Jewish community out of the Baltic States with a Jewish population of 155,000 which made up 6.2 per cent of the countries' total population. ORT had thirteen trade schools in Lithuania and 528 pupils. The only Jewish trade schools were run by ORT and the

ORT schools in Kovno were considered to be among the best in the country.

While the situation for the Sudeten and Czech Jews was deteriorating fast, according to Scharf: 'The economic condition of the Jew had always been considered to be better in Romania than in other Eastern European Countries ... Its commerce and industry, where the Jews are engaged chiefly, is not highly developed.'[45] By 1936 ORT had already set up twenty-nine institutions in Romania and had a total of 1,638 pupils. In Latvia, ORT established and ran eleven out of the country's twelve vocational institutions with a total of 450 pupils.

In the years preceding the outbreak of the Second World War, World ORT union continued its work across Europe. One example is ORT's 'Artisanship Programme' which operated successfully between 1920 and 1939.

> ORT realised that in order to help the Jewish artisan and to allow him to face competition (mainly from industry), it was on one hand important to increase his technical proficiency and on the other hand to grant him the financial means to make use of the newly acquired skills, namely to help him purchase tools, machines, etc.[46]

During the 1930s World ORT Union also found itself having to protect Jewish artisans against various government decrees which tried to limit their right to work. In 1935 most of the existing Guild Laws across Europe were changed to include a clause that stated that only artisans with a diploma would be allowed to join a Craftmen's Guild. This meant that everyone else would be at a substantial disadvantage. The race was now on to pass, or at least give the impression of having passed, a course and receive a diploma. More than ever, an ORT course was of great value to Jews across Europe, and the World ORT Union diploma and certificate took on a new importance – one that would become even more significant inside the ghettos of eastern Europe.[47]

In Romania at least 50 per cent of Jewish artisans were unable to produce the required documentation. In many cases the local ORT school was able to assist. They enabled the artisans to pass courses and, in some cases, to buy their certificates.

During the late 1930s the situation across Europe became more acute as the Nazis tightened their grip in Germany and more anti-Jewish legislation was passed in other countries. According to a 1938 World ORT

Union report, 'The Progress of our Work and our New Institutions in Eastern and Central Europe', the situation for ORT schools in Eastern Europe became almost unworkable.

> The accentuation of the anti-Semitic and totalitarian tendencies in Eastern Europe became a menace to the legal existence of the ORT organisations and institutions. The danger was particularly acute in Romania, after the installation of the Goga regime.[48]

It was not only in Eastern Europe that World ORT Union was trying to expand and offer aid to as many Jewish refugees and potential students as possible. In France and Germany, ORT continued its work, trying to arm as many people as possible with skills, certificates and qualifications. While unaware of how important a practical trade was to be in the years to come – literally a matter of life or death in the ghettos – ORT's foresight in this matter was considerable. Although the majority of reports relating to the ORT schools originate from ORT itself, the value and quality of their work is backed up in the countless testimonies of those who took part in their courses. When discussing the Berlin school, the 1938 report records that: 'Its equipment, personnel and number of pupils are unrivalled by any other Jewish institutions of juvenile training in Germany.'[49] In the light of all this information, the 1930s should be viewed as a pioneering time in the history of World ORT Union. According to Norah Scharf,

> The Assistance to German Jews – in and outside Germany cannot be measured by its quantitative extent only, but by the pioneering first step made by WOU and by the way in which the WOU, through its experiments, opened [the way] for the general work in aid of German Jewry.[50]

The ORT school in Berlin was opened in 1937 under the leadership of Werner Simon. The Ministry of the Interior oversaw all educational and vocational institutions and it was only once they had given their approval that the Berlin ORT school could be opened. Mr Klementinowsky who ran the Berlin office of the World ORT Union was in charge of negotiations with the Ministry of the Interior. Permission was granted and after a visit to Klementinowksy's office by Adolf Eichmann, the school was opened. Eichmann had granted permission on the understanding that the school was to be attended solely by Jews who were planning to emigrate.

From its origins there was a close relationship between the ORT school in Berlin and British ORT. Aware of the increasingly precarious situation for Jews in Germany, it was decided that all machinery and tools for the Berlin school be bought under the name of British ORT so they could not be confiscated by the Nazis as German Jewish property.

In 1937 Heinrich Stahl, the president of the Jewish Community in Berlin, wrote a letter in which he praised the work carried out at the Berlin school:

> Have you had a good view of the ORT school? Must not one be proud indeed of this wonderful creation of the ORT, of the enthusiasm of pupils and teachers? I know of no better Jewish Trade School in Germany. You may rest assured that the Jewish Community in Berlin will continue, as soon as circumstances permit, to support and to further the ORT school.[51]

By July 1938, the Berlin school had a total of 215 pupils and was offering a variety of courses over a three year curriculum. In addition to the main classes on offer, there were two courses for adults to train as either electricians or plumbers. Both of these courses ran for 18 months. The main part of the school was divided into six departments: locksmiths, blacksmiths, plumbers, electricians, mechanics and welders.

The relationship between the Berlin school and British ORT, while not offering diplomatic protection, acted as a safety net during the November 1938 pogrom. The Nazis feared foreign intervention if they were to attack or destroy property belonging to another country so they kept away from the Berlin school. According to Scharf, '[it] was the only institution which remained unaffected by the violent events of November 1938'.[52] Joseph Heller, a student at the Berlin ORT school at the time of Kristallnacht writes:

> I remember very well I stayed away from the ORT school for about at least three weeks until things started to sort of 'normalise again' because my father had been taken away to a concentration camp and my mother was by herself. With only my help, we tried to carry on as well as we could under the circumstances.[53]

ORT continued its work in Germany after Kristallnacht and the reputation and intake of the Berlin school grew. At the end of 1938, William Graetz recorded:

> The ORT technical school in Berlin is at present (December 1st, 1938), according to the unanimous opinion of all authoritative Jewish leaders in Germany, the best Jewish school, not only in Berlin, but in the whole country. It has a rich equipment which fills the two big floors of a factory building, and it possesses also a splendid staff of teachers and foremen collected with very great effort, after a long and extensive search, since it is exceedingly difficult at present to find in Germany highly qualified Jewish technicians and foremen.[54]

Graetz describes how fortunate the school was to have attracted so many skilled teachers and professionals onto its staff. Among those he mentions are Professor Rupert, head of a State Technical Institute in Germany, Regierungsrat Heiborn who, prior to the Nazis coming to power, had worked as an advisor of the State Patent Office, and Civ. Engineer Wiener, one of the chief engineers of the General Electric Corporation in Germany. The school's board was headed by Civ. Eng. Behrend.

According to a World ORT Union Budget Report from 1939,

> After the demolition of the Jewish Trade Schools and retraining institutions during the tragic events of the first half of November 1938, our Berlin School, as one standing under the protection of a British Organisation (British ORT Society), is the only Jewish institution of vocational training in Germany which continues its work without interruption and with an intact equipment. It must therefore be anticipated that the influx of new pupils will considerably exceed the high figures of the proceeding years.[55]

Building on the association between British ORT and the Berlin school, the heads of both institutions came up with a plan to transfer the Berlin School to the United Kingdom. Werner Simon, the head of the Berlin school, was prominent in the move to the UK. Simon worked tirelessly to ensure the safety of the Berlin pupils and was responsible for obtaining their visas. In total he was able to provide papers for 104 pupils and seven teachers and their spouses. Throughout this process Simon worked closely with Lieutenant-Colonel J.H. Levey of British ORT and the *Organisation Secour aux Enfants* (OSE) – The Organisation to Save the Children. The OSE had formed a partnership with World ORT Union and were responsible for the transfer of the Berlin school.

The British Ministry of Labour and the Home Office both agreed to the move on the understanding that the school be set up in Leeds and that the equipment from Berlin be sent with the boys and staff. The Home Office agreed to supply the necessary permits without passports. Lord Marley, chairman of the Parliamentary Advisory Council of the World ORT Union, worked on this transfer, with the help of the Leeds community and a host of other organisations who ensured the safe arrival of the Berlin teachers and pupils in England on 29 August 1939.

Simon was closely involved up to the last minute and it was only because of his, 'fearless negotiations with the Gestapo' that the boys were finally granted their visas.[56] When the time came to leave, Simon went with the pupils and teachers to Charlottenburg station helping them onto the crowded train. Simon and his family chose to remain in Berlin as he believed there was still work to be done in the city. Lou Raphaelson, who was among those at Charlottenburg station, describes the scene: 'The train station was unbelievable. There were people from all over Germany trying to get home before the war. It's amazing that we were able to push through. We got into trains through the windows.'[57]

Hans Futter also describes the farewells in Berlin. He explains that it was not until a few months after their arrival in Britain that the boys missed their parents. For the parents, however, the pain of saying goodbye to their children was over-whelming.

> We were very young and the immediate future seemed very exciting. Our parents were very distressed indeed. They realised that our goodbyes would probably be forever and were hoping that the inevitable war would soon end Hitler's power.[58]

Henry Lippmann remembers the leave-taking at the station. He recalls:

> When, in August 1939, many of us said goodbye to our people we did not realise that we would never see them again ... I don't think any of us will ever forget the scene on the crowded platform of Bahnhof Charlottenburg, the journey to Cologne, the crossing of the border.[59]

Max Abraham, one of the Berlin ORT teachers who travelled with the boys explains: 'The main thing was coming out of Germany – that was really the important thing. We were really, really delighted.'[60]

Henry James, one of the boys who came to England, spent his first night in England in Whitechapel in London where he was housed in a hostel in Rowton Street. He recalls the view from his window being 'like a scene from Dickens'.[61] The hostel in Rowton Street was a down and out house. Hans Futter describes this first night in London: 'We had to stay there for one night. We had to pay one shilling for one night there. We were sitting there playing cards surrounded by all the drunks.'[62]

After their night in Rowton Street they were sent by bus to the Kitchener Refugee camp in Sandwich. While waiting for the buses, Futter recalls:

> I still remember how the following morning the news had got out that the boys from Berlin had arrived. Jewish women from the east end were outside crying as they knew we were the boys that had had to leave their parents and did not know anybody here. They gave us chocolate, sweets and sandwiches. They were relatively poor people who did not have much. They were very sweet to us and we were very taken aback by that.[63]

Although the boys from Berlin had been granted their exit visas on the understanding that they were being transferred to an ORT school in Leeds, the school was still in the process of being built. David Cohn explains how they stayed in the Kitchener Camp until the new school was ready in December 1939. He recalls:

> We stayed in the camp until December 1939. By then hostel accommodation had been found in Leeds and a site for the new school had been located. I remember that each time we went to the school we carried two bricks to help with the building work.[64]

Max Abraham, who joined the Berlin ORT school as a teacher in 1938, describes life in the Kitchener camp:

> We had had a lovely time there, I can't complain. I went into the department where carpentry was made and I learnt a little carpentry – I enjoyed it thoroughly. We had enough to eat and that was

good enough. Whether it was good or bad didn't come into it really. The boys were really good – they behaved very well.[65]

The Kitchener Camp eventually housed about 4,000 German and Austrian refugees.[66] Although they were eager to get on with their new lives, it was here that their thoughts turned to home. Hans Futter describes the contact the boys had with their parents: 'We were allowed to write a letter a month through the red cross. But I was lucky in that respect having a brother who was also allowed to write. So we could both write letters but you had to be careful what you wrote.'[67]

Once the school in Leeds was established it carried on the work and training that had begun in Berlin. It was divided into the same six categories: locksmiths, blacksmiths, plumbers, electricians, mechanics and welders. The boys and teachers were housed in two hostels in Chapeltown Road in Leeds. Abraham recalls, 'I was made a hostel master. We had two hostels and about, there must have been fifty boys sleeping there. We stayed there too. We had a big room, a bathroom and a kitchen. The boys slept 6 to a room in bunk beds.'[68]

The school was run on a strict schedule with Colonel Levey imposing military discipline. The Leeds authorities were concerned that the local population would forget the 'Jewishness' of the refugees and see them only as German and thus as the enemy. To combat this, a stringent set of rules were imposed upon the boys. The pupils' Jewish identity and the fact they had fled Germany was overlooked. The document, 'Regulations of the Leeds ORT Technical and Engineering School', laid out the rules to be followed. It opened by saying:

> Although you have passed the Tribunal, you are, in the eyes of the Leeds Christian people, members of an enemy country at war with England. *DO NOTHING* at any time, to arouse the slightest hostility, and do not attract attention. The *Jewish_Community* of Leeds expect you to show a splendid example of respect and thankfulness to the people of the City of Leeds, for accepting you here in time of war.[69]

The list of regulations consisted of twenty-six points. Number one, which was seen as the most important, read: 'Never speak German in the streets, so that you can be *heard.* Try not to speak German *at all* if you can help it, and in any case speak very *quietly.*'[70] Abraham also remembers how: 'Levey came to the school every Sunday morning. He was very much involved.

The boys had to have a certain kind of haircut. A one inch haircut. He would check everyone and he told us off in no uncertain terms ... we had to make our beds like in the army.'[71]

Although the regulations were strict, the school did its best for the Berlin ORT boys. Even though many of those who came to England from Berlin were later interned as enemy aliens, the ORT school in Leeds attempted to follow the progress of its pupils.[72] They were keen to support them in their future endeavours and quick to supply references where they could. On 18 August 1941, F. Heilborn head of the ORT school in Leeds and Colonel Levey, the director of the Joint British Committee ORT/OSE wrote a reference for Henry James, formerly Heinz Jacobius 'To Whom it May Concern':

> In August 1939, Jacobius was transferred from the ORT Technical School, Berlin, to England and continued his work in the Mechanics Department of the Leeds School, until July 1940, when he was interned. He was interested in his work and always keen on learning. During his training, he proved himself hard working and his behaviour was very good. He is honest and trustworthy and there have been no complaints about his character. We wish Jacobius success in his future life.[73]

Although the majority of the Berlin school had been transferred to England, according to Jack Rader,

> What was left at the truncated school in Berlin did not dissolve. Its enrolment actually increased as other channels available to Jews virtually disappeared. Incredibly it continued into the war and even beyond the July 1942 Nazi decision for the final extermination of European Jews.[74]

Recalling the last days of the Berlin school, Rader draws on the testimony of one of the survivors of the Berlin ORT.

> On June 10, 1943 at 10 o'clock before noon, a squad of the SS in full battle array occupied the premises. All present, numbering some 100, were lined up in the hall. Identification was taken from each one. Only a very few of us were released. All the rest were immediately deported to Auschwitz. Three were sent to Theresienstadt.[75]

Werner Simon and his wife were two of those who were deported from Berlin to Theresienstadt. They were sent on transport I/96 which left Berlin on 17 June 1943.[76] They remained in Theresienstadt until 23 October 1944 when they were deported to Auschwitz and killed.

NOTES

1. World Ort Archive (hereafter WOA), d00a0133: Norah Scharf, *From Despair to Hope, 1933-1960* (Geneva: World ORT Union, 1979-80), p.23.
2. The Pale of Settlement was an area of Russia marked out by Catherine the Great in which all Jews were forced to live and work. They were to be separated from non-Jews in order to try and create a non-Jewish working class in Russia. The Pale remained in existence until the First World War. It was abolished by a Provisional Government decree in March 1917.
3. WOA, d05a089: Solomon F. Bloom, 'ORT - Fifty Years of Jewish Relief in Eastern Europe', *ORT Economic Review*, 5, 2 (December 1945) (New York: American ORT Federation, 1945), p.6.
4. Ibid., p.7.
5. Ibid., p.8. This concept of 'Relief through Work' is explored in greater detail in the following chapter which focuses on ORT's work inside the Ghettos of Eastern Europe.
6. Ibid., p.11.
7. WOA, d07a008: William Graetz, 'ORT's Work in Germany', in *Material and Memoirs* (Geneva: World ORT, 1955), pp.35-6.
8. WOA, d05a088, David Lvovitch, 'L.M. Bramson and World ORT', *ORT Economic Review*, 4, 2 (November 1944), p.11.
9. Ibid., p.12.
10. Ibid., p.24.
11. Ibid., p.25.
12. Graetz, *ORT's Work in* Germany, p.37.
13. Ibid.
14. For information on the birth of the *Centralverein* see, Pierre Birnbaum and Ira Katznelson (eds), *Paths of Emancipation - Jews, States and Citizenship* (Princeton, NJ: Princeton University Press, 1995), pp.59-93; Peter Pulzer, 'The Response to Antisemitism', in Michael Meyer (ed.), *German-Jewish History in Modern Times: Volume 3. Integration in Dispute 1871-1918* (New York: Columbia University Press, 1997), pp.252-80; Ismar Schorsch, *Jewish Reactions to German Anti-Semitism, 1870-1914* (Philadelphia: Jewish Publication Society of America, 1972).
15. Graetz, *ORT's Work in Germany*, p.39.
16. Ibid., pp.39-40.
17. For detailed description of the relationship between German Jewry and the SPD see Donald Niewyk, *Socialist, Anti-Semite and Jew: German Social Democracy Confronts the Problems of Anti-Semitism 1918-1933* (Baton Rouge, LA: Louisiana State University Press, 1971).
18. For information on antisemitism during the Weimar Republic, see Niewyk, *Socialist, Anti-Semite and Jew*; Donald L. Niewyk, *The Jews in Weimar Germany* (Baton Rouge, LA and London: Louisiana State University Press, 1980); Dan Cohn-Sherbok, *Anti-Semitism* (Stroud: Sutton Publishing, 2002), pp.231-66; Klaus P. Fischer, *The History of an Obsession - German Judeophobia and the Holocaust* (London: Constable, 1998), pp.119-53; Albert S. Lindemann, *Essau's Tears - Modern Anti-Semitism and the Rise of the Jews* (Cambridge: Cambridge University Press, 1997), pp.461-97; David Bankier (ed.), *Probing the Depths of German Anti-Semitism - German Society and the Persecution of the Jews, 1933-1941* (New York: Berghahn Books, 2000). For antisemitism in schools and universities see: Niewyk, *Socialist, Anti-Semite and Jew*, pp.92-4; for churches see ibid, pp.49-50 and 164-5; for the police force see ibid., pp.156-7; and for the legal system see ibid., pp.86-90 and 152-5.
19. For background on the early years of the Nazi Party and Hitler's rise to power see Neil Gregor, *Nazism* (Oxford: Oxford University Press, 2000); Michael Burleigh, *The Third Reich: A New*

History (London: Macmillan, 2000), pp.27-148 and 219-80; Ian Kershaw, *Hitler: 1889-1936: Hubris* (London: Allen Lane, 1998), pp.221-54, 255-312, 313-76 and 377-428; Ian Kershaw, *Hitler: 1936-1945: Nemesis* (London: Allen Lane, 2000). For Austrian and Czech Nazi parties and their recognition of Hitler see: Kershaw, *Hitler: 1889-1936: Hubris*, pp.221-54.

20. For information on Anti-Jewish measures and antisemitism in the Third Reich see Avraham Barkai, *From Boycott to Annihilation - The Economic Struggle of German Jews 1933-1943* (New England: Brandeis University Press, 1989); H. Graml, *Antisemitism in the Third Reich* (Oxford: Blackwell, 1992); M. Burleigh and W. Wippermann, *The Racial State: Germany 1933-1945* (Cambridge: Cambridge University Press, 1991); Fischer, *The History of an Obsession*, pp.233-91 and 292-330. For Jewish responses in Palestine see Benny Morris, 'Responses of the Jewish Daily Press in Palestine to the Accession of Hitler, 1933', *Yad Vashem Studies*, 27 (1999), pp.363-408.
21. Fortunoff Video Archive (hereafter FVA) testimony: 0946, Löre Löwenthal.
22. Ibid.
23. From February 1933 the Nazis rounded up political enemies, including Jews, and placed them in *Schutzhalttager* - protective-custody camps. See Abraham J. Edelheit and Hershel Edelheit (eds), *History of the Holocaust - A Handbook and Dictionary* (Boulder, CO and Oxford: Westview Press, 1994).
24. Victor Klemperer, *I Shall Bear Witness. The Diaries of Victor Klemperer 1933-41* (London: Weidenfeld and Nicolson, 1998), Vol.1, p.7. See Daniel Johnson, 'What Viktor Klemperer Saw', *Commentary*, 109, 6 (2000), pp.44-50.
25. Ibid.
26. Barkai, *From Boycott to Annihilation*, pp.13-53.
27. These were those Jews who had during the previous years arrived from Eastern Europe. On 14 October 1933, Germany withdrew from the League of Nations.
28. For Nuremberg Laws see Richard Lawrence Miller, *Nazi Justiz - Law of the Holocaust* (Westpoint, CT: Praeger, 1995); Cornelia Essner, *Die Nürnberger Gesetze oder Die Verwaltung des Rassenwahns, 1939-1945* (The Nuremberg Laws and the Management of Racial War 1939-1945) (München: Schöningh, 2002); Andreas Rethmeier, '"Nürnberger Rassengesetze" und Entrechtung der Juden Zivilrecht' ('The Nuremberg Race Laws and the Deprivation of Jewish Civil Rights'), in *Rechthistorische Reihe* 126 (Frankfurt am Main: Peter Lang, 1995); Ingeborg Hecht, *Invisible Walls - To Remember is to Heal - Encounter Between Victims of the Nuremberg Laws* (Illinois: Northwestern University Press, 1984).
29. Lucy S. Dawidowicz, *The War Against the Jews 1933-45* (London: Penguin, 1990), p.113.
30. For information on Austria in the years prior to the Anschluss see Eoin Bourke, *The Austrian Anschluss in History and Literature* (Galway: Arlen House, 2000); Kurt von Schuschnigg and Richard Barry, *The Brutal Takeover: The Austrian ex-Chancellor's Account of the Anschluss of Austria by Hitler* (London: Weidenfeld and Nicolson, 1971); Burleigh, *The Third Reich*.
31. United States Holocaust Memorial Museum (hereafter USHMM), Oral History Archive testimony: RG - 50.106.07, Ernst Kolben.
32. For the establishment of The National Representation of the Jews in Germany see O.D. Kulka, 'The Reichsvereinigung of the Jews in Germany - Problems of continuity in the Organisation and Leadership of German Jewry under the National Socialist Regime'. In *Patterns of Jewish Leadership in Nazi Europe 1933-1945. Proceedings of the Third Yad Vashem International Historical Conference - April 1977* (Jerusalem: Yad Vashem, 1979), pp.45-59; 'The Establishment of the "Reichsvereinigung der Juden in Deutschland" and its Main Activities', *Yad Vashem Studies*, 12 (1968), pp.19-38.
33. Barkai, 'Shifting Organizational Relationships', in Meyer, *German-Jewish History In Modern Times. Volume 4*, p.258.
34. Ibid., p.265.
35. For general information on the life and work of Rabbi Leo Baeck see Albert H. Friedlander, *Leo Baeck, Teacher of Theresienstadt* (New York: The Overlook Press, 1968); Albert H. Friedlander, *Leo Baeck - Leben und Lehre* (Leo Baeck - Life and Teachings) (Munich: Kaiser Taschenbücher, 1990); Leonard Baker, *Days of Sorrow and Pain - Leo Baeck and The Berlin Jews* (Oxford: Oxford University Press, 1978).
36. Barkai, 'Shifting Organizational Relationships', p.268.
37. WOA, d00a010: Norah Scharf, (ed.), *Between the Two Wars: (1919-1939) II. The Thirties B*

(Geneva: World ORT Union, 1979-80), p.36.
38. Scharf, 'Fourth ORT Congress, Paris 1937', in *Between the Two Wars: II: B*, p.3.
39. WOA, d07a149: *The Problem of Vocational Adaptation of the Refugees – Memorandum submitted to The International Refugees' Conference at Evian-Les-Bains, by the Central Executive of the 'ORT'* (Paris: 1938).
40. Ibid., p.1.
41. Ibid.
42. Ibid., p.5.
43. Ibid., p.15.
44. For information on the Munich Agreement see Maria Dowling, *Czechoslovakia* (London: Arnold, 2002), pp.39-57.
45. Scharf, 'ORT in Rumania', in *Between the Two Wars II: A*, p.44.
46. Scharf, 'The Artisanship Programme of ORT 1920-1939', in *Between the Two Wars II: B*, p.3.
47. See Chapter 3.
48. Scharf, 'The Progress of our Work and our new institutions in Eastern and Central Europe', in *Between the Two Wars, 1919-1939, II The Thirties B*, p.1.
49. Scharf, 'ORT Work in Western and Central Europe', in *Between the Two Wars, 1919-1939, II The Thirties B*, p.61.
50. Scharf, *From Despair to Hope*, p.7.
51. Ibid., p.23.
52. Ibid., p.18.
53. WOA, d07a166: Joseph Heller, *Joseph Heller Comments on ORT Berlin Photo Album*, 24 August 1999, p.2.
54. Graetz in Scharf, *From Despair to Hope*, p.25.
55. WOA, DC/0109: *The Financing of the Work of the ORT Union in 1939 (Expose and Budget Forecast)* (Geneva: World ORT Union, 1939), p.9.
56. WOA, d04a010: H. W. Futter, *Memories of ORT Old Boys*, 30 September 1966, p.1.
57. WOA, d07a173: Christine Stutz interview with Lou Raphaelson, *Saved by ORT*.
58. Futter, *Memories of ORT Old Boys*, p.1.
59. Lippmann, WL unpublished memoir no: 4014, p.1.
60. Max Abraham interview with Sarah Kavanaugh, 5 March 2007.
61. Henry James in Alan Gill, *Interrupted Journeys – Young Refugees from Hitler's Reich*, (Australia: Simon and Schuster, 2004), p.218.
62. Hans Futter, interview with Sarah Kavanaugh, 12 March 2007.
63. Ibid.
64. David Cohn, *British ORT Report*, Edition 4 (London: British ORT, 2001), p.9.
65. Max Abraham interview with Sarah Kavanaugh.
66. For information on the Kitchener refugee camp see WL document collection: document no: 644/1 Kitchener Camp. See also WL, OSP921: Elaine Bentley, *Reception in the United Kingdom of Jewish refugees with special emphasis on the role of the Kitchener Camp, 1938-1939* (Doctoral Thesis: Polytechnic of Central London, 1989).
67. Hans Futter interview with Sarah Kavanaugh.
68. Max Abraham interview with Sarah Kavanaugh.
69. WOA, d07a154: Col. J.H. Levey, *Regulations of the Leeds ORT Technical and Engineering School*, 27 November 1939, p.1.
70. Ibid., p.1.
71. Max Abraham interview with Sarah Kavanaugh.
72. For information on internment and the Dunera see Cyril Pearl, *The Dunera Scandal: Deported by Mistake* (London: Angus and Robertson, 1983).
73. WOA, d07a169: Reference for Henry James from Lt. Col. Levey and F. Heilborn, 18 August 1941.
74. Jack Rader, *By the Skill of Their Hands* (Geneva: World ORT, 1970), p.50.
75. Ibid.
76. For details of all those deported from Berlin to Theresienstadt see *Theresienstädter Gedenkbuch: die Opfer der Judentransporte aus Deutschland nach Theresienstadt 1942-1945* (Theresienstadt Memorial Book) (Prague: Institut Theresienstadter Initiativ, 2000).

ORT's Work during the Second World War and Life in the Ghettos

> Like a cry from heaven the rumour spread among the Jewish population that the ORT workshops were to be reopened ... The excitement of the people at this news is indescribable.[1]

The outbreak of the Second World War in September 1939 was to have a dramatic effect on all relief organisations, social work and educational and vocational programmes relating to Jewish Life in Europe and World ORT Union was no exception. In *The World ORT Union and the American ORT Federation: A Study Made under the Auspices of the Budget Research Committee*, Mark Wischnitzer claims:

> The war dislocated Jewish social work in Europe. The efforts of overseas Jewish organisations were directed to immediate relief, sheltering and clothing of the uprooted people, and to refugee and immigration work.[2]

The 1930s had proved a decade of substantial upheaval for the World ORT Union. They were forced to relocate their headquarters as well as move and close several of their schools. Having already moved from Berlin to Paris in 1933, the declaration of war in 1939 forced the World ORT Union headquarters to move again, this time to Vichy. In January 1940 it moved back to Paris but returned to Vichy once more in June of the same year.[3]

In 1934, once the World ORT Union HQ was in Paris, a five man executive committee was established to run it. In 1937 the World ORT Convention elected a Central Board which consisted of fifty-two members from nine countries and an executive board of fourteen members who were all based in Paris. The chairman of the last pre-war executive was Dr Leon Bramson and his vice-chairmen were Dr Lvovitch and Dr Syngalowski. Dr Bramson, who had been executive head of the World ORT Union from 1911 to 1914 and then again from 1921 to 1941, subsequently died in March 1941, leaving Syngalowski and Lvovitch to take over as co-chairmen.

At a press conference held by World ORT Union during its time in Paris in 1940, Syngalowski spoke about the plight of Jewish refugees and the subsequent role of Jewish relief agencies. He announced,

> Refugees ... Everywhere they have become a permanent social class and almost a stable one. They have formed a sort of fourth estate. But among them there is a group that is forced to seek constantly new asylums. All can imagine how difficult is the task of the Jewish organisation these days.[4]

The new social climate created by the outbreak of war prompted Syngalowski to seek an evolution in World ORT Union's mission and methods. He claimed that this new era necessitated a fresh direction in relief work, inspired by a new philosophy of social involvement. He continued,

> ORT's aid to refugees must be oriented in two directions: give refugees vocational training, and secure for them the right to work. For the stateless and homeless work means not only material help, but also the kind of help that will give him a chance to gain the respect of his fellow man.[5]

This statement shows that Syngalowski, among others working in the sphere of Jewish educational and social work, was keenly aware of how anti-Jewish legislation across Europe had already affected the community and how Jewish education was being eroded. Already in 1940, thoughts were turning to how Jews might be affected by long-term legislation of this kind and the vital role that education and rehabilitation would play in the post-war years. Syngalowski recognised that practical, physical rehabilitation would be needed in addition to psychological aid and sustenance.

After World ORT Union made the move back to Vichy in June 1940, an ORT report records how, 'ORT leaders reaching Vichy, in the summer of 1940, organized vocational training programs in unoccupied France with the cooperation of newly-established local committees.'[6] However, by November 1940 it was no longer viable for the World ORT Union HQ to remain in Vichy and it was forced to make a further move to Marseilles. After the move to Marseilles, a Central Committee for ORT in 'Unoccupied France' was established and branches of this were opened in several cities.

As the war progressed, communication between the World ORT Union and national branches of ORT in other countries became increasingly difficult. Prior to the war the American ORT Federation had always allocated funds to the Central Board in Europe. The realities of the conflict in Europe made a relocation to the relative safety of the US a logical course. On 19 May 1942, an Emergency Committee for World ORT Union Affairs was established in New York. This consisted of members from the ORT Central Board which had by this time moved from Marseilles to New York. The chairman of the new Emergency Committee was Baron Pierre de Gunzbourg and the vice-chairmen were Alexander Halpern and Murray Levine. The Emergency Committee lasted until the post-war ORT Congress of 1946.

During the early years of the war, while its headquarters had been based in France, the World ORT Union was able to play an important role in the lives of refugees fleeing to that country. In addition, ORT France also played an extremely active role in the lives of the Jewish community at this time. The primary beneficiaries of the work of ORT France were not the French Jewish community but those Jewish refugees who had fled Germany and Austria and now found themselves interned as 'enemy aliens' in France. ORT came to the rescue of these refugees.[7] It fought for their release as internees and placed them in agricultural training projects. These projects were situated in La Roche, Cambes de Pujols and Les Angiroux.

When ORT France was unable to secure the release of groups of internees, they sent teachers and other representatives into the internment camps to set up workshops. Vladimir Akivisson, who worked as an interpreter to the head of the internment camp at Meslay-du-Maine, claimed that before ORT officials arrived, 'The people were literally perishing behind the barbed wires because they were doomed to the involuntary idleness'.[8] However, once the courses were established, the internees were kept busy, equipped with useful skills, and had ORT staff on hand to ensure their good treatment.

Within months of their establishment, the popularity and size of the internment camp workshops had increased beyond recognition and they were even opened to soldiers who were keen to gain extra skills. These soldiers, who were housed in nearby military barracks and camps, were given permission by the French authorities to attend the ORT classes.

According to Wischnitzer's report,

> When France entered the war, ORT programs in Paris had to be adjusted to war-time needs. The facilities of war-related courses were expanded and new ones established. The number of adults and youths trained in ORT schools in April, 1940, was 1,425. The two ORT schools of metallurgy in Paris as well as ORT courses for adults in electricity and metalwork continued to operate after the Nazi occupation (June, 1940).[9]

Jack Rader also discusses the schools which were operated by ORT France:

> [They] remained in operation and were well-attended, although greatly handicapped by the deportation of many instructors and pupils as well as the general persecution to which Jews were subjected ... Many who were not arrested, lived in constant fear of arrest and had to interrupt their courses to hide. Sometimes they were helped by ORT.[10]

ORT France had its successes during the occupation but these should be set against the overwhelmingly bleak tenor of the time. Inevitably it was unable to help with the majority of cases. Shapiro discusses how ORT France was able to run for as long as it did during the war and he comes to the conclusion that, 'That ORT was able to conduct an extensive program in occupied France is explained by the fact that the ORT centre remained in France for several years'.[11] How did the fact that the World ORT Union headquarters were based in France benefit the work and success of ORT France? The war had a huge impact on communication and the dissemination of information and, unlike ORT in other countries, ORT France was able to communicate with and access the World ORT Union headquarters which was now located in the same country.

On 15 July 1943, Jacob Blaustein, the Chairman of the World ORT Union Budget Research Committee wrote in detail on the impact of the war in relation to the dissemination and collation of ORT material. Blaustein explained, 'Problems of administration, accounting and reporting arising from the war made the task of assembling material on ORT difficult'.[12] Blaustein continues, 'There is evidence of programs being continued by the hard-pressed Jewish populations in some of the Axis occupied areas, but definite record thereof will probably have to await the end of the war.'[13]

Wischnitzer wrote extensively about how much World ORT Union had changed since the beginning of the war in September 1939.

> The ORT has undergone considerable changes since the war. At the present time, there are no ORT committees in Poland, Lithuania, Latvia and Germany, but they still exist in Rumania, Bulgaria, Hungary, England and Switzerland. A central committee for 'unoccupied France' was organized in Marseilles, 1940, with branches in various cities.[14]

The wartime activities of World ORT Union that are under discussion in this report are described by Blaustein as, 'training refugees as artisans, industrial workers and farmers in order to prepare them for conditions overseas'.[15]

When discussing how ORT has changed and how many pupils were being trained in various countries, Wischnitzer records how the present political climate affected the Jews of Europe. Wischnitzer concludes:

> A total number of 10,637 youths and adults was provided with trade education and training in 1939 by ORT Committees in the following countries: Poland 7,349, Rumania 2,044, Lithuania 619, Latvia 661 ... Under present conditions, it is impossible for the Jews in these countries to emigrate but efforts by the Jewish groups still there, including local ORT committees, to promote industrial and agricultural training in the hope of future emigration continue.[16]

Having discussed the administrative set-up of the World ORT Union in France and of ORT France, it is important to examine the work of ORT in other countries in Europe. What was happening further east and how was World ORT Union adapting on a national scale to the war in Lithuania, Hungary, Romania and Bulgaria? In Lithuania there was a series of agricultural and horticultural training programmes for refugees which were set up during 1940 under the leadership of Jacob Oleiski. These were established primarily in response to the arrival of refugees from Poland and were set up in Kovno and Vilna. The Lithuanian ORT recruited the help of local farmers in the training. ORT's work continued in these areas into 1941 and,

> During the Russian occupation, 1940–41, the ORT Trade School in Kaunas continued to function, with the partial support from the ORT Union. No information is available about the fate of the institution since the Nazi occupation of Lithuania in July, 1941.[17]

Shapiro also discusses how ORT Lithuania sought to assist the newly arrived Polish refugees. He writes how, 'There were ORT training programs in Vilna, Shavli, Vilkoviski, and Kovno (Kaunas) in Lithuania and in Riga, Libau, and Dvinsk in Latvia, most of them geared to the needs of refugees from Poland.'[18]

In Romania, there were four trade schools which continued to function during the early part of the war offering adult education. These were located in Bucharest, Galatz, Iasi and Constanta. By 1941, these schools had a combined register of 900 students. Shapiro writes, 'Throughout, ORT organizations, operating under harsh conditions and suffering from lack of funds, strove to bring some measure of relief to the Jews of Rumania.'[19]

In Hungary, the ORT Committee in Budapest was able to continue with its vocational training work and news of its operations continued to reach headquarters until January 1943. Shapiro writes, 'Sporadic ORT efforts were maintained in Hungary, which, in 1938, had annexed part of Slovakia and Sub Carpathia in cooperation with Nazi Germany, contributing to the destruction of Czechoslovakia.'[20] In Bulgaria, where the Jewish Trade School in Sofia was taken over by ORT in 1940, a training project that consisted of gardening, agriculture and cattle-raising was established.

During the war it was not only in Europe that World ORT Union made its mark, expanded and evolved. World ORT Union also expanded geographically, broadening its reach across the globe. During and after the Second World War, ORT schools could be found in all the countries to which Jews were forced to flee. An example of a refugee ORT school can be seen in the city of Shanghai.[21]

This International city became after 1938 a haven for Jewish refugees. Up to 1941, about 25,000 refugees reached Shanghai. A number of persons formerly connected with ORT in Europe established a committee on June 16, 1941. Workshops opened in September, 1941, provided six months training in building trades, electricity, locksmithing and carpentry.[22]

In March 1949, looking back on seven and a half years of work in Shanghai, M. Rechenberg, the director of ORT in Shanghai wrote, 'During their transitory stay in Shanghai, more than 3,000 Refugees obtained vocational training through "ORT". They represent more than 15% of all the Refugees in Shanghai.'[23] Rechenberg explains how ORT's work in Shanghai went far beyond providing vocational training: it also supplied psychological and moral support to those traumatised by the war.

> Our training, however, was more than a mere teaching of a trade. Many of our pupils had suffered and undergone great hardships, and often have broken down under this strain. We tried to assist them morally, we tried to give them a new outlook and a new way of thinking, and thus to build up their character and personality.[24]

Several ORT leaders who had either been forced to leave Europe or who chose to leave while they still could, migrated to America. Keen to maintain as much contact with those who remained in Europe, they established *European Friends of ORT* under the presidency of Baron de Gunzbourg. This was set up in New York in 1940. Their purpose was two-fold. First, to help fundraise for the World ORT Union and secondly, to carry on vocational training for newly arrived refugees in New York. In the winter of 1941 a vocational training school was set up in New York and was officially opened in March 1942.[25]

The changes wrought by the outbreak of war affected World ORT Union's work in its pre-war sphere of influence and in the new territories as its work evolved both inside and outside Europe. But World ORT Union changed its role most dramatically when it made its way inside the ghettos of Eastern Europe. Since its origins in Russia in 1880, never before had World ORT Union's work been so closely associated with issues of life and death and never before had an ORT certificate taken on such importance.

At the outbreak of the Second World War the Jews formed roughly 10 per cent of Poland's population. These 3.3 million Jews were the heirs to a fabulously rich spiritual and cultural tradition. In September 1939 Germany attacked Poland and within a few weeks the country was partitioned between the Third Reich and the Soviet Union, whose forces invaded from the east by agreement with the Nazis. About 2.3 million Jews lived in the area occupied by the Germans. Several hundred thousand found themselves in districts annexed to the Third Reich and re-designated the Wartheland, east Upper Silesia and east Prussia. The vast majority were in the region dubbed the General Government. Everywhere they came under the sway of the SS and the Nazi security apparatus. In September, SS General Reinhard Heydrich issued instructions for the treatment of the Jews. They were to be concentrated temporarily in large cities with major Jewish populations, near to railway lines, pending a permanent solution. Each Jewish community was to be placed under a Jewish Council, whose members were appointed by the Germans. At the same time, Jews were ejected from public life, stripped of their property, businesses and assets. All Jews were compelled to wear the yellow star on their outer clothing and hundreds were rounded up on the streets for forced labour.

Although initially the main fury of the German occupation fell on the Poles, claiming around 60,000 victims, thousands of Jews were randomly murdered by SS units in the first weeks. During 1940, about 600,000 Poles were brutally displaced from the regions annexed to Germany to make way for the settlement of ethnic Germans brought in from the Baltic states and the Balkans. At the same time, the Jews were evicted from their homes and forced into ever smaller districts of Poland's cities. There was massive overcrowding as Jews were compressed into slum areas demarcated as 'Jewish living quarters'.

Enforced unemployment and poverty quickly led to starvation and disease. By the spring of 1940 the Jewish districts were afflicted by a variety of epidemics. Yet the 'solution' heralded by Heydrich never materialised. The attempt to create a 'reservation' for Jews in the area around Lublin ran into trouble after Hans Frank, governor of the General Government, objected to the influx of Jews into his territory and the army protested against the establishment of a Jewish colony in a sensitive border zone. This was not the only obstacle. The same SS agencies charged with the deportation of Jews to the 'reservation' were also responsible for ethnic cleansing and resettlement. It was too much to handle, even for the fanatics serving Heydrich, and the plan was cancelled in October 1939.

Thus, more by accident than by design, the Nazi administrators in occupied Poland began to create ghettos. Their aim was to separate the

Jews from the surrounding population, especially German military personnel, to prevent the spread of diseases. They also hoped that by refusing to supply the ghettos with food, fuel and medicines except in return for cash or gold, that they would be able to squeeze the Jews for their mythologised wealth.

The first ghetto was created in Piotrkow, near Lodz, in the annexed region known as the Wartheland, in October 1939. Lodz itself, with a Jewish population of 160,000, was ghettoised in April 1940. A huge exchange of population was necessary to create the ghetto. The Germans attempted to create a Jewish quarter in Warsaw in October 1939. The task was too complex so Warsaw remained one of the last cities to be ghettoised.

Each ghetto was run by a Jewish Council, Judenrat, appointed by the Germans and answerable to a German civil official and security commander. The Jewish Councils gained a bad reputation after the war because of their role in the deportation of Jews to the death camps. But in the first period of their existence they had a different aspect. The Germans tended to select Jewish 'elders' who held administrative positions in the pre-war Jewish community. These men were conscientious and capable. They faced an awful task. The Jewish quarters teemed with Jewish refugees from the countryside with no livelihood or homes. So the councils set up soup kitchens and found accommodation for the incomers. They struggled to maintain sanitation and hygiene and to prevent epidemics. They were responsible for setting up schools for the children and taking care of orphans, the sick and the elderly. To pay for these operations the councils levied money from well off Jews and used relief funds sent from American Jews while America remained neutral.

From time to time, the Germans ordered the Jewish Councils to supply teams of able bodied men for forced labour. Most controversially the councils, with German assent, set up a Jewish police force. It was initially composed of decent men and was deployed to enforce sanitation rules, maintain order in the ghetto, guard labour teams and prevent smuggling. This was a perennial problem because it aroused German wrath by frustrating their aim to starve the ghettos. It also undermined the efforts of the councils to control the distribution of food and ensure some fairness. However, precisely because the Germans wanted the Jews to starve, smuggling was seen as a form of resistance and the Jewish police were often complicit in the illegal importation of foodstuffs.

Although they were superficially similar, the ghettos in Poland varied widely and their leaderships were no less different. In Warsaw, Adam Czerniakow presided over the largest Jewish population and headed an intricate administration that ran communal canteens, schools, children's homes, hostels, employment agencies, cultural activities and an archive. Czerniakow kept many intellectuals and artists alive by giving them jobs with the Jewish Council. One consequence of this was the astonishing record of day-to-day life compiled by the Oneg Shabbat cultural organisation under the historian Emmanuel Ringelblum. Much of what we know about the Warsaw ghetto comes from papers and diaries buried in milk churns by Oneg Shabbat activists so that future generations would learn what happened to the Polish Jews.

During 1940–41, Czerniakow faced a catastrophic situation. The Germans allowed the Jews 180–220 calories a day in rations (as against 670 for Poles and 2,613 for Germans). As a result the old, the infirm, the very young, and those without connections fell victim to malnutrition. In one year, 43,000 people died – 10 per cent of the entire ghetto population. In desperation, Czerniakow encouraged Jewish workers and entrepreneurs to use any scrap of metal or wood or material to produce goods to exchange for food. The results impressed the Germans who believed, according to their own propaganda, that Jews were idle parasites with no manufacturing skills. By the end of 1940, the German ghetto administration agreed to set up a *Transferstelle*, transfer agency, to manage economic relations between the ghetto and the outside world. The *Transferstelle* supplied raw materials and food for the ghetto and marketed its products. It employed the Jewish workforce and oversaw a number of enterprises inside the ghetto itself. In March 1941 the Nazis allowed several German entrepreneurs to set up large scale manufacturing ventures in the ghetto. Although tens of thousands of Jews died in the harsh winter of 1941–42, by the following spring the population had stabilised. The weak and the vulnerable had died, eventually totalling 61,000, leaving those with access to a breadwinner employed legitimately in the ghetto industries or by the Jewish council, or connected with the underground economy of smuggling and the black market.

In Lodz, the Jewish Council was led by Chaim Rumkowski. He developed a policy of ruthless centralisation and set the Jews to work for the Germans in the belief that this was their best hope of survival. After all, Lodz was a major industrial centre and the Jews were a skilled labour force. By October 1940 the German ghetto commander realised that the ghetto could be useful for the war effort and supplied Rumkowski with the food and raw materials he needed to turn it into a major production centre. Rumkowski ran the ghetto in dictatorial style. When Bundists led protests against food shortages in the summer of 1940, he had them imprisoned by the ghetto police. Yet he, too, treasured cultural activities and kept a ghetto diary that, when it was recovered from its hiding place, became a major source for understanding this period.

On 22 June 1941, the German army launched 'Operation Barbarossa' and rolled into the eastern part of Poland that had been occupied by the Soviet Union in September 1939. *Einsatzgruppen*, mobile task forces of Waffen SS and police units, commenced the slaughter of tens of thousands of Jews who were rounded up from towns and cities in eastern Poland. Their targets included Vilna, where 40,000 Jews were murdered in the Ponar forest in just a few weeks, Brest and Grodno. The surviving Jews were plundered and herded into temporary ghettos. Once the first wave of pogroms and mass shootings had passed the surviving Jews took stock. A few young Jews in each ghetto, mainly Zionist youth or socialists, resolved to escape into the forests and to resist as partisans. Gradually news of the *Einsatzgruppen* massacres filtered back to the ghettos in western Poland. The news brought by Jewish couriers was hard to believe. In any case, the Jews in the old-established ghettos were now a part of the German war effort. They could not imagine that the Germans would wipe out such a useful labour force. However, the Nazi leadership was planning exactly that.

In the build up to the invasion of the Soviet Union and during the first months of successful blitzkrieg, the Nazi officials in Poland were elated at the prospect of deporting the Jews to the wastes of Siberia after the Russians were defeated. But it did not work out that way. While the German advance stalled before Moscow there was pressure on the Nazi ghetto commanders to accept Jews deported from the Reich. To 'make room' for these Jews in the overcrowded ghetto they resolved to adopt the methods employed against the Jews of the USSR, but with a significant variation. Mass shooting was too public and wearing on the killers. So the SS drew on the experience of their 'experts' who had been conducting the mass murder of the disabled in the Reich over the previous year. The SS constructed a camp at Chelmno, near Lodz, where Jews could be murdered using poison gas. At Chelmno they used 'gas vans' which had been so adapted that the poisonous exhaust fumes were piped back into the cargo compartment into which 40–60 Jews had been crammed. Gassings at Chelmno commenced on 8 December 1941.

A few weeks later in the Wannsee suburb of Berlin, Reinhard Heydrich convened a meeting of senior SS officers, Nazi Party and state officials to coordinate the European-wide genocide against the Jews. State Secretary Buhler represented Hans Frank at the meeting. He and Frank had previously resisted SS incursions into the General Government, but now they were eager to sign up to Heydrich's master plan. Indeed, Buhler's major contribution to the discussion was to demand that the General Government be the first to be 'cleansed' of Jews.

Over the following months three more camps were constructed in Poland, each near to centres of Jewish population. Belzec, Sobibor and Treblinka were each equipped with several gas chambers using carbon monoxide piped from internal combustion engines. Gas chambers were also added to the concentration camps at Majdanek, near Lublin, and Auschwitz (Ozwiecim). The latter camps used Zyklon B gas, a pesticide that was lethal to humans. During the spring and summer of 1942, police and SS units, augmented by battalions of Latvian, Lithuanian and Ukrainian collaborators, surrounded the Polish ghettos one after another. The Jewish Councils were told that non-essential Jews were to be 'resettled in the east' and they were given daily quotas to meet. As an incentive, the Jews were told that if they went voluntarily to the embarkation points they would receive extra rations.

The deportations were carried out with terrifying ferocity. First the Germans ordered the Jewish Council to issue special identification cards to those with essential jobs. It was obvious that such an ID was a key to survival and there were bitter struggles to get real or imaginary work permits. In many ghettos the 'working Jews' were physically divided from the Jews deemed surplus. To begin with, 'surplus Jews' were lured to the assembly points by the promise of food. But as fewer responded to these blandishments and rumours spread about mass murder the Jewish police were charged with routing out the necessary numbers each day. When more and more Jews hid, heavily armed teams of SS and auxiliaries stormed through streets, courtyards and buildings grabbing anyone they found and using sniffer dogs to uncover hiding places. The ghettos echoed with screams and shooting and the streets resembled a charnel house.

The deportations to Belzec commenced in mid-March 1942 and halted in mid-May while the gas chambers were enlarged. The killing resumed in mid-July and continued until the end of December 1942. About 600,000 Jews were murdered at Belzec, including Jewish men, women and children from Piotrkow, Lublin, Radom, Lwow, the many shtetls of eastern Galicia, and the Cracow area. Sobibor operated from May to July 1942, paused while the rail line serving the camp was strengthened to take the unusual volume of traffic to which it was being subjected, and continued from September 1942 to October 1943. It is estimated that 250,000 Jews were murdered there, including Polish Jews from the Lublin, Vilna and Lida ghettos. After a false start in August 1942, Treblinka was active continuously from September 1942 to August 1943. No fewer than 870,000 Jews were killed there. In addition Jews from Radom, Siedlice, Minsk-Mazowieski, Radom, the Lublin region, and 107,000 from Bialystok were transported to Treblinka.

Majdanek accounted for 125,000 Jews who were gassed and shot. During one 'Aktion' on 3 November 1943, the so-called 'Harvest Festival', 17,000 were shot to death. Auschwitz-Birkenau used improvised murder facilities until March 1943 when large purpose-built gas chambers and crematoria were built. Amongst the 1.1 million Jews from all over Europe who were murdered in Auschwitz-Birkenau between May 1942 and October 1944 were the Jews of Upper Silesia, formerly part of Poland, and Lodz. The 70,000 Jews from Lodz who were transported to the gas chambers in August 1944 were the last major community of Poland to be destroyed in this way.

The onslaught against the ghettos was so sudden and brutal that it was hard for the Jews to respond effectively. The Nazis initially demanded that the Jewish Councils select 'useless mouths' which could not assist the war effort. They never said how many would be removed so the Jewish Councils always hoped that each transport would be the last. Jewish resistance is a vexed issue. After the war praise was heaped on those who fought back in the forests or in the ghettos. By contrast, the Jewish Councils were condemned and ordinary Jews denigrated for 'going like sheep to the slaughter'. Much later, after historians had assimilated the extraordinary conditions under which people had lived, the view changed. It was realised that because the Nazis set out to break the spirit of the Jews and dehumanise them, every effort to retain dignity and to maintain Jewish traditions was a form of defiance. Schools, theatres, songs, artworks and hidden prayer rooms were all ways of resisting Nazi aims. Keeping a record, collectively or individually, defied the Nazi aspiration to hide their crimes and wipe out even any memory of the Jews. Because the Nazis wanted to starve the Jews, food smuggling was a form of resistance. The strategy of the Jews was '*iyberlebn*', to survive or overcome, which in the face of genocide was resistance.

After the horrors of the great deportation wave in 1942 the survivors in the shrunken ghettos re-evaluated previous strategies. In Warsaw, a movement for armed resistance coalesced around the Zionist youth, led by the charismatic Mordecai Anielewicz, the Bundists and right-wing Zionists. The most sustained ghetto revolt took place in Warsaw in April–May 1943. It is estimated that after the great deportation of 1942, 25,000 Jews fled the Warsaw ghetto and found refuge on the 'Aryan side'. There were many other ghetto revolts and military actions – including Bedzin, Czestochowa and Cracow – and Jewish partisans fought throughout Poland where there were favourable conditions. However, the chances of survival of Jewish fighters and Jews in hiding were so poor that barely 50,000 Jews were alive on Polish soil when the Red Army finally drove out the Germans.

Prior to the outbreak of the Second World War, Warsaw was the centre of Jewish cultural and social life in Poland. It had a pre-war Jewish population of more than 300,000 which made up 30 per cent of the city's total population. This made it the largest Jewish community in Europe.

German troops entered Warsaw on 29 September 1939 and within days the Jewish population were ordered to wear the Star of David. Although anti-Jewish legislation was implemented immediately, it was another year before the ghetto was established. The order to set-up the ghetto was issued on 12 October 1940. All Jews were informed that they would be ordered to move into the designated area which would be sealed off from the rest of the city. A total of 113,000 Poles were forced to leave their homes in central Warsaw and 138,000 Jews from around the city took their place. When the ghetto was finally sealed in November 1940, it held 400,000 people behind 11 miles of wall ten feet high. One third of Warsaw's population was jammed into 2.4 per cent of its area with a density of 9.2 persons per room. A further 130,000 Jews uprooted from the countryside were forced in. At its peak in March 1941, the Warsaw ghetto contained 445,000 souls.

As in all the ghettos during the war, the fear of deportation clouded every other consideration. In Warsaw, the first deportations left for Treblinka in July 1942 and by 6 September 300,000 Jews had been deported from the ghetto. In January 1943 the second series of deportations began and this time a further 5,000 people were deported. On 16 May 1943 the third and last group of transports left the ghetto. The total number of Jews deported from Warsaw to Treblinka was approximately 310,000.

Due to the devastation wrought by the deportations, small groups of resisters sprang up all around the ghetto. They soon joined forces, began to build underground bunkers and shelters and prepared themselves for large scale resistance in the face of future deportations and the final liquidation of the ghetto. On 19 April 1943, the Germans entered the ghetto with the intention of emptying it of all remaining Jews. For almost a month the Jews of the Warsaw Ghetto resisted the Nazis but were finally defeated on 16 May 1943, when all those remaining were deported to Treblinka.

The Jewish council of the Warsaw ghetto was housed in buildings on Grzybowska Street which was located in the southern part of the ghetto. In addition to the men of the council who went out of their way to assist the ghetto population, various Jewish organisations attempted to ease the life of those imprisoned there. There were several relief and welfare organisations working in the ghetto. These included: the Federation of Associations in Poland for the Care of Orphans, the Jewish Mutual Aid Society, and ORT.

ORT's classes and workshops constituted a vital part of ghetto life. Prior to the discussion of the actual classes held by ORT Warsaw, it is important to discuss the role of work in the ghettos in general. What did it mean to have a work placement inside the ghetto rather than a place in a labour gang outside its walls? What could and did the ghetto organisations do for their workers? Could they secure extra rations, a warm place to work, the company of friends and family and in some cases exemption from deportation? Finally, why did the men who ran the Jewish councils set up and organise work that would aid the German war effort and what role did ORT play in this?

According to Lucy Dawidowicz,

> the idea of ghetto industry originated out of the needs of the ghetto itself and of its inhabitants. Cooperatives in traditional Jewish trades were set up by Judenrate in Lwow, Cracow, Radom, Siedlce, ... often in conjunction with remnant trade-union groups or with ORT, the agency for vocational training and rehabilitation: in men's and women's clothing, shoes, hats, carpentry, brushes, bakeries.[26]

The idea that work could mean salvation began to evolve in the ghettos across eastern Europe soon after communities were incarcerated. The concept of 'rescue through work' has since been explored in detail. Raul Hilberg writes, 'The Jewish Councils, West and East, tried to postpone disaster ... and sought ways to create work projects that would make as many Jews as possible indispensable to the war economy.'[27]

It was preferable to have work inside the ghetto rather than outside and this is where the ORT classes and workshops played a prominent role. Inside the ghetto the workers avoided long and strenuous walks to factories and worksites several kilometres away and were often able to procure additional rations.

Isaiah Trunk discusses the morally complex policy of 'rescue through work'. He claims,

> Charges concerning the ultimate ineffectiveness of the policy of 'rescue through work' as a method of extending the life of the ghettos and its inmates have overshadowed the moral problem involved.[28]

He goes on to define this 'moral problem':

> The problem was a simple one: How could such service, offering considerable help to the Germans, be justified when the laborers' compatriots were engaged in a moral fight with their employers as army regulars or resistants? With the Jews, the problem had a difference: the Jews had been extirpated from the economic life of the countries of their residence, and unable to create a self-sustained economy in the conditions of ghetto life; the only alternative to 100 percent unemployment lay in serving the enemy employer.[29]

As laid out by Trunk, there was really no alternative to the policy of 'rescue through work' as it was one of the few ways to avoid slave labour gangs or deportation. It also helped to ease the appalling ghetto conditions and improve the quality of life for those who found a place within the workshops.

When the Nazis occupied Warsaw in September 1939, the Jewish Vocational School in Warsaw was shut down. However, as documented by Wischnitzer,

> In August 1940, permission was granted by the Nazi authorities to open and equip trade courses in Warsaw. In September 1940, the Warsaw ORT Committee transferred its school building and equipment to the vocational training commission of the Jewish Community Council. ORT school instructors became members of

the commission. In December 1940, an agreement was reached with the Community Council whereby ORT undertook to finance the schools.[30]

This relationship between ORT, the Jewish council and established members of the Jewish community was neither a new ghetto phenomenon nor one that was specific to Warsaw. Before the outbreak of war and the establishment of the ghettos, members of ORT Poland had often worked closely with prominent members of Jewish communities and council men in various locations. Trunk writes,

> In Piotrkow Trybunalski before the war six councilmen were simultaneously active in the labour unions, in ORT (Organisation for Rehabilitation and Training) and TOZ, and in the vocational school, and also served on the executive committee of the Yiddish school.[31]

Trunk explains how the relationship between the Jewish Council, the ORT and the other Jewish organisations in the ghetto worked. He writes, 'In Warsaw, the TOZ, Centos and the ORT were active independent of the Jewish Council and became part of the JSS when it was established there. For a long time, they operated as autonomous institutions.'[32] Trunk continues, 'Moreover, as a socially oriented body the JSS enjoyed the cooperation of personalities who before the war had been active in the TOZ, Centos, ORT, the interest-free loan banks etc, and who now preferred to give their time and efforts to the JSS, which was better equipped to meet the immediate needs of the Jewish masses than were the Jewish councils.'[33] Trunk explains how pre-war organisations like ORT had to be officially included within the Jewish Councils thereby constituting a department inside the larger organisation. He concludes by adding that,

> In a number of ghettos, as a result of collective or individual initiatives, associations whose aims were philanthropic, professional, or religious, were created, which did not belong to the Judenrat's structural framework, but were partly subsidized by the Councils. They assisted the Judenräte, particularly in the field of social welfare.[34]

Trunk describes the relationship between ORT and the councils, citing the example of Wlodzimierz Wolynski, in which five of the councilmen were also active in ORT.

When Warsaw fell and the Germans entered the city, Jewish life stopped. All education ceased and all vocational training schools and workshops were shut down. Within a couple of weeks, however, the situation changed once more and within a month, the ORT workshops were fully functioning. Rachel Gourman, a survivor of the Warsaw Ghetto and a former ORT employee, describes how news of the workshops' re-opening breathed life into the demoralised and desperate Jewish population of Warsaw. She recalls:

> Like a cry from Heaven, the rumour spread among the Jewish population that the ORT workshops were to be reopened ... The excitement of the people at this news is indescribable ... This enabled them to earn at least a little something almost immediately, so that they could buy a loaf of bread or a head of cabbage.[35]

Gourman explains how it was possible that ORT was able to re-open at this time despite the war-time conditions and the lack of funds and supplies. She writes,

> With the outbreak of war, ORT in Warsaw was cut off from the World Union and was left without funds. However, we collected the necessary monies, quite substantial sums for the purchase of objects required for the artisans' exhibition in Krakow. Then dozens of courses opened for which all necessary material had been procured.[36]

When, in September 1940, the ORT courses revived under the leadership of Joseph Jashunsky there was a glimmer of hope for those who were fortunate enough to have a place on a course or a position as a teacher. In addition to running ORT within the ghetto, Jashunsky was a member of the Warsaw Judenrat and the former head of ORT Poland from 1935 to 1942.

Gourman stresses the importance of gaining a place on an ORT course and explains how this could help with securing work:

> life in the ghetto became more and more difficult. The Jews tried to 'escape' by setting up workshops in order to work for the Germans. Unbelievable sums of money were paid to enter workshops. People stood in queues for days and nights. Those in possession of ORT certificates were employed by any workshops.[37]

It is important to stress that the ORT vocational training school was the only school in the Warsaw Ghetto at this time so it was of huge educational importance. Although the Nazis had given permission for the ORT courses and ghetto workshops to re-open, they insisted that they only cover technical training and not a more general curriculum, as all forms of Jewish education were now illegal. Shapiro discusses how they had to be extremely careful to conceal any deviation from this command as, 'The Commission for Vocational Training, which included representatives of the Jewish Council and Warsaw ORT, was accountable to the Nazi authorities'.[38]

On 22 July 1942 the mass deportations to Treblinka started from the Warsaw ghetto. Due to the huge reduction in the population at this time, workshops were closed and entire streets in the ghetto were laid to waste. Unable to remove all their machinery from the newly emptied workshops, ORT was forced in many respects to start again. It opened new workshops in an attempt to save lives. Those running the ORT courses knew that anyone with an ORT certificate could get a place in a ghetto workshop and that, most importantly, those in the workshops were registered as legal workers at the German Labour Office and therefore less likely to be deported. Gourman writes how, 'Again a glimpse of light entered the shops. Naked people received clothes and the barefoot were given shoes. Whoever managed to escape from the camps, went directly to ORT.'[39] This shows that ORT's extraordinary reputation was not merely confined to the ghetto. Anyone who escaped the concentration camps and made their way to the Warsaw Ghetto knew about ORT's work and tried to secure a place on one of their courses inside the ghetto workshops.

An ORT certificate not only gave workers a legal status in the ghetto, but could also secure extra rations as well. The scarcity of food inside the ghetto meant that nearly all the population were on starvation rations. Abraham Lewent describes the horrific hunger that was prevalent in the ghetto, he recalls:

> The hunger in the ghetto was so great, was so bad, that people were laying on the streets and dying ... And every day thousands and thousands died just from malnutrition because the Germans didn't give anything for the people in the ghetto to eat. There was no such thing. You can't walk in and buy anything, or getting any rations. It's your hard luck. If you don't have it, you die, and that's what it was.[40]

If these starvation rations could be supplemented in any way, chances of survival increased dramatically. Gourman writes, 'It was known in the Ghetto that at the ORT workshops, people received a plate of soup and 100g of bread each day. People came to get a bit of food and to forget their sorrows for a moment.'[41] She describes how it was not only physical sustenance that ORT supplied to its workers but also intellectual nourishment. She explains:

> In ORT offices one could forget the nightmare of reality and find new courage to live: the offices became a kind of a literary and political circle. In addition to many teachers and instructors of various courses, other 'habitues' who passed through Lezno Street, began to drop in for a chat and a glass of tea.[42]

Several reports that comment on ORT's work in the ghetto claim that an ORT identification card was protection against deportation. While nothing could guarantee survival in the ghetto, ORT certainly did save lives in several cases. On a couple of occasions ORT pupils were released having been rounded up on the streets of the ghetto. Gourman writes, 'Whereas several persons were nabbed on Lezno Street, no one ever entered the ORT premises at No.13'.[43]

One of the most renowned ORT courses in Warsaw was the course for the manufacture of clothing and underwear which opened on 10 March 1940 inside the Jewish orphanage. The ORT orphanage workshop had a total of twenty seamstresses who were aged between 14 and 24. The orphanage which was located on Krochmalna Street was run by Dr Korczak. When the ghetto was established the orphanage was engulfed by its walls and when the children of the orphanage were included in a deportation, Korczak chose to go with them rather than save his own life.

By the summer of 1941, the work of ORT in the ghetto had expanded from the early, almost experimental, courses into a wide array of vocational training programmes. There was a total of twenty-four courses on offer for 832 boys and twenty-four courses for 818 girls. In addition there were sixteen mixed courses for 681 pupils which made a total of 2,331 pupils. Bernard Goldstein, a survivor of the ghetto, remembers ORT courses in 'tailoring, hatmaking and corsetry'.[44]

By May 1941 a total of 1,195 people in the ghetto had completed ORT courses in locksmithing, auto mechanics, optical work and candymaking. By the end of August 1941 ORT had a total of 4,000 pupils.

Because Warsaw had been Europe's largest Jewish community, there was no shortage of teachers. The ghetto was full of eminent professors excelling in subjects across the academic spectrum: 'Experienced engineers, architects, mechanics, electricians, chemists, draftsmen and other specialists, who had been ousted from their posts by the Nazi administration, served as lecturers and instructors.'[45] Trunk describes the wide array of courses on offer inside the Warsaw Ghetto, 'In time vocational courses on the lyceum or nearly college level were established with extensive programs such as the nurses' school with 250 students who worked professionally at the Jewish hospital.'[46]

Due to the stringent laws on education and cultural activities inside the ghettos, most of the courses had to be taught in secret. Trunk explains however, that some teachers were allowed to continue their work on 'the condition that no subjects in humanities would be included in the curriculum, except those relating to Judaism'.[47] This proved impossible for the authorities to police so most subjects continued to be taught in secret.

In addition to teaching clandestine academic subjects and carrying out specific vocational training, ORT focused on gardening and agriculture in the ghetto as well. As noted by Trunk, ORT was keen to, 'create within rubble-covered areas some green spots, "lungs for the ghetto"'.[48] In order to make this possible, they joined forces with the pre-war Society for the Promotion of Agriculture, known as TOPOROL.

News of ORT's work inside the Warsaw Ghetto reached England in November 1943 when Eduard Warszawski, an escapee from the ghetto, was interviewed by the *Jewish Chronicle*. He wrote how, inside the ghetto,

> many training courses were organised, and the majority of the people worked as skilled craftsmen. Jews were taught to till the soil, and vegetable gardens were found on every vacant plot of the ghetto, while gardens were laid out for the children in the courtyards of the tenements.[49]

He goes on to discuss other aspects of ghetto existence but returns to the subject of education. He concludes by saying that, 'Very good schools for the young and professional courses were established' in the ghetto.[50]

The deportations to Treblinka from Warsaw continued and on 18 January 1943, Joseph Jashunsky, Director of ORT in Warsaw, was deported with his family. Rachel Gourman describes his dedication to ORT and his tireless work in the ghetto:

> Up to the last day of his life he did his work. Exhausted and depressed, he would arrive at his office early in the morning and do everything necessary so that things might go on normally ... Sometimes he arrived with broken glasses, his face covered with blood. Because of his near-sightedness, he would not notice a German coming his way and so would not leave the pavement, or take off his hat, or would be guilty of committing some other 'offence'.[51]

Jashunksy's dedication to the people of the Warsaw Ghetto and to the work of ORT although remarkable, was not unique. Those who ran the workshops of the Kovno Ghetto exhibited the same values and inspirational behaviour as Jashunsky.

In addition to Jashunsky, other prominent ORT teachers inside the ghetto were Dr Meyer Meisner, Eng. Kielin and Jeshie Greenberg, the Chief Instructor in the ghetto. Professor Zentnerschwer was placed in charge of all ORT chemistry courses in the ghetto. The staff of the ORT girls' school, such as Edzie Wollman, Branie Birnzweig, Channe Kowarski and Tolie Wettlaufer, also worked unstintingly on behalf of their pupils. M.R. Zweifuss, the former head of artisans' union in Warsaw was also a member of ORT inside the ghetto.

According to Jack Rader, Emmanuel Ringelblum, the Warsaw ghetto historian and diarist, wrote about the work of ORT. On 1 March 1944, just days before his death, his diary entry mentions various welfare and educational groups in the ghetto, concluding, 'The ORT also developed a many-sided program. The lives of tens of thousands of adults as well as children were saved by the aid of these institutions.'[52]

Similarities can be seen between the Warsaw and the Kovno ghettos and the importance of the ORT schools within both of them. In 1939, Kovno was Lithuania's largest city with a Jewish population of approximately 37,500. This made up about a quarter of the city's population. Kovno, like Warsaw, had a vibrant Jewish community and was an important centre of Jewish learning as well as a prominent centre of Zionist thought. The Soviet Union occupied Lithuania in June 1940 and life for the Jewish community changed overnight. There was a series of arrests and the majority of the city's Jewish organisations were disbanded. A huge propaganda drive followed which flooded the city with antisemitic literature turning many Lithuanians against their native Jewish cohabitants.

On 22 June 1941 Germany invaded the Soviet Union and within two

1 WOA: psa0731
Foundation of World ORT Union. Delegates at the first ORT Congress in Berlin, July 1921.

2 WOA: p05a178
Delegates at the 1923 ORT Union Congress in Danzig. Photography: Verra and Blaschy, Danzig.

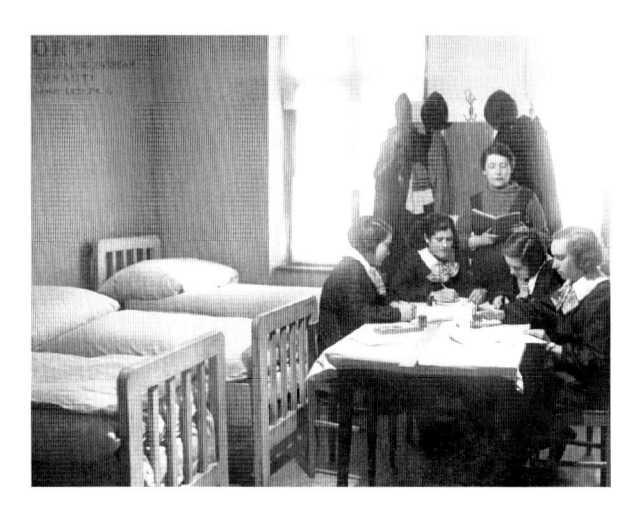

3 WOA: psa1006
Dormitory at the ORT boarding school for girls in Czernowitz [Cernauti], Romania, 1937.
Photography: Foto-Sternschein, Cernauti.

4 WOA: p00a022 Dr David Lvovitch.

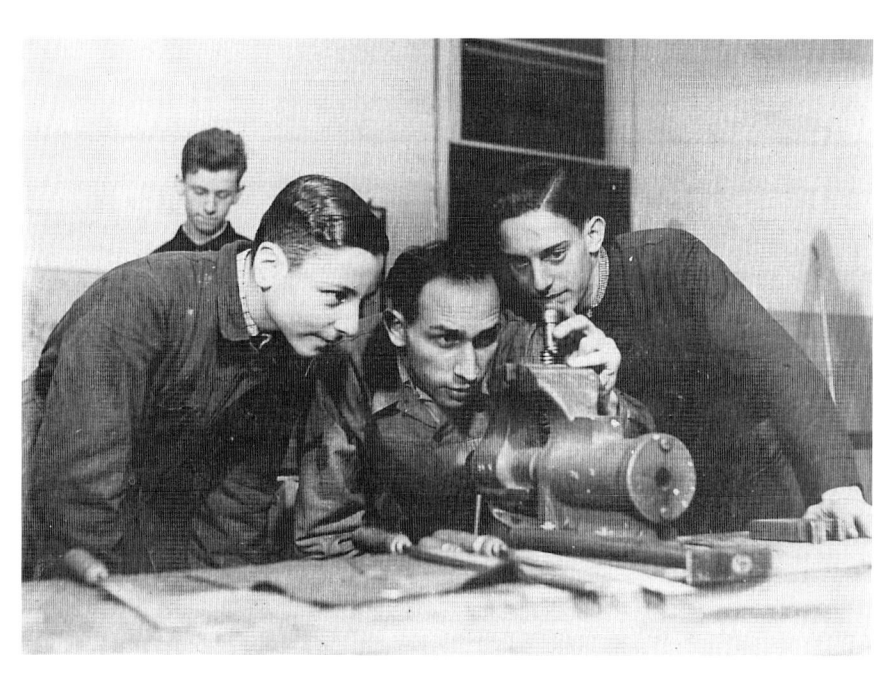

5 WOA: p00a018 Dr Leon Bramson.

6 WOA: OW/PA49/ Page 2 Instructor Max Abraham with students at the ORT Berlin School, November 1938. Photography: Lilli Szkolny.

7 WOA: p03a542 Lt. Colonel Joseph Henry Levey, instrumental in transferring the Berlin School to England in August 1939.

8 WOA: psa1732 German refugees in Lithuania. Vocational course for young German Jewish refugees, 1933–34. Photography S. Bajero.

9 WOA: psa0039 ORT France cinema projectionist course for German refugees, Paris, 1939.

10 WOA: psa1809 ORT Upholstery course in Zbaszyn Camp on the German-Polish border, 1939. The camp was used to hold Jews of Polish nationality, who were expelled from Germany between October 1938 and August 1939.

11 WOA: p00a031 Farming community run by ORT in Kybartai, Marijampole County, Lithuania, May 1940.

12 WOA: p00a448 ORT leaders welcome François de Tessan (centre), back from a fund-raising mission in the USA, 1939. On Tessan's right are Dr Bramson, William Graetz (standing behind him), former President of ORT Germany, and Mr J. Blum. On Tessan's left are Kaplan (back row), Leites and Efros.

13 WOA: p05a155 ORT basket making course in Uzhorod, Hungary, November-December 1943.

14 WOA: psa0061 ORT course in the Warsaw Ghetto, 14 March 1941.

15 WOA: p00a038 Jacob Oleiski.

16 WOA: p00a455 Dr Syngalowski and agronomist Osher Malkin, visiting the ORT farm in La-Roche, France, 1942.

17 WOA: d00a003 Postcard written in Theresienstadt on 22 November 1943 by Dr Werner Simon, Director of ORT Germany. Bearing the postmark of the Third Reich and a stamp portraying Hitler, it was posted in Berlin in February 1944. Simon and his family were deported to Auschwitz on 23 October 1944.

18 WOA: psa0531 Tile making course in Bialystok, Poland, June 1939.

19 WOA: psa0864 ORT driving course, Shanghai, China, 1940s. Photography: Photo Willinger, Shanghai.

20 WOA: a018012 Illustration showing ORT operations in the six administrative sections of the US Zone of Germany, from an ORT report, *ORT US-Zone Germany*.

21 WOA: a079000 Cover of *ORT Vocational School in Bergen-Belsen 1945-1947* pamphlet. The illustration shows the ORT school arch, erected in the camp's Freedom Square, by carpentry and electro-technician ORT students.

22 WOA: d06a123 Identity card from Landsberg DP camp, dated 3 August 1945. The card belonged to an auto-mechanics ORT student, Mordechai Aisen [Eisen]. Reproduced by kind permission of Stan Eisen

23 WOA: d06a121 Military Government US Army pass allowing ORT personnel and students passage to and from the Landsberg DP camp barracks, August 1945. Reproduced by kind permission of Stan Eisen

24 WOA: d06a078 ORT certificate for cinematography course, Zurich, Switzerland, 1945.

days the Soviet forces fled Kovno. The German troops arrived on 24 June 1941 sparking a series of anti-Jewish attacks carried out by pro-German Lithuanians. In the wake of the German troops came *Einsatzgruppe A*, one of the four Nazi mobile killing units, which together, were responsible for shooting over one million Jews in Eastern Europe. *Einsatzgruppe A* started killing Jews in the old military forts that surrounded Kovno. These executions were mainly carried out at the Ninth Fort and within a period of six months about half of the Jewish population of Kovno had been murdered.

In July 1941 the order was given to establish a ghetto for the remaining Jewish population of Kovno. The ghetto was set up in an area known as Slobodka and consisted of two parts. As with the Warsaw Ghetto, both parts of the Kovno Ghetto were secured by barbed wire enclosures surrounded by armed guards. These were sealed on 15 August 1941.

The size of the ghettos and thus the amount of living space allocated to each person was constantly reduced. Each time this happened the housing and sanitary conditions worsened and the mortality rate rose. The smaller of the two ghettos was completely destroyed on 4 October 1941 with nearly all those housed there being shot at the Ninth Fort in the weeks that followed. On 29 October 1941, the 'Great Action' took place, when 9,200 Jews were killed in one day at the Ninth Fort. In the autumn of 1943 the Kovno ghetto became the Kauen concentration camp. On 8 July 1944, the Germans emptied the camp and the majority of those remaining were deported to Dachau and Stutthof concentration camps. On 1 August 1944 the Soviet army liberated Kovno.

The Jews of the Kovno Ghetto were employed as slave labourers at various locations outside the ghetto. The majority of the forced labour was based at a military airport outside Kovno and the work on labour gangs started at the age of 13. In addition to the forced labour battalions which worked outside the ghetto, the Jewish council set up a series of workshops inside the ghetto. It was in these workshops that the members of the Jewish council hoped to save the lives of the Kovno Jews. Little could be done to aid those who were forced to work outside the ghetto but the council hoped that if they could convince the Nazis that the workshops contained workers essential to the war effort some might be saved.

Dr Elkes, the head of the Kovno Judenrat, believed that it was only through work that the council might be able to save the people. When discussing his father's views on the policy of 'rescue through work', his son Joel writes,

> Work meant food, and the extra rations, although meagre, were extremely important ... Work in the Ghetto could serve people who were too weak to march five or six miles to work and still be able to stand the rigors of manual labor. The Council, therefore, decided to give the establishment of workshops the highest priority. If the Germans allowed such workshops to be developed, it would increase the workforce of the Ghetto substantially.[53]

Once this decision had been made, the Kovno Judenrat began to implement these plans straight away. Joel Elkes writes, 'The Council started preparations immediately. A building on Krisciukacio Street, a place where thousands of homeless Jews were housed before the Big Action, was assigned as a place for the workshops.'[54] In addition to the actual workshops, he writes how, 'a department of Culture and Education was in charge of both the Kindergarten and the elementary/secondary schools, headed by Dr Nachman Shapiro. A Vocational School under Dr Jacob Oleiski was also established.[55]

The winter of 1941-42, which followed the mass executions of the Kovno Jews at the Ninth Fort, was a period of uncertainty and forced labour for those who remained. The main focus of the uncertainty and anxiety was on the ghetto young. How were the parents, carers and teachers in the ghetto to attempt to keep them safe? How could they ensure that the children would be viewed as key workers and be given a place within a workshop?

Jacob Oleiski, the former head of ORT Lithuania, began to think about how he could help the ghetto's youth. Oleiski had been appointed Director of ORT in Lithuania in 1927. He was originally offered the job on a one year approval scheme by Dr Leon Bramson, the Chairman of the World ORT Union in Berlin, but by the time the Kovno ghetto was established, Oleiski held three important positions in Lithuania. He was head of the ORT agricultural school, head of the Kovno Trade School and head of all ORT activities in Lithuania.

Recalling the early days of the ghetto, Oleiski wrote:

> Then I got the idea for a trade school in the ghetto, which, I reasoned would keep youngsters away from slave labour at the airport, prevent their physical collapse, teach them vocations that would get them places in the workshops in town, and provide them with cultural interests and a learning environment that would help to save them from a breakdown in morale.[56]

When the school was opened there were 500 children in the ghetto aged between 12 and 15. Although the official starting age for forced labour was 13, Oleiski recorded how, 'Often, even younger children went to work ... as "angels", substituting for a parent, or a stranger for pay'.[57] It was Oleiski's belief that if he could keep them working inside the ghetto walls, he might be able to save at least some of them.

Oleiski discusses the early days of the school and how it opened with courses in 'locksmithy and carpentry for boys and dressmaking for girls'. As in the other ghettos there was little space and no equipment but as Oleiski explains, they were lucky as they could rely on, 'some former instructors from the Kovno ORT school'.[58] 'Former ORT personnel had hoped that this chance to resume their occupations would be a link with the past, and I took on the management of the school – a veritable ORT institution in the tragic circumstances of the Ghetto of Kovno.'[59] This solved the problem of teaching staff while the lack of equipment was tackled due to the ingenuity and bravery of those in the ghetto. Tools were smuggled into the ghetto inside bundles of wood, sometimes even instead of food. These former ORT workers who were desperate to set up the school in the ghetto were risking their own lives and those of their families in order to bring the tools in. The vocational school in the Kovno Ghetto was finally inaugurated at the end of March 1942: 'Within three months, by Purim, 1942, we had a school with 40 pupils. We had 20 vices, a sewing machine, a small lathe and some smaller implements.'[60]

Oleiski was fortunate to be able to draw on the expertise of former teachers who were now imprisoned in the ghetto. Iser Feldman and Yitzhak Appleboim, both former employees of the Kovno ORT, taught on the trade courses while Eng. Shimon Ratner was in charge of academic studies. Elly Gotz, who was moved into the ghetto with his parents in 1941, remembers being taught by Yerachmiel Feldman on the locksmith and metalwork courses:

> I loved the experience! I learned first the tools of the trade, how to file, measure precisely and shape metal with hammer and chisel. Later we scrounged some machines, a lathe, mechanical drills, and I learned how to use them. Theory was taught in the afternoons, together with Jewish subjects ... I was a good student.[61]

In addition to providing vocational training to men and women, the ORT school also became a refuge to the children and adolescents of the

Kovno Ghetto. The tireless work of those who taught in the school and those who cared for the children, according to Oleiski, 'won the admiration and love of all the population of the ghetto'.[62]

In addition to the vocational courses on offer, the school opened a library in which it taught the ghetto's youth. It was here in the library that, 'the threat of extermination which hovered over the ghetto, was forgotten for a while and youngsters were given a chance to spend at least part of the day in human conditions'.[63] Elly Gotz remembers how in addition to his learning a skill, 'We put on a play by Peretz, we discussed history and we played chess. As I look back now I must give credit to those dedicated and inspired teachers. Life in the Ghetto was miserable and the school was a place of respite.'[64]

On 26 August 1942 a new commandant, Köpen, arrived at the ghetto. Soon after his arrival he ordered that all youth education be shut down. This included the primary school, the vocational school, the yeshiva and the synagogues.

> This order fell on the youngsters like a thunderbolt on a clear day. Parents were alarmed over the fate of their children. Youngsters were again included in the work gangs of the ghetto, the workshops closed down but continued to exist underground and a nucleus of Jewish youngsters from the ghetto rallied around the closed vocational school.[65]

Although life under Köpen was uncertain, his rule was to be short lived. Deeply concerned over the closure of the schools in the ghetto, the Jewish Council began to discuss the possibility of opening a new vocational school. On 13 September 1942, Avraham Tory recorded in his diary that there was 'A meeting of the Council on the subject of schools in the Ghetto: the plan is to set up a vocational training school with an expanded program of study which would include general subjects.'[66] Martin Gilbert writes that,

> The official function of the vocational school was to train youngsters for the workshops; in practice, it was an ordinary primary school, which also taught technical studies, as a means of compensating for the closing down of Ghetto schools that August.[67]

This was of vital importance. If all other schools were shut down, an

ORT vocational school in the ghetto would be the only place of education for the children.

Once opened, the school was quick to expand and, on 10 October 1942, Tory wrote that 'The vocational training school opened courses in baking'.[68] He describes the growth of the school and recorded on 25 February 1943 that courses for sewing and gardening had been established. By this time, the school had 350 pupils and more staff had been added. Mrs Muscat headed the Arts and Crafts section while Professor Shapiro ran seminars for 14–16-year-olds. The ORT choir was conducted by B. Gerber and Wolf Luria organised the children's cultural evenings. The fact that so much was on offer at the ORT school meant that it became both an educational centre for the ghetto young and a refuge for the adults too.[69] Oleiksi described it as 'the spiritual centre of the Ghetto. Our initiative had made it possible for it to function also as a forum for lectures for adults, and thus bring some solace to our miserable lives.'[70]

Commandant Köpen was succeeded by Miller in November 1942. He did not object to the vocational school on the understanding that it trained ghetto inhabitants exclusively for work in work gangs. The other schools in the ghetto remained closed so it became of the utmost importance that the vocational school lowered its age of entrance to allow children into its classes.

During Miller's time in power, the ORT school grew to accommodate 350 pupils. It expanded so it could include children aged 10 and hired primary school teachers in order to help with their education. According to Oleiski, children aged between 10 and 13 learned

> arithmetic, Hebrew, Yiddish, botany, history and in addition, practical work in the school workshop. Girls were taught dressmaking and handicraft. Boys could choose between locksmithy, carpentry and tinsmithy. Mr. Strelecki, the former pedagogic headmaster of the ORT school in Kaunas was appointed pedagogic headmaster of the school.[71]

Dr Shapiro who had been in charge of the ghetto's primary and secondary education prior to closure was now working within the ORT school.

April 1943 was an important time in the life of the school as the ghetto celebrated Passover. Tory describes how the ghetto marked the occasion and how all workplaces outside the ghetto were closed as Passover coincided with Easter. On 26 April 1943 Tory wrote,

> Yesterday a third Passover seder was held at the vocational school ... Between forty and fifty young boys, aged from twelve to fifteen, were seated around long tables set for the Passover meal. Each boy had his Passover Haggadah in front of him, from which to read and sing. The girls and the boys were dressed in their best clothes, their faces beaming, their eyes shining.[72]

As it is unusual for Jews in the Diaspora to celebrate the third night of Passover, the fact that the vocational school marked that evening with a third seder is interesting. With no direct religious connections this third night's celebration should be seen as being symbolic as well as political. As Tory explains,

> The boy interspersed the Haggadah passages with commentaries about contemporary Egypt and the contemporary Egyptians; about the next Exodus: about building up our homeland; about the historical generation of the desert; and about the Ghetto today. He also spoke about today's youth, their hopes, and their yearnings for redemption and freedom.[73]

The themes of freedom and redemption that underline the Passover celebrations would have seemed especially pertinent inside the ghetto and perhaps this is why those organising the festivities thought it necessary to celebrate with a third seder.

The vocational school in Kovno had a dual purpose and a dual identity. Tory describes the two 'identities' and how they came about. He describes the official and practical work of the school:

> The declared objective of the vocational training school – which was set up after the closing of all educational institutions in the Ghetto – was to train skilled workers for various workplaces. After a short period of education and vocational training, the school is able to graduate carpenters, construction workers, cobblers, tailors.[74]

Thanks to the appointment of a fairly 'lenient' director to run the Labour Office, the school was able to carry out more clandestine work too. When discussing the new director, Tory writes: 'On account of his numerous duties, he practically never intervenes in the affairs of the school or the activities of its students.'[75] This meant that those running the school could choose how they wished to educate the ghetto young. Tory explains, 'We make sure that Jewish children will, in addition to the vocational training, receive a Zionist education in the spirit of the Jewish heritage and our national aspirations.'[76]

At the third Passover seder, Jacob Oleiski rose to speak. Oleiski delivered a speech which backed the Zionist teaching of the school and explained how his own feelings on Zionism and the Diaspora had changed. He claimed, 'I have sinned. I have been in error. I have sought redemption in the ideal of universal humanity – in distant lands – and I have failed. We must have our own land, our own life. The land of Israel is the one and only truth.'[77]

As was the case in other ghettos, the Kovno ORT workshops and vocational courses were occasionally able to save lives by guaranteeing workplaces and supplying increased rations. In July 1943, the factories outside the ghetto which used slave labour started to cut back, no longer wanting Jews on site. Although the work was strenuous and the journey to and from the factories exhausting, as long as the factory needed the labour, the Jews would not be deported. Hence the cutbacks in demand for labour marked a turning point and represented a substantial blow to ghetto security. Inhabitants began to fear that the liquidation of the ghetto was imminent and that they would be deported to concentration camps. On 7 July 1943, Tory recorded that it had been decided that, 'Younger children will stay in the Ghetto and study in vocational training schools'.[78] This was a critical development as it meant that the ghetto was not to be liquidated immediately and that the young would be spared, at least for the moment.

On 8 September 1943 Geke replaced Miller as ghetto commandant and a new era began. With Geke came an increased SS presence and it was under his rule that the ghetto was changed into a concentration camp. On 26 October 1943, 2,700 people were deported from the ghetto with fifty being taken from the vocational school. The men were taken to slave labour camps in Estonia while the women and children were sent to Auschwitz. According to Oleiski,

> After this deportation the Ghetto looked like the aftermath of a pogrom. Its streets were strewn with possessions of victims sent to their deaths; survivors wandered about shocked and dazed, overwhelmed with what they had seen. Yet, there was no time to indulge

in these feelings, for we soon had to return to forced labor and the basic problem of daily survival.[79]

On 1 November 1943, soon after these deportations, the ghetto was transformed into a concentration camp by the SS. However, according to Oleiski, 'we inmates continued to call it "Ghetto"'.[80]

During the winter of 1943-44 the school suffered a series of devastating blows as their community was reduced daily due to illness and deportations. However, in February 1944 the school had 440 pupils and had, in a desperate attempt to save the lives of the young, started accepting children as young as 8-years-old. Oleiski explains how they would issue the younger children with work cards claiming they were 12-years-old, thus hoping to save them. He writes how mothers would accost him in the street having dressed their children in adult clothing: 'Mothers, pointing out how mature their children looked, begged me to take their young into the school and issue them cards. "Save my child!" they would plead.'[81]

On 27 March 1944 a further 1,000 people were sent to Auschwitz, including 700 children. The news that this further group were to be deported sent many people into hiding. The day after the transport left the ghetto the SS returned to the ghetto in order to find more people to deport. Their deportation lists did not tally so they were convinced people were in hiding. They searched the ghetto with dogs, finding a further 300 people, including 200 children. They were all taken from the ghetto and shot at the Ninth Fort later that day. Out of these additional 200 children who were killed in the 'Children's Action', fifty-four had been pupils at the ORT school. The scale of these deportations and the fact that they had taken so many children sent shock waves through the ghetto. Parents were panic-stricken, and, in an attempt to ease their anxiety, those running the vocational school decided to move it inside the confines of the adult workshops in April 1944.

Throughout its time in operation, the vocational school in the Kovno Ghetto was subject to random visits by the SS. The purpose behind these visits was to ascertain whether the young employed there were sufficiently useful to the war effort. As the unwanted visitors approached the classrooms and workshops,

> a pupil on duty would issue a warning agreed in advance and all the children, even the 9 year old ones, would begin to use their

sharpeners and wield their hammers vigorously. The children always wore a serious expression and they behaved like disciplined soldiers. Whenever the hangman left the workshops, they would come to me 'Well, Mr. Oleiski, how did this impress them? Were they satisfied today? Will they leave our workshops alone?'[82]

The final liquidation of the ghetto began on 8 July 1944 and, 'Of the hundreds of pupils in the vocational school of the ghetto, only close to twenty survived'.[83] The remaining Jews of Kovno were taken to various concentration camps in Germany. Elly Gotz elaborates: 'I worked in the Ghetto Fachschule till the very end, when the Ghetto was liquidated and the remaining people were sent to Germany in cattle cars – the women to Stutthof and the men to Dachau Concentration Camp.'[84]

Although the loss and devastation caused by the deportations from the ghettos in eastern Europe was immense and to some extent incalculable, the important part played by the ORT workers inside the ghettos should not be overshadowed. As stated by Wischnitzer in the *ORT Economic Review* of 1948,

> The ORT ideology lived, as in Warsaw and Vilna, until the last dying gasp of the Ghetto. To know a skill, to be a worker, or even a master craftsmen often helped young Jewish people to save their lives from a dreadful death, or at least to prolong life to have a chance of surviving Nazism.[85]

Wherever and whenever possible ORT protected the Jews inside the ghettos of Eastern Europe. It cast its net as wide as possible, hoping to save as many people from starving in the ghettos and from being deported east. As was often the case in both the ghettos and the concentration camps, the main emphasis was on trying to save the young. In the case of the ghettos, this was an almost impossible task as they, together with the elderly, were among the first to be included on any transports east. However, in the Warsaw Ghetto, Gourman recalls how, 'one has to remember that during all that period there was not a single incident of anybody being taken away from ORT and deported to Treblinka'.[86]

NOTES

1. Rachel Gourman, 'In the Ghetto of Warsaw: ORT Under the German Occupation', in WOA, d07a008: N. Scharf (ed.), *Material and Memoirs Chapters for the History of ORT* (Geneva: World ORT Union, 1955), p.51.
2. WOA, d07a001a: Mark Wischnitzer, *The World ORT Union and the American ORT Federation: A Study Made under the Auspices of the Budget Research Committee* (New York: Council of Jewish Federations and Welfare Funds, Inc., July 1943), p.23.
3. For information on Vichy see Richard Vinen, *The Unfree French: Life Under the Occupation* (London: Allen Lane, 2006); Peter Jonathan Davies, *France and the Second World War: Occupation, Collaboration and Resistance* (London: Routledge, 2001); Julian Jackson, *France: the Dark Years, 1940-1944* (Oxford: Oxford University Press, 2001); Donna F. Ryan, *The Holocaust and the Jews of Marseilles: the Enforcement of anti-Semitic Policies in Vichy France* (Urbana, IL: University of Illinois Press, 1996).
4. Wischnitzer, *World ORT Union*, p.14.
5. Ibid., p.15.
6. Ibid., p.25.
7. See WOA, d00a014c: Vladimir Akivisson, 'ORT's Work in the French Internment Camps', in Norah N. Scharf (ed.), *The Fateful Years 1938-43* (Geneva: World ORT Union, 1979-80) , pp.57-63.
8. Ibid., p.58.
9. Wischnitzer, *The World ORT Union*, p.25.
10. Jack Rader, *By the Skill of Their Hands* (Geneva: World ORT, 1970), p.53.
11. Leon Shapiro, *The History of ORT: A Jewish Movement for Social Change* (New York: Schocken Books, 1980), p.194.
12. Blaustein in Wischnitzer, *The World ORT Union*, p.i.
13. Ibid., p.ii.
14. Wischnitzer, *The World ORT Union*, p.13.
15. Blaustein in Wischnitzer, *The World ORT Union*, p.iii.
16. Wischnitzer, *The World ORT Union*, p.7.
17. Ibid., p.24.
18. Shapiro, *The History of ORT*, p.195.
19. Ibid., p.194.
20. Ibid.
21. For more information on Shanghai during the Second World War see Berl Falbaum, *Shanghai Remembered: Stories of Jews who Escaped to Shanghai from Nazi Europe* (Michigan: Momentum Books, 2005); Sigmund Tobias, Michael Berenbaum, *Strange Haven: A Jewish Childhood in Wartime Shanghai* (Urbana, IL: University of Illinois Press, 1999); James R. Ross, *Escape to Shanghai: A Jewish Community in China* (New York: Free Press, 1994).
22. Wischnitzer, *World ORT Union*, p.27.
23. WOA, d02a001b: M. Rechenberg, *ORT Shanghai: Society for Promotion of Handicrafts and Agriculture for Jews in East Asia*, p.26.
24. Ibid., p.27.
25. For more on the New York school see Shapiro, *The History of ORT*, p.226.
26. Lucy S. Dawidowicz, *The War Against the Jews 1933-45* (London: Penguin, 1990), p.287.
27. Raul Hilberg, *Patterns of Jewish Leadership in Nazi Europe 1933-1945. Proceedings of the Third Yad Vashem International Historical Conference - April 1977* (Jerusalem: Yad Vashem, 1979), p.38.
28. Isaiah Trunk, *Judenrat: The Jewish Councils in Eastern Europe Under Nazi Occupation* (Lincoln, NE: University of Nebraska Press, 1972), p.xli.
29. Ibid.
30. Wischnitzer, *The World ORT Union*, p.23.
31. Trunk, *Judenrat*, p.33.
32. Ibid.
33. Ibid.
34. Trunk, *Patterns of Jewish Leadership in Nazi Europe 1933-1945*. Proceedings of the Third

Yad Vashem International Historical Conference, April 1977 (Jerusalem: Yad Vashem, 1979), pp.24-5.
35. Gourman, 'In the Ghetto of Warsaw', p.51.
36. Ibid., p.52.
37. Ibid.
38. Shapiro, *The History of ORT*, p.192.
39. Gourman, 'In the Ghetto of Warsaw', p.53.
40. Abraham Lewent, USHMM, survivor testimony - Warsaw Ghetto.
41. WOA, d00a014c: Rachel Gourman, 'ORT's Activities in Nazi Dominated Europe', in Norah N. Scharf (ed.), *The Fateful Years 1938-43* (Geneva: World ORT Union, 1979-80), p.71.
42. Ibid.
43. Ibid.
44. Bernard Goldstein, *Five Years in the Warsaw Ghetto* (Edinburgh: AK Press, 2005), p.72.
45. Ibid., p.23.
46. Trunk, *Judenrat*, pp.200-1.
47. Ibid.
48. Ibid.
49. Eduard Warszawski, article from the *Jewish Chronicle*, 5 November 1943, p.11.
50. Ibid.
51. Gourman, 'In the Ghetto of Warsaw', p.53.
52. Rader, *By the Skill of their Hands*, p.63.
53. Joel Elkes, *Values, Beliefs and Survival: Dr. Elkhanan Elkes and the Kovno Ghetto: a Memoir* (London: Vale, 1997), p.36.
54. Ibid.
55. Ibid., p.68.
56. I. Posner (ed.), *Jacob Oleiski: A Man's Work* (Israel: ORT Israel, 1986), p.41.
57. Ibid.
58. Ibid.
59. Ibid.
60. Ibid., p.42.
61. Elly Gotz, 19 March 2007, 'My Story of how ORT influenced my life'. Personal testimony sent to author.
62. Posner, *Jacob Oleiski*, p.45.
63. Ibid., p.47.
64. Gotz, 'My Story'.
65. Elkes, *Values, Beliefs and Survival*, p.71.
66. Avraham Tory, *Surviving the Holocaust - The Kovno Ghetto Diary*. Introduction by Martin Gilbert (London: Pimlico, 1991), p.134.
67. Ibid.
68. Ibid., p.140.
69. See similar organisations and cultural havens in other ghettos - especially Theresienstadt. For more on this see R. Rovit and A. Goldfarb (eds), *Theatrical Performances during the Holocaust: Texts, Documents, Memoirs* (Baltimore, MD: John Hopkins University Press, 1999). Also see Elena Makarova, Sergei Makarov and Victor Kuperman, *University over the Abyss: The Story behind 489 Lectures and 2309 Lecturers in K2 Theresienstadt 1942-1944* (Jerusalem: Verba, 2000).
70. Posner, *Jacob Oleiski*, p.44.
71. Ibid.
72. Tory, *Surviving the Holocaust*, pp.307-8.
73. Ibid., p.308.
74. Ibid., p.307.
75. Ibid.
76. Ibid.
77. Ibid., p.309.
78. Ibid., p.447.
79. Posner, *Jacob Oleiski*, p.45.

80. Ibid.
81. Ibid., p.46.
82. Ibid., p.47.
83. Ibid.
84. Gotz, 'My Story'.
85. Wischnitzer, *The World ORT Union*, p.23.
86. Gourman, 'In the Ghetto of Warsaw', p.51.

The Liberation of the Concentration Camps and the Arrival of the ORT Missions, 1945-46

> Whenever I spend time in training workshops or visit vocational classes and look into the eyes of former concentration camp inmates, my faith grows stronger and stronger ... Indeed it is only through productive, creative work that we can lessen our anger at having lost so many years.[1]

The end of the Second World War left Europe with an immense set of challenges. But it also allowed World ORT Union to fulfil its mission like never before. As reported in the *ORT Economic Review*,

> Perhaps at no other time and at no other place in the world have the objectives of ORT been so dramatically demonstrated and justified as in the DP camps in Germany. Established and organized amid the ruins of a broken, bombed-out land, for men, women and children who had gone through seven years of hell – people without a country, still hated by the Germans who had persecuted them, still harbouring one major desire, that of getting away from the scene of their misery and getting on, somewhere, somehow, to a happier land.[2]

Thousands of Jews were transported from the ghettos to the extermination camps of Auschwitz-Birkenau, Treblinka, Sobibor, Belzec and

Majdanek where they were killed on arrival. In addition to these, hundreds of thousands died slow deaths at the many concentration and slave labour camps that covered Nazi-occupied Europe.

When the Allied troops advanced across Europe they began to uncover the horrific truth about the Nazi concentration camps and the mass murder of the Jews. Thousands of prisoners were discovered by the Allies inside Germany after they had been forced to march west from the camps. Those being liberated were in an advanced stage of starvation and many were suffering from typhus and other infectious diseases.

Most of the concentration camps were liberated before the end of the war. The Soviet troops reached Majdanek, near Lublin in Poland, as early as July 1944. In an attempt to hide the evidence, the Nazis destroyed many of the camps – blowing up buildings, setting fire to paperwork and killing or evacuating large numbers of prisoners. In addition to Majdanek, the Soviets also uncovered the sites of former extermination camps at Belzec, Sobibor and Treblinka during the summer of 1944.

On 27 January 1945, the Soviets liberated the vast complex of Auschwitz-Birkenau. Only a few survivors remained, as most prisoners had been forced west on death marches as the Russians approached. In *The Drowned and the Saved,* Primo Levi describes how he felt when he first saw the Russians enter the camp and how the Russians reacted to what they witnessed inside Auschwitz-Birkenau:

> They did not greet us, nor did they smile; they seemed oppressed not only by pity but by a confused restraint, which sealed their mouths, and kept their eyes fastened on the funereal scene. It was the same shame which we knew so well, which submerged us after the selections, and every time we had to witness or undergo an outrage: the shame the Germans never knew, the shame which the just man experiences when confronted by a crime committed by another.[3]

Although the retreating Nazis destroyed much of the infrastructure of Auschwitz, some substantial evidence was left behind. The personal belongings of tens of thousands of victims were found by the Soviets on arrival – the suitcases, the shoes and the masses of human hair of those killed all told their own stories.

After Auschwitz the Soviets went on to liberate Stutthof, Ravensbruck and Sachsenhausen. The final camp they liberated was Theresienstadt on 10 May 1945. Edith Kramer who was liberated in Theresienstadt explains that for many, liberation was not the joyful experience they had longed for: 'But hardly had the first excitement passed than it appeared that the energy used so far for self-preservation would be necessary for a new struggle ... Many felt not up to the new struggle, and even amongst my four room-mates two committed suicide.'[4]

In addition to the Soviets, the U.S. and British forces were also responsible for liberating several concentration camps. The Americans liberated Buchenwald, Dachau and Mauthausen. Col. Edmund M. Fortunoff was a First Lieutenant in the 65th Infantry Division of Patton's Third Army and was present at the liberation of Mauthausen. He recalls:

> The thing that, I think, impressed all of us immediately was the horrible physical condition of most of the inmates ... most of them in very, very bad shape. Some of them actually looked almost like living skeletons ... I would estimate their average weight might have been probably eighty-five, ninety pounds.[5]

Buchenwald was liberated on 11 April 1945, only a few days after the Nazis began to evacuate the camp. On arrival the American troops found more than 20,000 prisoners. Dr Harold Herbst describes what they found on entering Buchenwald:

> And as I walked by a little window that probably was one foot square or thereabouts, I heard a voice and I turned around and I saw a living skeleton talk to me ... Did you ever talk to a skeleton that talked back? ... And later on I saw mounds of these living ... I mean these skeletons that the Germans left behind them.[6]

On 15 April 1945, just four days after the Americans liberated Buchenwald, elements of the 11th Armoured Division of the British Army entered the concentration camp at Bergen-Belsen.

Hagit Lavsky describes what was found when the camp was liberated: 'Entering Bergen-Belsen, the British troops found two camps. In Camp One there were 45,000 people, most of them barely alive, and some 10,000 corpses piled in the yards. The 15,000 inmates of Camp Two were in better shape, having only recently arrived at Belsen.'[7]

Lieutenant-Colonel R.I.G. Taylor, Commanding Officer of the 63rd Anti-Tank Regiment recorded his first impressions on entering the camp:

> A great number of them were little more than living skeletons with haggard yellowish faces ... many of them were without shoes and wore only socks or stockings ... There were men and women lying in heaps on both sides of the tracks. Others were walking slowly and aimlessly about – a vacant expression on their starved faces.[8]

Alan Zimm from Kolo in Poland was liberated in Belsen. He recalls the moment when the prisoners first realised that they were 'free': 'The people were jumping and hugging and kissing. And everybody was running to the jeep ... And still people did not believe. There were a lot of people still afraid.'[9]

In order to assess the community that was liberated in Belsen in April 1945 it is important to understand how the Nazis used the camp and who had been sent there and why. Bergen-Belsen was first established in 1940 in the Hannover area of Germany, 11 miles north of the town of Celle as a prisoner-of-war camp. Initially it housed Belgian and French POWs but after 1941 it also was home to Soviet POWs. On 4 February 1943 the Nazis began discussing the option of exchanging prisoners and on 30 April 1943 SS Reichführer Heinrich Himmler gave the order to set up a 'residence camp', inside the POW camp at Belsen, as a facility for exchanging prisoners. The idea was that individuals imprisoned there could be swapped for German citizens held hostage or interned in foreign countries – very few were actually exchanged. On 29 June 1944, the Nazis allowed 220 prisoners to leave for Palestine in exchange for German citizens interned by the British while on 6 December 1944 approximately 1,600 Hungarian Jews were sent to Switzerland in return for money.

Until March 1944 the conditions in Belsen had been of a slightly better standard than in other camps. However on 27 March 1944, Belsen became the collection point for prisoners from other concentration camps who were deemed unfit for work. These sick and injured prisoners were housed in the 'hospital camp' at Belsen. When the hospital camp became too crowded the women were removed and placed in the 'tent camp'. This women's camp was set up on 7 June 1944. Other areas of Belsen designated for specific purposes were the 'neutrals camp' for several hundred Jews who were citizens of neutral countries and the Hungarian camp which was built in July 1944 for 1,600 Hungarian Jews.

In December 1944 the Nazis decided that Belsen should become a fully functioning concentration camp. This decision was marked with the appointment of Hauptsturmführer Josef Kramer as camp Commandant on 2 December 1944. Kramer replaced Adolf Haas as Commandant and camp conditions deteriorated fast. The situation was made worse by the arrival of thousands of prisoners from the east.

As the Allied forces advanced in late 1944 and early 1945 the concentration camps were evacuated and forced on death marches heading west. These death marches brought thousands of prisoners to Belsen. In February 1945 the camp housed approximately 22,000 prisoners but by 15 April 1945 the population had reached 60,000.

In addition to the 60,000 prisoners who were liberated at Belsen on 15 April 1945, the liberators discovered the bodies of thousands of unburied corpses. A further 10,000 survivors died soon after liberation. As soon as the camp had been evacuated, the buildings were burned down to avoid the further spread of disease. During its four year existence approximately 50,000 persons died in Belsen.

As soon as the British troops were established inside the camp they handed over all relief work to Brigadier H.L. Glyn-Hughes, the Deputy Director of Medical Services for the British Second Army. Glyn-Hughes was faced with the enormous job of feeding and housing the surviving prisoners. The first deliveries of food and fresh water arrived on 16 April, only one day after liberation but due to their advanced state of starvation, thousands of prisoners continued to die. The average death rate continued at 300–400 people a day. On arrival in the camp the British had discovered 13,000 bodies and during the following month a further 14,000 people died. The first distribution of food did not bring relief but further deaths. The survivors' bodies were in such appalling condition that their weakened digestive systems could not handle the sudden intake of food.

The days following the liberation were chaotic and it was vital that order be established in the camp as soon as possible. According to Hagit Lavsky, people not only died of starvation after liberation but many were also killed. She writes:

> Liberation was scarcely felt on the day the British arrived, and the shooting, the murders continued as if nothing had happened ... Over the next three days, dozens of starving prisoners were shot, mainly by the Hungarian soldiers who guarded the kitchen and manned the watchtowers under British supervision.[10]

It took two weeks to bury the corpses found at Belsen. During this time all survivors were transferred in groups of 1,000 to the nearby military camp – Camp III – which was approximately three miles from the former concentration camp. The transfer of the prisoners was completed on 19 May and on 21 May, the remaining barracks of Camp I were set on fire:

> the main camp of the Belsen complex was evacuated and burned down a little over a month after the British Army moved in. The internees were moved to smaller camps at the *Wehrmacht* barracks, a mile or so down the road. This new site, named Höhne by the British authorities after a nearby German village, eventually became a centre for Jewish displaced persons.[11]

Once the Second World War had ended, the full extent of the devastation it had caused was laid bare. Vast expanses of land lay in ruins and the Jewish community of Eastern Europe was all but destroyed.

The Yalta Conference which was held between 4 and 11 February 1945 and the Potsdam Conference which ran from 17 July to 2 August 1945 were to decide the fate of Germany. The Allies divided the defeated Germany into four military zones of occupation. The British zone was in the Northwest, the French in the Southwest, the American in the Southeast and the Russian to the Northeast. Eastern Prussia and Silesia were ceded to Poland while Konigsberg in East Prussia was annexed to the Soviet Union. The Germans living in these territories, terrified of the Soviet forces, fled westwards.

The Potsdam Conference also decided on the movement of 7 million Germans from Poland, the Soviet Union, the Sudetenland, Hungary, Romania and Yugoslavia. Although the decision to move all these people was made in August 1945, many did not relocate until the 1950s. In total, approximately 12 million ethnic Germans were forced to leave eastern Europe.

The four occupation zones fell under the authority of the Allied Control Council. Each country ran their own sections but would consult on issues which affected Germany as a whole. Berlin, which was located in the Soviet zone was further divided into four sections. The sections occupied by the Western powers became West Berlin and the Soviet section became East Berlin.

After nearly six years of war, the German infrastructure was in ruins.

According to Reilly, '[It] had been devastated by the war: in the British zone in May 1945, only 650 out of 8,000 miles of railway track were open to traffic; the roads were badly damaged; and the Rhine and the canals were almost all out of use.[12] In addition to the obvious task of rebuilding the German infrastructure, the Allies placed huge emphasis on the 'denazification' of Germany and of the German people. Adding to the allies' challenge was the presence of hundreds of thousands of DPs.[13]

The winter of 1946 was harsh, further damaging the crumbling European economy and postponing reconstruction. Soon it became clear that without substantial financial input, the economy of what had been German-occupied Europe would not survive. On 5 June 1947, Secretary of State George C. Marshall spoke on this subject at Harvard University. This speech became the foundation of the Marshall Plan, guaranteeing financial aid to Europe. Marshall said: 'I need not tell you gentlemen that the world situation is very serious'.[14] He continued:

> The truth of the matter is that Europe's requirements for the next 3 or 4 years of foreign food and other essential products – principally from America – are so much greater than her present ability to pay that she must have substantial additional help, or face economic, social, and political deterioration of a very grave character.[15]

Marshall argued that such deterioration, aside from causing further devastation in Europe, would not be in the interests of the United States. The outcome of Marshall's speech at Harvard was that America offered Europe $20 billion on the understanding that the European countries decided together how this money was to be used. Initially the Soviet Union was to be included in the plan but Stalin refused to take part. The plan was successful and by 1953 the US had pumped $13 billion into Europe and the economy was once again sustainable.

While the Americans invested in the European economy, the start of the Cold War in 1948 permanently changed the relationship between the occupying powers in Germany. The Soviets, who were against the US aid, withdrew from the four power set-up and initiated the Berlin blockade in March 1948. They blocked all access between Western Germany and west Berlin forcing the Western allies to airlift supplies to west Berlin for ten months until the blockade was eased.[16]

On 23 May 1949, the Federal Republic of Germany was established with Bonn as its capital. The new Republic covered the Western zones of occupation. In response to this and the introduction of a separate currency in the Western zones of occupation, the Soviets set-up the German Democratic Republic on 7 October 1949 claiming East Berlin as its capital. Berlin became a complex and divided city; West Berlin was completely enclosed by East Germany although its inhabitants were West German citizens. West Germany was allied with the United States of America, the UK and France. East Germany was occupied by, and later allied with, the Soviet Union.

Having liberated the concentration camps and set up the zones of occupation in Europe, the Allied Occupation forces realised they had to address the situation regarding the mass of refugees and DPs roaming war-torn Europe. According to Mark Wyman,

> Finding a solution to the DPs' plight became one of the major policy issues confronting the victorious Allies ... More than for most of the world's human population in 1945, the past guided and limited the present for the DPs.[17]

Wyman describes how the time spent in the concentration camps was to affect the survivors for the rest of their lives. He concludes: 'Some carried memories so searing that they would forever be unable to lead normal lives.'[18] Dr Paul Friedman, an American psychoanalyst working in the field of rehabilitation, claimed that the process of rehabilitation should be viewed as more than simply helping the individual: 'It is a project that has significance for the whole world; it is, indeed, a reassertion of our belief that the civilising forces in man may yet win to victory.'[19] It is this 'project' that will now be examined.

How were the Allied Occupational Forces to address this situation? Who was going to supply relief and aid to the thousands of displaced persons and where were they going to be housed? Before these questions could be answered the Allies first had to agree on who qualified for DP status and who was 'merely' a refugee. There was much disagreement on this matter.

As soon as the war had finished, the responsibility for all displaced persons was handed over to The United Nations Relief and Rehabilitation Administration (UNRRA). This had been created at a conference held at the White House on 9 November, 1943. Its goal was to give economic assistance to Europe after the Second World War and to help with the repatriation of refugees and displaced persons. The organisation came under the authority of the Supreme Headquarters of the Allied Expeditionary Forces (SHAEF) in Europe and had, during its four year term, three American directors. The first Director-General was Herbert Lehman, former Governor of New York. The second was Fiorello La Guardia who took over in March 1946 and in early 1947 Major General Lowell Ward became the third and final director.[20]

UNRRA was responsible for the repatriation of millions of refugees in 1945. In addition it managed hundreds of displaced persons camps in Germany, Italy and Austria. It provided healthcare to the DPs and was responsible for education and vocational training as well as running considerable cultural programmes. It oversaw the work of twenty-three voluntary aid agencies, including the Joint Distribution Committee (JDC), World ORT Union, and the Hebrew Immigrant Aid Society (HIAS). By the end of 1945, the various DP camps and the prominent agencies working within them, began to act independently of UNRRA and by 1947 UNRRA was taken over by the International Refugee Organization (IRO).[21] Although UNRRA had overseen the repatriation of hundreds of thousands of DPs, when the IRO took over there were still 643,000 displaced persons in Europe.

According to Reilly, 'By mid-1944 a DP Branch had been set up at SHAEF and as the Allies advanced, new assembly centres were established on the major transport routes to deal with the ensuing "crescendo of refugees"'.[22] By the summer of 1945 the situation was so extreme that the east and west occupational powers began to exchange their DPs in forced repatriations: 'exchange points were established on the British/Russian zonal border. SHAEF transports carried Russian DPs, formerly in western hands, over to the eastern zone and returned with West European DPs.[23]

From the very beginning, World ORT Union worked closely with UNRRA. As explained by Dr Lvovitch in his address, 'Work Done in the Western Hemisphere and Certain Other Countries', UNRRA from the outset had very similar goals to those of World ORT Union. He claimed, '[UNRRA] adopted the slogan which ORT had preached and practiced for so many decades, "help them to help themselves". It was only natural that we made every effort to cooperate with this organization, which at that time was headed by an old friend of ORT, Governor Herbert H. Lehman.'[24]

The early policy of the British and American occupational forces was to attempt to repatriate as many displaced people as possible. The idea that many DPs, especially Jews, would not want to return to their country of origin did not feature in this policy. As Reilly writes, 'The first premise of the Allied repatriation policy had been the belief that all liberated peoples in Europe desired to return home. The slow realisation that this was not the case for many forced the military to review their policies.'[25]

The situation for all the DPs in Europe was severe but, as described by Lavsky, 'For German Jews, the problem was compounded'.[26] She continues,

> Those who had been liberated from concentration camps were recognised as victims of the Nazis, but the liberated Jews, who were usually older and in worse health than their German counterparts, had no families to whom to return, no sources of income, and no special connections to assist them. In addition, there were some German Jews who had survived in their hometowns, without being deported. As such, they were not included in the 'victims' category and were treated as ordinary Germans.[27]

This final point is important as only those who had been through the camp system were compensated and given the status of 'displaced person' and 'victim'. This excluded all those who had managed to survive the war in hiding and who had also lost everything.

This distinction of who was 'German' and who was 'Jewish' was to cause problems for the authorities and considerable distress for the DPs. This difficulty had its origins in the British approach to the entire DP situation. It was the British policy to prioritise nationality over ethnicity, race and religion, causing the Jewishness of the DPs to be overlooked. Lavsky explains how the British, 'adopted a policy whereby the Jews were treated just like all the others – in terms of their nationalities – and this was true even in respect to German Jews'.[28]

The British decided that all DPs should be housed according to nationality, irrespective of ethnicity, race or religion. This approach was to cause huge problems for the Jewish DPs who often found themselves living side by side those who only months before were attempting to kill them.

The rationale behind the British policy was that the Nazis had persecuted the Jews because they saw them as being ethnically and racially different and inferior, and, if the British were to categorise the Jews on racial grounds, they too would be open to charges of discrimination. The British claimed they were also anxious not to cause further antisemitism by giving the Jews 'preferential' treatment. 'It was acknowledged that the Jews had suffered in the concentration camps but then so had other groups. The idea of special treatment was a notion unacceptable to British liberal monoculturalism.'[29] Reilly describes how the firm line of the British policy 'sanctioned further Jewish suffering'.[30] This was compounded when some concentration camp survivors from Axis countries were classed as enemy nationals rather than Jews who had suffered at the hands of the Nazis.

The British refused to change their policy insisting that they would not class the Jews as a separate race, though they failed to address the underlying problem. Reilly explains, 'It is clear that the claim of the Jewish DPs for a distinctive handling of their situation in Germany was not based on a claim that they were a separate race, but on the fact that because designated as a race, they had suffered particular persecution'.[31]

Lavsky sees the British policy towards the Jewish DPs as an expression of their latent antisemitism concluding,

> The policies in the British zone were really a continuation of deep-seated animosity toward the Jews ... total disregard for the unique sufferings of the Jews under the Nazis was a subtle expression of their feelings, which had found expression in British war and immigration policy since the 1930s. The policy toward the Jews in occupied Germany was just more of the same.[32]

The British policy only exaggerated the feelings of loss and exclusion felt by the Jews in the British zone of occupation.

Mark Wyman examines the various types of accommodation that were available for the refugees and DPs, identifying three primary types of housing. First, old military structures which needed converting in order to house the refugees. Secondly, former slave labour and concentration camps and thirdly, domestic houses. Within this third category entire villages were made over to refugee housing, such as the village of Meerbeck in Germany. In larger urban areas, sections of cities were cleared and the DPs and refugees were housed there. In Salzburg, Austria, an area of refugee housing became known as 'New Palestine'. According to Wyman, 'Most displaced persons knew at least two of these basic types intimately, plus numerous variations that defied classification'.[33]

Desperate for assistance with housing the refugees, the occupying forces turned to UNRRA.

> Official responsibility for administering DP camps in the American Zone of Germany was handed over to the UNRRA on 1 October 1945. By the end of the year the organization was running 227 centres in the western zones of Germany and 25 in Austria; this increased by June 1947 to 762 DP centres; 8 in Italy, 21 in Austria, 416 in the U.S. Zone of Germany, 272 in the British Zone, and 45 in the French Zone. The UNRRA workload was still increasing.[34]

An average sized DP centre housed approximately 3,000 people and had a team of 13 UNRRA workers positioned there. A standard thirteen-person UNRRA team consisted of a director and a deputy, a doctor and nurse, a cook, a stenographer, two welfare officers, two drivers, a supply officer, a mess officer and a warehouse officer. Once the decision to house the non-repatriable DPs according to nationality had been made, they were divided and placed in country specific camps. Belsen became one of the main centres for non-repatriables. It was also to become one of the exclusively Jewish DP centres. Others in this category were: Landsberg, Feldafing and Föhrenwald. These centres were all set up in former German military barracks.

Once inside the camps it became obvious that the British policy could not work and that it was vital to separate the Jewish DPs from the non-Jews. As Angelika Königseder and Juliane Wetzel explain,

> The Jews' sharing of quarters with non-Jews caused major psychological problems for the Jewish survivors, especially since many non-Jewish DPs made no secret of their anti-Semitism and worked to make life in the camps as difficult as possible for the Jews, who were in a weakened state and desperately trying to find out whether any of their relatives were alive.[35]

Having examined the DP policy of the British forces and how the DPs were divided and housed, it is important to look at the experiences of the DPs themselves. Many of the issues that had plagued those imprisoned in the concentration camps continued to trouble and endanger the DPs:

Initial camp activities for incoming DPs centred on immediate dangers – protecting the larger group from infectious diseases and satisfying the individual's hunger. The UNRRA camp reception process began with registration, then shifted immediately to delousing, medical inspection, the first meal, and finally giving out soap, blankets, and cooking and eating equipment.[36]

Conditions in some of the DP centres and camps were initially appalling and supplies in short demand, but by the spring of 1946 UNRRA had stemmed the flow of infectious diseases and the threat was substantially reduced.

Although there was more food available in the DP camps than there had been in the concentration camps, it remained in short supply. Wyman comments that, 'A U.S. Army camp director reported that over half the complaints he received in his Italian camp centred on food – its quality, quantity, and serving size (servers were accused of giving more to members of their own nationality).'[37]

Clothing also proved contentious. There was little available and many DPs still wore their camp uniforms or were offered the clothing of former concentration camp guards. Wyman describes how, 'An Estonian recalled that he wore but one pair of shoes for the first three years after the war, and the touring UNRRA director discovered that leaflets distributed to refugees were not being read – they were used to patch clothing.'[38] The fact that the DPs were hungry, poorly clothed and inadequately housed paled into insignificance next to the pressing and relentless mission of locating relatives and loved ones. In their weakened state and with little or no transport available, survivors travelled vast distances in an attempt to discover living relatives. 'Walls all over Europe were now covered with messages as wives sought husbands, parents sought children, nephews sought uncles.'[39]

For many survivors, liberation did not bring feelings of freedom and relief. On the contrary, it brought with it the horrific realisation of the loss they had suffered and many were fearful of what lay ahead. How could they imagine a future without their loved ones? Shortly after liberation, having been placed in a DP camp, one concentration camp survivor remembers asking herself, 'Why am I alive? Why am I alone? Maybe it's a punishment?' While another states: 'It's better to be a conquered German than a liberated Jew'.[40] Königseder and Wetzel comment on the post-liberation trauma:

> After liberation, their pain and suffering were far from over. Living with the past proved to be extremely difficult and in some cases impossible. Many freed prisoners became depressed and had nightmares. Uncertainty during the weeks following liberation was an additional burden ... Would they, like some non-Jewish displaced persons, be forcibly repatriated and sent back to countries that were no longer home to them? What was the fastest way for them to obtain information about their families? Where would they live and where would they get food and clothing in the midst of this chaos, inside a country destroyed by war?[41]

These feelings of fear and dread brought about by the liberation, and the difficulty of making a transition from survivor to displaced person, are backed up in the testimony of many survivors. Vera Schiff, who was liberated in Theresienstadt writes, 'The first post-war year was the single most unhappy one for me ... I was gathering information about the extermination camps and accumulating a long, hopeless list of murdered relatives.'[42]

Although the physical needs such as housing, food and clothing were to be met fairly soon, the psychological scars proved much harder to heal. The feelings of loss that accompanied the survivors did not go away and it was only after several months and in some cases years that they were able to contemplate their future. The relief agencies played a helpful part in this process. Desperate to do something to keep them busy and make them feel useful, the DPs turned in their hundreds and thousands to the agencies that offered them any form of education.

World ORT Union's work in the British zone of Germany began in the former concentration camp of Bergen-Belsen during December 1945 and by 1946 a plan had been drawn up to train 3,000 DPs. Mr Ambrose Vear was put in charge of ORT's work in the British zone which covered five primary sites. These were located at Belsen, Hanover, Northeim, Ahlem and Neustadt.

The site at Belsen was the largest and best equipped out of the five. Within a few months of its establishment, ORT Belsen had 303 pupils and offered twelve different courses. These consisted of machine shop, auto mechanics, carpentry, electric engineering, building and plumbing. There were also several courses which covered clothing and design, these included men's clothing, dressmaking, corsetry, shoemaking, men's underwear and cap making. In addition to all these there was also a dental school at Belsen.[43]

In Hanover there were two centres which offered a more limited training programme with a choice of six subjects. The Ahlem centre was dedicated to agriculture and was aimed at those who planned to emigrate to Palestine. By May 1947 it had fifty-seven pupils, all of whom were DPs. The school at Neustadt was designed for maritime trades, whereas the school at Northeim focused on dressmaking, carpentry and dentistry.

Prior to examining ORT's work inside the DP camp at Belsen it is important to explain how the liberated concentration camp of Bergen-Belsen became the Belsen-Höhne DP camp. Belsen was divided into four areas: Camp I, the former concentration camp, had been entirely emptied by 21 May 1945 and was burned down. Camp II had been used as an overflow facility by the Nazis when Camp I was too crowded. Camp III contained an SS training school and SS housing, and Camp IV was home to the SS officers. The new DP facility was located across camps II, III and IV. The DPs were not to be housed in the old concentration camp barracks but in the former Wehrmacht and SS buildings.

The DP camp at Belsen provides interesting insight into the experience of survivors in the immediate post-war years. 'The history of Belsen in the five years after the war is the history of this Jewish remnant, the community they established and the difficulties they encountered.'[44]

More Jews were liberated at Belsen than in any other western camp. Reilly explains, 'Indeed by September 1945 the great majority of internees were Jews of Polish origin. There were a number of Jews of other nationalities and also a contingent of non-Jewish Poles; the latter lived in a separate section of the DP camp.'[45]

By the summer of 1945 there were approximately 10,000 to 12,000 Jews in Belsen, constituting two thirds of the camp population and making it the largest community in the British zone. This community almost unanimously refused to be repatriated, and, as a result was declared to be stateless. According to Lavsky, 'There was an exceptionally high ratio of women; and of youngsters and children – about 500 who apparently were brought there just before liberation, from Buchenwald and Theresienstadt'.[46]

The major concerns facing the Belsen population continued to be those of food, clothing and housing. In addition, however, was an overriding sense that they were still not free. They had been released from the concentration camps, but remained in cramped conditions, often under guard behind high walls and barbed wire enclosures. Reilly explains that, 'The general level of supplies and basic necessities in

Belsen improved greatly over the course of 1945. Yet, conditions in the Displaced Persons centre were generally substandard throughout most of the five years of its existence.'[47]

Although shortages continued throughout the DP period, what seemed to bother the DPs most was this lack of personal freedom. Often unable to leave DP camps when they wanted, the DPs were constantly reminded of their time in the concentration camps, and indeed, Belsen was surrounded by Polish guards.

In the days immediately following liberation the survivors in Belsen were quick to form self-help groups – these were strictly divided by nationality. These national groups identified their primary goal as a return to their country of origin. The Jewish DPs stood in opposition to this and to the British policy on DPs as they had no desire to return home.

The Jewish DPs in Belsen were politically active and were quick to organise themselves. By the end of April 1945 Josef Rosensaft, a 34-year-old Polish Jew, had set up a committee to represent Jewish interests in Belsen. Joanne Reilly discusses the success of this early committee. She claims it was able to achieve so much because its members were in relatively good health and had a clear plan for their future. 'These factors enabled them to serve as the leadership of the weak and exhausted survivors, to offer a vision for the future and to establish an organisational model.'[48]

Rosensaft's committee was Zionist in outlook but represented all political parties among the Jewish population of Belsen. The committee was committed to Zionist goals, a desire to unite the Jewish survivors across the British zone of occupation and to the presence of a thriving cultural and educational life within the DP camps.

The first Congress of the Jewish survivors in the British zone was held in Belsen between the 25 and 27 September 1945. It was at this Congress that the Central Committee of Liberated Jews was formed in order to represent the interests of all Jews in the British zone of occupation. Josef Rosensaft, due to his earlier work on the provisional committee, was the natural choice for President.[49] According to Lavsky:

> The Congress set the stage and gave direction to the survivors' struggle for freedom, which was closely bound up with the Zionist struggle for independence. On both fronts Britain was the source of antagonism, as the occupation authority in Germany, and the mandatory power in Palestine.[50]

Major C.C.K. Rickford of the British Policy Division covered the Congress in a confidential report. Of particular interest to the authorities were the sections of the conference which dealt with British Policy towards the DPs and with Palestine. Major Rickford records, 'Despite a few enthusiastic anti-Zionists the meeting was overwhelmingly in favour of the opening of Palestine to such as wished to go there, and of immediate segregation into Jewish Camps.'[51] Rickford's report concluded, 'Pending a statement of policy on the Palestine question, it is quite certain that a good deal of agitation may be expected regarding the conditions and treatment of Jewish DPs.'[52] The British authorities kept a close eye on the work of Rosensaft and refused to officially recognise the Committee of Liberated Jews. As the Committee was openly dedicated to the Zionist cause, the British could not recognise it without legitimising their aims.

Soon after the liberation, the British decided that they should change the name of the Belsen camp. Reilly explains, 'The name 'Bergen-Belsen' was a useful publicity tool in itself, a detail which did not escape the Central Committee. In June 1945 the British authorities, having burned down the main Belsen camp, decided to call the new Displaced Persons' centre Höhne Camp.'[53] This change in name was deeply resented by the Jewish Committee at Belsen who, 'did not want to sever connections with the name ... Höhne meant nothing to anybody. If they were not to be forgotten, the Jewish Committee knew they had to keep the name of Belsen alive.'[54]

One of the early achievements of the Central Committee of Liberated Jews was securing separate barrack accommodation for Jewish DPs inside Belsen. Contrary to their policy of housing DPs by nationality, the British issued a directive on 30 November 1945 to allow separate housing just for the Jewish DPs.[55] They had been pushed towards this decision by Rosensaft and his committee in addition to the American authorities and the publication of the Harrison Report.[56]

The 'Jewish Congress' took place between 25 and 27 September and it was here that it was decided that the young were in desperate need of education and vocational training and that a school should be established within the confines of the former camp.[57] The 'Resolutions' of the Congress stated: 'This congress urges that opportunities be created for training the survivors for productive life in Palestine.'[58]

> Education in Belsen was felt to be of crucial importance and a great deal of attention was given to it. The first school, in fact, was

established just six weeks after the liberation of the camp. The children were classed not according to age or ability but according to their first language.[59]

It was not only the children who needed to fill the gaps in their education. The adolescent and adult communities were also in desperate need of education and stimulation. It was primarily the 17-25 year olds that were in need of training.

In November 1945, Dr Lvovitch, by then Chairman of World ORT Union and the man responsible for the DP programme, made an agreement between World ORT Union and UNRRA for vocational schools to be set up wherever possible in order to aid the DPs. It was obvious from the beginning that the most urgent need was for tools and machinery, as well as raw materials. In order to help with distribution a central supply office was set up in Arolsen by Vladimir Grossman. Within days of being established, twenty-nine cases of tools and forty sewing machines were sent to Belsen.

While Lvovitch was running the DP programme from Paris, Syngalowski had the responsibility for other areas of World ORT Union's work including Eastern Europe which he oversaw from Geneva.[60]

In February 1946, a reporter for the Belsen newspaper, 'Unzer Stime' recorded that,

> My first visit was to the office of the School where a register was kept of 250 trainees aged between 13 and 35 ... As soon as the students became aware of the fact that a correspondent of the paper came along in order to acquaint himself with their work and achievements they surrounded me and begged of me to write to ORT and to ask them to send tools and machinery to help the students to make up for time lost in the Nazi Camps.[61]

Once established, Reilly claims that, 'The school was strongly backed by the Central Jewish Committee and by UNRRA as both bodies recognised not simply an educational opportunity but also a "potent instrument for real rehabilitation"'.[62]

World ORT Union's mission inside the DP camps was to equip the DPs for the future and Belsen was no exception. Not only were they equipping them with a new skill but with the confidence to imagine a future in which they could use it. The success of the ORT school was twofold: it tackled the immediate problems inside the camp, those of apathy and dissatisfaction, while also encouraging the survivors to face the future with hope as well as trepidation. On completion of any ORT course, the Belsen pupils received an ORT certificate which would prove to be a valuable document for those seeking to emigrate. It is interesting to note that in addition to equipping the students with useful skills, 'the instructors would find useful work to do in maintaining the camp and surroundings. The building of a wall around the cemetery of mass graves where Camp 1 had stood was one such project.'[63]

The ORT school made arrangements with skilled workers in Belsen who might act as instructors for them. It was decided that they would be paid later in a currency of their choice once they had settled in another country. For now, they were to receive higher rations.

Even though supplies were now being shipped to the training centres and ORT had sourced instructors nevertheless, to start with, pupils were scarce. More programmes were set up and slowly ORT began to attract the younger people in the camp. However, the instructors were still impeded due to lack of equipment. According to one source, 'In the first few months, adequate teaching could not be achieved for the simple reason that every-day requisites such as pencils, scissors, pins and needles were not available'.[64] However, progress was made and the courses expanded encouraging more and more young people to join them.

The students in Belsen and the other centres in the British zone were not the only ones to benefit from the teachings of World ORT Union. World ORT Union was also able to enter DP camps and establish courses in the US zone of occupation.

In the immediate post-war period there was no difference between the British and the American treatment of the Jews. All this was to change with the publication of the Harrison report. Earl G. Harrison was sent as President Truman's envoy to the DP camps during the summer of 1945. His mission was to assess the situation of the DPs. Harrison filed an interim report after having visited thirty DP camps in which he urged the US to recognise the unique position of the Jewish DPs. He suggested to Truman that he immediately allow 100,000 Jewish DPs to enter Palestine. Truman was quick to address the situation and contacted Attlee who flatly refused the request, insisting that Jewish immigration to Palestine remain at 1,500 a month.

The Harrison report was sufficiently damning to force the US to change its policy. The British, however, remained firm and did not alter their approach until several months later, insisting that the report did not accurately reflect life for the DPs in the British zone.

The Harrison report examined four specific areas. First, the current living conditions of the DPs in Austria and Germany; secondly, the needs of these DPs; thirdly, whether or not these needs were being met; and fourthly, where the DPs thought they might live in the future. In his covering letter, Harrison writes, 'As my report shows they [Jewish DPs] are in need of attention and help. Up to this point they have been 'liberated' more in a military sense than actually.'[65] He goes on to say that the Jewish survivors have not been given the attention they deserve. He concludes, 'they, who were in so many ways the first and worst victims of Nazism, are being neglected by their liberators'.[66]

In response to the Harrison Report, President Truman issued the following directive:

> The grave dislocation of populations in Europe resulting from the war has produced human suffering that the people of the United States cannot and will not ignore. This Government should take every possible measure to facilitate full immigration to the United States under existing quota laws.[67]

Reilly claims: 'There is no doubt that the Harrison Report was in part exaggerated and unfair to the military; to compare the Allied armies to the SS was unjustified. Nevertheless, for the first time a figure with political standing (the importance of the fact that he was a non-Jew should not be underestimated) had spoken to the Jews.'[68] On a second point she concludes: 'Neither was it entirely correct to claim that the Jews in Belsen were living in an ex-concentration camp. The concentration camp proper had been burned to the ground and the internees moved to the improved, if still grossly over-crowded, Panzer Training School barracks.'[69]

The Harrison Report called for a change in policy and could hardly be ignored by the British authorities. However, they chose not to accept its findings. The British government concluded: 'Mr. Harrison's report is not in accordance with the facts, at any rate as far as the British zone is concerned.'[70] The Harrison Report and the subsequent change in US policy was to shape the DP camps in the US zone of occupation.

Officially, World ORT Union's work in Germany did not start until November 1945 when Dr Lvovitch arrived in Munich from America. In

25 GMCRO: DPA 1934/8. ORT school at Landsberg Displaced Persons Camp, Germany, September 1945. From the Documentary Photographic Archive. Reproduced by kind permission of Greater Manchester County Record Office.

26 GMCRO: DPA 1934/16. ORT school at Landsberg Displaced Persons Camp, Germany, September 1945. From the Documentary Photographic Archive. Reproduced by kind permission of Greater Manchester County Record Office.

27 WOA: p00a039 Students of the ORT school in the liberated Bergen-Belsen concentration camp, 7 December 1947.

28 WOA: p04a001 Sewing course at the Bergen-Belsen DP camp, in the British zone of Germany, c.1947.

29 WOA: p04a002 Carpentry course at the Bergen-Belsen DP camp, in the British zone of Germany, c.1947.

30 WOA: p04a256 ORT School for Maritime Trades in Neustadt in the British Zone of Germany, 1947. Photography: Foto. A. Druvins.

31 WOA: p05a131 Sewing course at the Bergen-Belsen DP camp, in the British zone of Germany, 1947.

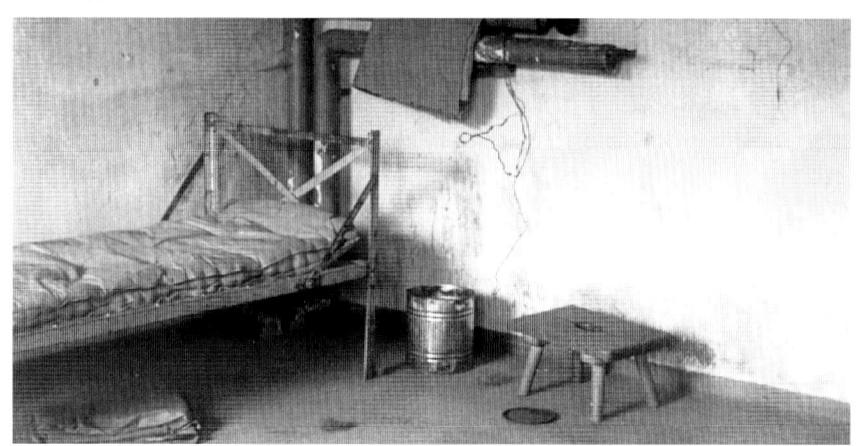

32 WOA: p06a070 ORT student's room in Neustadt, Germany, c.1947–48.

33 WOA: p06a087 Transporting equipment for ORT schools in Germany, c.1947–48.

34 WOA: p06a088 Mechanics workshop at the Bergen-Belsen DP camp, in the British zone of Germany, 1947.

35 WOA: p06a095 Typewriter repair workshop at the ORT Munich school in the US zone of Germany, c.1947-48. Photography: Charles T. Reyner.

36 WOA: d07a259 ORT diploma awarded to Moniek Choyne, a graduate of the ORT Munich school, February 1947. Reproduced by kind permission of Alan Choyna.

37 WOA: p07a098 ORT workshop for children, Florence, Italy, 1940s.

38 WOA: p02a770 ORT student weaving a rug featuring the emblem of the State of Israel at the ORT Ramleh school for rug making, c.1950.

39 WOA: p02b395 Young students with their work at the ORT cabinet making school in Jaffa, Israel, c.1950.
Photography: Mirlin Yaron Press Photography, Tel Aviv.

40 WOA: p05a055 Rug making at the ORT Sofia school, Bulgaria, c.1948. Former ORT Bulgaria students were among the first to attend ORT courses in Israel, where some of them completed ORT courses begun in Sofia. Bulgarian students also participated in a rug making course in Ramleh, where one of the teachers was a former instructor at the ORT school in Sofia.

41 WOA: p06a115 Electrical engineering course at the Exodus Camp ORT School in Emden, in the British zone of Germany, January 1948.

42 WOA: p06a116 View of Exodus Camp, Emden, in the British zone of Germany, February 1948.

43 WOA: p07a102 Dr Syngalowski visiting the first ORT carpentry school in Jaffa, Israel, 1949.

44 WOA: p07a101 ORT School for Carpentry at the Youth Aliyah Home, Bex, Switzerland, 1949.

45 WOA: p07a099 ORT workshop for children, Florence, Italy, 1940s.

46 WOA: p03a389 ORT pilot training course, Italy, 1948. Graduates of the course joined the newly established Israeli air force.

Ten Years of Jewish Reconstructive Work, Sussia Goldman describes how Lvovitch, 'signed an agreement with the JDC, according to which all work in favour of the D.P.s in the field of vocational training was transferred solely to ORT'.[71]

Unofficially, the first ORT training course had begun in the Landsberg DP centre in October 1945, under the auspices of Jacob Oleiski 'and a number of ORT instructors from various Eastern European countries, themselves former inmates of concentration camps, who served as its pioneers and guides'.[72]

The Lvovitch agreement was made permanent in March 1946 when Vladimir Grossman was appointed Director of ORT activities in the American and British zones of occupation. This agreement 'made it possible to extend ORT's vocational training activities to the entire American Zone, as well as to the British and French Zones of Germany'.[73]

World ORT Union's activities in the American zone of occupation were divided between four districts. The main centres in each of the four areas were: I. Stuttgart, II. Kassel-Frankfurt, III. Regensburg and IV. Munich. The Jewish DP centre at Landsberg was in district IV which had Munich as its centre.

In October 1945, A.C. Glassgold was assigned to the Landsberg DP camp as an UNRRA Director. He recalls:

> Though I had heard and read about the tragic lives of these people in German concentration camps, I was not quite prepared for the shock of seeing the tattooed blue numbers on their left forearms ... It was here in Landsberg, that I witnessed the miracle of the human spirit; saw it revive from the ashes of the gruesome past to rise above the obstacles of the present and soar above the bleak promises of the future.[74]

In his article on the ORT school in Landsberg, Glassgold recalls the make-up of the Landsberg population:

> By the middle of June, 1945, there were over 7,500 people bursting the walls of the former German artillery barracks which had been designated as a DP camp. There were Poles, Dutch, Latvians, Lithuanians, Russians, Greeks, Frenchmen, Rumanians – people from every land ravaged and despoiled by the Nazis. The DP

> population was a constantly shifting one. As transports of men, women and children were dispatched to their homelands, new arrivals ... poured through the gates of the Landsberg Center.[75]

Although the original military buildings were designed to house 2,500 soldiers, thousands of DPs were crammed into them. However, by the autumn of 1945 one million had already been repatriated. During his description of the camp, Glassgold recalls a 17-year-old Polish survivor called Joe Pilzer. He writes:

> The Jewish DP's almost to a man refused repatriation. I once asked Joe, why he didn't return to Poland: Was he afraid? 'No, I'm not afraid to go back. But what should I go back to? I've lost my family, I haven't any friends there. The only people I know are here in Landsberg.'[76]

By October 1945, 4,500 DPs remained in Landsberg out of which all but eight were Jewish, mainly Poles. Glassgold concludes, 'Of the eight non-Jews, two were Catholics married to Jewish wives; one was a Hungarian Catholic woman married to a Lithuanian Jew, and two were Greek Catholic men.'[77]

Although during the autumn of 1945, thousands of refugees, known as 'infiltrees' entered the US zone from Poland, the Landsberg centre only contained DPs. According to Glassgold, 'The 4,500 residents of the Landsberg Jewish Center were strictly displaced persons. All had served terms in Nazi concentration camps, work camps, or slave factories, and had been liberated in Germany. The Landsberg Jewish Center was literally a city of souls snatched from slaughter.'[78]

Major Irving Heymont of the United States Army who was based at Landsberg, wrote a series of letters to his wife detailing his time there. On 19 September 1945 he recorded,

> The camp is filthy beyond description. Sanitation is virtually unknown. Words fail me when I try and think of an adequate description. The camp is run by an **UNRRA** team and a few representatives of the American Joint Distribution Committee. With a few exceptions, the people of the camp themselves appear demoralised beyond rehabilitation. They appear to be beaten both spiritually and physically, with no hopes or incentives for the future.[79]

The following day he continued with his description of the appalling conditions at Landsberg, writing, 'The toilets beg description ... In the washrooms, most of the sinks were out of order ... The two bright spots of the inspection were the camp hospital and the camp schools'.[80]

Although conditions were bad in Landsberg, Heymont does recall the remarkable work that was being carried out in the area of education. He commented,

> The schools of the camp were impressive. Under the leadership of Dr. J. Oleiski, a graduate of a concentration camp, Landsberg has developed a remarkable school system ... Children are now learning to read and write. Adolescents, for the first time, are learning trades. Instruction is offered in a great variety of skills, including garment making, all phases of shop working, auto mechanics, radio and repair and construction, and many others. Nor were the adults neglected. Former shopkeepers and salesmen are learning to work with their hands. A variety of evening courses in cultural subjects is also offered.[81]

Jacob Oleiski who had run ORT Lithuania and been so prominent in the Kovno Ghetto went on to set up the ORT school in the Landsberg DP camp. The drive and determination he had brought to the workshops inside the Kovno Ghetto, he now applied to the school system within the Camp. On 1 October 1945 he gave a speech marking the opening of the Landsberg ORT:

> We must give camp residents a purpose; we must reorganize their daily lives and introduce them to every possible kind and aspect of work. They must have the feeling that everywhere there are things to do. This is the only way we can prevent our fellow sufferers from letting their minds atrophy and become even more demoralised.[82]

In these few sentences, Oleiski summed up exactly what was required in the DP camps. He had assessed the situation and as a fellow sufferer instinctively knew how his co-inhabitants were feeling. He continued:

> Whenever I spend time in training workshops or visit vocational classes and look into the eyes of former concentration camp inmates, my faith grows stronger and stronger ... Indeed it is only

through productive, creative work that we can lessen our anger at having lost so many years.'[83]

Describing Oleiski, Heymont writes: 'Before Hitler, this remarkable man had been a trained agronomist in Lithuania, working for the ORT organisation ... Now, he is preaching and putting into practice his credo of salvation through work'.[84]

It was the combination of Oleiski's personal drive and determination and the influence and capabilities of the World ORT Union that lay behind the success of the ORT school in Landsberg. In December 1945, fully realising the potential of this alliance, Vladimir Grossman wrote in the *ORT Economic Review,* 'Immediate relief in the form of training skilled and semi-skilled workers must be given, particularly where there are remnants of destroyed Jewish communities who want to start life on their own.'[85]

While Oleiski and World ORT Union were combining forces to improve the situation in the Landsberg camp, the Jewish Committee for Relief Abroad (JCRA) was deciding on who it was going to send into the Allied zones of occupation. The JCRA had been established on 23 January 1943 at a conference held by the Board of Deputies of British Jews in London.[86] This, 'Jewish Conference on Immediate Relief in Europe' laid the groundwork for all post-war relief efforts. The conference had a five-point programme: first, to select volunteer agencies for relief work; second, to make arrangements for training; third, to raise funds; fourth, to make arrangements for training with foreign agencies; and finally, to set up a central office and staff. On 2 October 1945 Vice-Chairman Leonard Cohen signed a document committing six JCRA workers to the Landsberg camp and additional men and women to other camps in the US zone. These included six workers being sent to Feldafing, four to Munich and a further four to Herrlingen Ulm.[87]

Although the Landsberg school was successful, progress was not straightforward. According to Königseder and Wetzel, 'ORT, of course, had to overcome a number of obstacles during its initial period of operation, similar to those encountered by those who built the camp school system, namely lack of sufficient equipment and a competent teaching staff.'[88] The influx of Jews from Poland proved a blessing as, 'ORT was able to make up for some of the teacher shortage, since many of the survivors were graduates of prewar ORT schools'.[89] As the Landsberg school grew it became impossible to run it from the camp itself and the headquarters were moved to Munich.

The Harrison Report strongly recommended separating the Jewish and non-Jewish DPs. This policy was picked up by Heymont in his letters; on 22 September he writes, 'It seems to me that some problems would be eliminated if the non-Jewish elements of the camp ... were transferred to other camps so that Landsberg could be made an exclusively Jewish camp ... The Jews differ strongly among themselves, but they have common basic interests.'[90] Intent on helping separate the communities inside Landsberg, Heymont visited the DP camp at Fohrenwald on 28 September 1945. The plan was that Fohrenwald, which was not nearly as crowded as Landsberg, would take on the non-Jewish DPs, leaving Landsberg as a purely Jewish camp.

Once the education system in Landsberg was in place, the news of its success spread across the US zone and soon Jews in the British zone began to hear of it. On 12 October Heymont was informed by the camp rabbi, Rabbi Rosenberg, that Landsberg had a reputation for being the best DP camp in Europe and that, 'according to him, Jews from all over Europe are drifting towards here'.[91]

Despite the successes of the education system, Landsberg still suffered the same ordeals as the other DP camps in Europe. On 14 November Heymont wrote: 'Our latest headache is the food situation. Previously, the food for the camp came from local sources. That system worked well here because Landsberg is a food exporting area.'[92] However, the system had changed and all food was now being sent in from Munich. 'This changeover has caused a great deal of resentment in all DP camps – not alone in the Jewish camps. The complaints are that the variety and quantity are now worse than under the old system.'

The letters of Major Irving Heymont come to an end on 15 November 1945 when he writes: 'The official word came through this morning. I am no longer responsible for the Landsberg camp.'[93] The US army had been informed that they were to withdraw from the camp as UNRRA was now in charge of the DP camp system.

While all this work and rehabilitation was taking place in the British and American zones, work was also being carried out by World ORT Union in the French zone of occupation in Germany, as well as in Austria and Italy. In the French zone, by the end of 1945, apprenticeship workshops for DPs had been established in Gailingen near the Swiss border. It had been decided that work in the French zone should be run from Switzerland, from where the first workshop equipment was sent. *The Work of the ORT in Europe January–May 31, 1946*, explains how,

'The Geneva Head Office tried and began some work in Gailingen hoping to be able to connect it later with the whole of the ORT activity in Germany.'[94] One of the leaders of the local Jewish community at Diessenhofen offered his assistance to the ORT project at Gailingen, showing a continuation of relations between Jewish leaders and World ORT Union, a relationship that had first developed in the ghettos.

It was not only World ORT Union that offered to help the DPs during this time. The JCRA wrote to UNRRA on 2 October 1945 to pledge their assistance.[95] According to William Haber, President of the American ORT Federation,

> Some turned to the schools simply to occupy themselves. Others were attracted by the great variety of activities in and about the schools. For practically all, learning a trade was conscious preparation for life elsewhere and therefore a step toward emigration.[96]

However, it was World ORT Union that was going to lead the way in the rehabilitation of Holocaust survivors. It hoped that its vocational courses would enable the DPs to face their future and as an organisation it felt up to the challenge that lay ahead. In December 1945, Vladimir Grossman wrote:

> As an organisation which, for the last sixty-five years, has been engaged in correcting and straightening out occupational deformities in Jewish life, the ORT should be the leader amongst the other organisations who are prepared to participate in large-scale rehabilitation work in the world.[97]

NOTES

1. Jacob Oleiski in Angelika Königseder and Juliane Wetzel, *Waiting for Hope: Jewish Displaced Persons in Post-World War 11 Germany* (Illinois: Northwestern University Press, 2001), p.110.
2. Franklin J. Keller, 'Miracle of ORT Among the DPs', in WOA, d05a093a: *ORT Economic Review, June-September 1948* (New York: American ORT Federation, 1948), p.3.
3. Primo Levi, *The Drowned and the Saved* (London: Abacus, 1989), p.54.
4. Edith Kramer in Ruth Schwertfeger, *Women of Theresienstadt - Voices from a Concentration Camp* (New York: Berg, 1989), p.114.
5. Testimony of Col. Edmund M. Fortunoff Video Archive for Holocaust Testimonies, Yale University, USA. HVT: 1219.
6. Testimony of Harold Herbst. United States Holocaust Memorial Museum (USHMM). Personal Histories Collection - Liberation.
7. Hagit Lavsky, *New Beginnings: Holocaust Survivors in Bergen-Belsen and the British Zone in Germany, 1945-1950* (Detroit: Wayne State University Press, 2002), p.42.
8. Testimony of Lieutenant-Colonel R.I.G. Taylor. USHMM. Personal Histories Collection -

Liberation.
9. Testimony of Alan Zimm. USHMM. Personal Histories Collection – Liberation.
10. Lavsky, *New Beginnings*, p.42.
11. Joanne Reilly, *Belsen: The Liberation of a Concentration Camp* (London: Routledge, 1998), p.78.
12. Ibid.
13. For information on the number of displaced persons and refugees in Europe at the end of the Second World War see Mark Wyman, *DPs: Europe's Displaced Persons, 1945-1951* (Ithaca: Cornell University Press, 1989), pp.15-37.
14. George C. Marshall. USA Congressional Record. 30 June 1947.
15. Ibid.
16. For more on the Berlin Blockade see Richard Collier, *Bridge across the Sky: the Berlin Blockade and Airlift, 1948-1949* (London: Macmillan, 1978); Michael D. Haydock, *City Under Siege: the Berlin Blockade and Airlift, 1948-1949* (London: Brassey, 1999); Ann Tusa and John Tusa, *The Berlin Blockade* (London: Coronet, 1989).
17. Wyman, *DPs: Europe's Displaced Persons*, p.36.
18. Ibid., p.37.
19. Ibid.
20. For more on UNRRA see Marvin Klemme, *The Inside Story of UNRRA: An Experience in Internationalism: A first hand report on the Displaced People of Europe* (Washington, DC: Lifetime Editions, 1949); Susan T. Pettiss, *After the Shooting Stopped: The Memoir of an UNRRA Welfare Worker Germany 1945-1947* (London: Trafford Publishing, 2004); UNRRA European Regional Office. Division of Operational Analysis, *U.N.R.R.A.: Displaced Persons Operation in Europe and the Middle East* (London: UNRRA European Regional Office, 1946); UNRRA, *UNRRA: Organisation, Aims, Progress. Instructions and Procedure* (Washington, DC: UNRRA, 1945).
21. For more on the JDC see Yehuda Bauer, *American Jewry and the Holocaust: the American Jewish Joint Distribution Committee, 1939-1945* (Jerusalem: Hebrew University of Jerusalem, 1981); Oscar Handlin, *A Continuing Task: the American Jewish Joint Distribution Committee, 1914-1964* (New York: Random House, 1994); Joseph Neipris and Ralph Dolgoff, *The American Jewish Joint Distribution Committee and its Contribution to Social Work Education* (Jerusalem: JDC Israel, 1992). For more on the IRO see International Refugee Organisation, *IRO: what it is, what it does, how it works* (Geneva: IRO, 1949); IRO, *Constitution of the IRO* (London: HM Stationery Office, 1950).
22. Reilly, *Belsen*, p.80.
23. Ibid.
24. Dr David Lvovitch, WOA, d05a091: *ORT Economic Review, Sept-Dec 1946* (New York: American ORT Federation, 1946), pp.23-9.
25. Reilly, *Belsen*, p.81.
26. Lavsky, *New Beginnings*, p.51.
27. Ibid.
28. Ibid., p.52.
29. Joanne Reilly, 'British Policy', in Menachem Z. Rosensaft and Irving Greenberg (eds), *Life Reborn: Jewish Displaced Persons 1945-1951: Conference Proceedings, Washington, DC. January 14-17 2000* (Washington, DC: United States Holocaust Memorial Museum, 2000), pp.108-9.
30. Ibid.
31. Ibid., p.109.
32. Lavsky, *New Beginnings*, p.54.
33. Wyman, *DPs: Europe's Displaced Persons*, p.43.
34. Ibid., p.47.
35. Königseder and Wetzel, *Waiting for Hope*, p.16.
36. Wyman, *DPs: Europe's Displaced Persons*, p.49
37. Ibid., p.52.
38. Ibid., p.54.
39. Ibid., p.55.
40. Testimony taken from, *The Long Way Home,* documentary film about the DP camps and the struggle to create the State of Israel. WL video collection. Film no: 1210. Written and directed by Mark Jonathan Harris.
41. Königseder and Wetzel, *Waiting for Hope*, p. 12.
42. Vera Schiff, *Theresienstadt, the Town the Nazis gave to the Jews* (Toronto: Lugus, 1998), p.150.

43. WOA, d05a014: *Report on the ORT Activities August 1946-July 1947* (Paris and Geneva: ORT Union, June 1947); and WOA, d05a022: *The Work of the O.R.T. in Europe - January-May 31, 1946 - Report presented to the members of the Executive Committee of the ORT Union at the meeting called in Paris June 2-4, 1946* (Geneva: ORT Union, May 1946).
44. Reilly, *Belsen*, p.81.
45. Ibid., p.82.
46. Hagit Lavsky, 'A Community of Survivors: Bergen-Belsen as a Jewish Centre after 1945', in J. Reilly, D. Cesarani, T. Kushner and C. Richmond (eds), *Belsen in History and Memory* (London: Frank Cass, 1997), p.164.
47. Reilly, *Belsen*, p.152.
48. Ibid., p.167.
49. For more on the Central Committee of Liberated Jews see Lavsky, 'A Community of Survivors', pp.162-77.
50. Ibid., p.169. The role of the British in Palestine will be examined in Chapter 5.
51. The National Archives of the UK (hereafter TNA) document: FO 1052/283, 'Report on "Jewish Congress" at Hohne Camp', p.1.
52. Ibid., p.3.
53. Reilly, *Belsen*, p.97.
54. Ibid., p.98.
55. See discussion by Königseder and Wetzel in *Waiting for Hope*, pp.170-6.
56. See next section on the US zone of occupation and US policy towards the DPs.
57. TNA: F01052/283: 'Report on "Jewish Congress" at Hohne Camp'.
58. Ibid., pt 2b, p.2.
59. Reilly, *Belsen*, p.178.
60. For more on the two men at this time and their relationship see Leon Shapiro, *The History of ORT: A Jewish Movement for Social Change* (New York: Schocken Books, 1980), pp.232-45.
61. WOA, d06a079: World ORT Union, *ORT Vocational School Bergen-Belsen, 1945-1947* (Geneva: World ORT Union, 1947), p.9.
62. Reilly, *Belsen*, p.179.
63. Ibid.
64. WOA, d06a079: *ORT Vocational School Bergen-Belsen*, p.10.
65. Covering letter to the Harrison Report to President Truman, July 1945. The Harrison Report was received by President Truman on 24 August 1945. United States Holocaust Memorial Museum website and online archive: www.ushmm.org/museum/harrisonreport.
66. Report of Earl G. Harrison, 'Mission to Europe to inquire into the conditions and needs of those among the displaced persons in the liberated countries of Western Europe and in the SHAEF area of Germany - with particular reference to the Jewish refugees - who may possibly be stateless or non-repatriable', United States Holocaust Memorial Museum website and online archive: www.ushmm.org/museum/harrisonreport.
67. President Truman's directive, 22 December 1945. Issues of immigration will be examined in Chapter 5 of this book.
68. Reilly, *Belsen*, p.90.
69. Ibid., p.91.
70. TNA: FO 1049/195/107: CCG to WO 6 September 1945.
71. WOA, d05a085: Sussia Goldman, *Ten Years of Reconstructive Work - ORT Activities 1945-55*, p.3.
72. WOA, d05a014: *Report on the ORT Activities August 1946-July 1947*, p.42.
73. Ibid.
74. A.C. Glassgold, 'The Spirit Will Rise: The Miracle of Landsberg', in WOA, d05a092: *ORT Economic Review, March 1947* (NYC, USA: American ORT Federation), p.12.
75. Ibid., p.13.
76. Ibid., p.14.
77. Ibid., p.15.
78. Ibid., p.16.
79. Irving Heymont, *Among the Survivors of the Holocaust - 1945. The Landsberg DP Camp Letters of Major Irving Heymont, United States Army* (Cincinnati: American Jewish Archives, 1982), p.5.
80. Ibid., p.11.
81. Ibid., p.12.
82. Königseder and Wetzel, *Waiting for Hope*, p.110.

83. Ibid.
84. Heymont, *Among the Survivors*, p.13.
85. Vladimir Grossman, 'First Aid and Personal Rehabilitation for Displaced Persons', in WOA, d05a089: *ORT Economic Review, December 1945* (New York: American ORT Federation, 1945), p.38.
86. Wiener Library. Henriques Collection, Microfilm reel 1. Document no. HA1 1/7.
87. WL. Henriques Collection. Reel 1, document no. 1-HA2/2/5/B.
88. Königseder and Wetzel, *Waiting for Hope*, p.112.
89. Ibid.
90. Heymont, *Among the Survivors*, p.16.
91. Ibid.
92. Ibid., p.93.
93. Ibid., p.95.
94. WOA, d05a022: p.23.
95. WOA, d07a006: Leonard Cohen, *JCRA Proposed Deployment of JCRA Personnel*, 2 October 1945.
96. Forward by William Haber, President of the American ORT Federation, WOA, d07a007: *ORT Rebuilding Jewish Economic Life* (New York: American ORT Federation, 1955), p.4.
97. Grossman, 'First Aid and Personal Rehabilitation for Displaced Persons', p.44.

Life in the DP Camps: ORT and the Mature Period of Work, 1946–48

> After 12 months of very energetic study I received my ORT diploma as a radio mechanic. All the while I took private lessons in mathematics and studied physics and a little chemistry on my own.[1]

The poor sanitary and housing conditions that had plagued the DP camps and their inhabitants during the early days continued to be a problem throughout 1946. Wyman explains:

> As had happened with other DPs, it was the contrast of wretched overcrowding in the camps with well-housed Germans nearby that put bitterness into the hearts of many, and led some in the UNRRA and IRO to urge major shifts in priorities. This was behind the publicized resignation of the Landsberg camp's welfare director in December 1945 and the resulting army investigation.[2]

The comparison between the plight of the DPs in the camps and the conditions of the local German community was indeed one that caused tension and conflict with the camp population. Wyman continues:

> The Landsberg director, Dr. Leo Srole, a sociologist, protested the overcrowding, underfeeding, and lack of adequate housing …, while expressing fear of impending epidemics, since outbreaks of cholera had been reported in Eastern Europe, the source of most of the infiltrees.[3]

As made clear by Dr. Srole's anxiety, the overcrowding was not only unpleasant for the DPs but also dangerous. The excessive density could lead to the spread of disease and potential epidemics.

In addition to overcrowding, the lack of food and poor sanitation led to the constant movement of the DP population. DPs were constantly on the move with some attempting to travel between camps in order to collect extra rations. This made it even harder to maintain control of the DP population and created an unmanageable situation for the UNRRA officers who were in charge. In Neustadt, an UNRRA welfare officer recorded that:

> There is no satisfactory control of the DP population in the camp, consequently the food is drawn on the strength of about 650, although the actual number of Jews in Neustadt is only around 400. There is constant movement of displaced persons in and out of the camp without any permit, which makes it possible for the same displaced person to be registered and collect food at Belsen and Neustadt at the same time.[4]

The UNRRA officer concluded his report with the following statement: 'The morale among the Jewish displaced persons is unsatisfactory. There is resistance toward any rehabilitative project and tendency toward isolation from the rest of the camp ... The present staff cannot cope with the situation.'[5] The lack of nutritious food continued to be a serious problem across the DP camp system. In Belsen the situation was critical. On 9 December 1946 a telegram was sent to London announcing,

> FOOD SITUATION IN BRITISH ZONE ESPECIALLY BELSEN = CATASTROPHIC. IMMEDIATE INTERVENTION NECESSARY IN ADDITION DIFFICULT SITUATION REGARDING REFUGEES WHO ARE HERE 4 MONTHS WITHOUT RATIONS FROM MILITARY OR UNRRA ... AWAITING IMMEDIATE REPLY.[6]

The food shortages became particularly acute because of the soaring camp population. Men and women in the camps, desperate for the comfort of relationships and wanting to replace lost loved ones, married in large numbers or cohabited. The result was an increase in pregnancies across the British and American zones. According to Lavsky, 'The most significant factor in establishing a feeling of normality in the camps was the forming of new families'.[7] Many of the survivors in the DP camps were men and women in their twenties and thirties – all of whom had lost loved ones and out of which only a small percentage were able to relocate any relatives. It was easier to form new relationships with someone else who had lost everything than with someone who had no understanding of what had been lost: 'They did not have to talk too much concerning the dark side of their recent past lives. They also shared a sense of pragmatism and scepticism which meant they did not expect to find eternal love in a new marriage.'[8] These new relationships led to a series of marriages in the camps during the latter months of 1945 and 1946 and to a baby boom across the zones of occupation in 1946 and 1947. Most of those who were married in the DP camps chose to have a Jewish wedding ceremony, including those couples who were not religious. This can be explained by an overwhelming desire to maintain links with Jewish tradition and a continuation of a lost past. One female survivor recalls: 'There was at least one wedding a day at Bergen-Belsen. People paired themselves because they had nobody. We got together out of loneliness.'[9] She continues:

> I felt so alone; alone. I got married and pregnant but wasn't ready to make commitments. Under normal circumstances we would never have married. My husband was a Polish survivor. He had nobody. Everybody had been killed. When we met we liked each other kind of ... so after four days he proposed and I accepted ... we lived happily for years.[10]

These weddings resulted in a post-war baby boom. By the spring of 1946 1,000 babies had been born in the British zone, 200 of which had been born in Belsen. The food shortages continued – especially shortages of nutritionally beneficial food. Lavsky writes:

> As the growing number of pregnancies and babies presented the welfare workers with a serious burden, mother and child care became a major focus of concern. Growing families and improvement of health contradicted each other. Due to the numerous pregnancies, births, and infants and the growing number of elderly people who arrived as refugees from Eastern Europe, looking after the sick and the children became a central occupation for the welfare agencies.[11]

In addition to the poor food, inadequate housing and sanitation, the fact that the British authorities stuck firm to their decision to divide the camps by nationality alone further angered the already disillusioned DP population. The classification of the DPs is important as it was only those who were accorded DP status that could then benefit from relief and rehabilitation organisations such as World ORT Union.

In November 1947 Colonel Solomon, the Special Advisor for Jewish Affairs in Germany, compiled a report, 'Representation of German Jews'. Having toured the British zone from 22–31 October 1947 at the request of Lord Pakenham, Solomon commented on the continued British policy of housing Jews by nationality:

> Jews are grouped according to nationality and there are the strongest reasons (extending far beyond the bounds of the German tangle) that this principle should be observed. Within the somewhat narrow confines of Jewish deliberation within the British Zone this important factor is often overlooked and there is a cry that Jews should be recognised 'as such' without their place of origin.[12]

Solomon explains how the Central Committee of Liberated Jews were in opposition to this policy and had strongly voiced this opposition. Due to this public opposition, Solomon states: 'It has been decided that the Central Committee cannot be recognised officially'.[13] This refusal by the British authorities to recognise the Central Committee would increase the divide between the Jewish population of Belsen and administering authorities.

In the post-war period, World ORT Union continued to offer courses, but who took them and what did they mean to the participants? Often survivors were still trapped behind barbed wire and could only leave the DP camps with special passes. Hagit Lavsky picks up on this point: 'Worst of all was being, "liberated but not free" as the survivors put it – forced to live in a camp under semi-military regulations, in over-populated barracks, with no privacy'.[14] The barbed wire that surrounded the DPs and the day-to-day restrictions placed on their lives acted as a constant reminder of their previous imprisonment inside the ghettos and concentration camps.

Due to the continuation of these difficulties and the lack of stimulation in the lives of the DPs, circumstances were right for ORT courses in the camps to flourish. World ORT Union was quick to recognise this and 1947 saw a dramatic expansion of its work inside the DP camps. According to Rader:

> By the end of 1947, ORT had become a network of over 700 courses located in the DP camps of Europe. The phenomenal number of 22,620 persons was enrolled that year, almost one-tenth of the DP population of the time. 934 teachers taught more than fifty trades, including metal machining, shoemaking and carpentry ... also automobile motor repairing, dental mechanics, millinery designing, typesetting, goldsmithing, watch repairing and such relatively complex fields as optics and surveying.[15]

Rader picks up on one of the most important aspects of World ORT Union's work inside the DP camps, in some ways even more important than the technical training itself; that of instilling an interest in learning and work into those who had previously had to perform slave labour and endure the concentration camps. Rader explains: 'If this generation was to be salvaged, it had to be taught a new set of life values. Beyond mechanical techniques, the ORT schools for youth sought to teach the positive significance and dignity of labor.'[16]

By May 1947 there were forty-four teachers and 583 pupils in ORT in the British zone of occupation, and, by the end of 1947, ORT was hoping to enrol 3,000 pupils.[17] By June 1947, the programme in the US zone had expanded to incorporate 229 schools with a total of 5,304 pupils. There were now forty courses on offer in the US zone which ran for between nine and eighteen months. In the light of possible emigration, several new trades had been introduced, including optics, refrigerator assembly, linotyping, orthopaedics, wireless operating and manufacture of medical instruments.

World ORT Union adjusted its tactics in response to the desperate desire of DPs finally to flee the camps. Once it had decided to set up training facilities in some of the larger cities World ORT Union laid out its plan to establish three schools for 3,000 pupils in larger cities to be overseen by the JDC. Dr. Zalman Grinberg who visited the DP camps picked up on the desire of the DPs to flee the camps and set up lives in the cities and abroad:

> Now that the problem of food no longer exists and the fear of death has been removed, they have reverted to their former status of human beings and now they have time to ponder ... lack of work

leads to demoralization ... it is inconceivable that thousands of human beings should remain sitting in the camps without a single, solitary thing to do.[18]

Grinberg saw the solution to this problem as lying 'primarily in one direction, and that is to supply them with a useful occupation. That this is true is evidenced by the fact that for the past eight months there has been a universal demand by the displaced persons for workshops, for training courses.'[19] According to *Rebuilding Jewish American Life,* published by American ORT:

> By 1947-48, the ORT DP network had grown to 712 workshops and vocational courses at a peak enrolment rate of over 18,000 a year in Germany, Austria and Italy alone; additional thousands were enrolled in Switzerland, France, Holland and Belgium. Fifty trades were covered ... 934 instructors had been put to work in classrooms and shops, almost all of them located among the DPs themselves.[20]

On 19 September 1947, H. Vredenburg, the chief for the DP division of the Central Control Committee for Germany and Austria wrote to London about the formation of a Jewish Advisory Committee to oversee Jewish organisations committed to rehabilitation and training. Listed among those asked to forward names of representatives was World ORT Union.[21]

On 17 November 1947, Vredenburg wrote (again) this time to Dr Otto Deutsch director of ORT in the British zone about setting up ORT schools in Emden and Seigwarden. The letter announces that the approval has been granted for the establishment of these schools under the following conditions:

a. that no accommodation suitable for living quarters will be used for school purposes
b. that classes will be limited to residents of the camp
c. that no financial obligation will devolve upon C.C.G
d. that the curricular will be submitted to the HQ through the usual channels
e. the directors of the school will furnish the respective DPAC commanders with normal rolls of staff of the school when required.[22]

The five conditions that had to be adhered to when setting up the ORT schools in Emden and Seigwarden were the same across the British zone of occupation. The establishment of the ORT school in Belsen was also subject to the same conditions.

The ORT vocational school in Belsen was part of a much larger educational system that flourished during the post-war years. Within Belsen there was a nursery, children's home,[23] Kindergarten,[24] the Jacob Edelstein Elementary School,[25] two Beth Jacob Girls Schools (Polish and Hungarian),[26] Yeshiva 'She'erit Israel',[27] Hebrew High School,[28] Beth Jacob Seminar,[29] ORT Vocational School,[30] Popular University,[31] Workshops in Kibbutzim,[32] Youth Movements[33] and three Halutz Houses.[34] Lavsky describes the various courses that were offered by ORT in Belsen:

> Vocational training was initiated by the camp organisations, the JRU, the JA, and the ORT, and was financed mainly by the JDC. In Belsen, various courses in different trades, such as automobile mechanics, auto driving, sewing and dressmaking, electromechanics, and carpentry, were started. These sporadic courses run by the camp inmates developed into a full-time vocational school that was taken over by the ORT, with Jack Weingreen of the JRU as the headmaster.[35]

She continues: 'During its first year of operation this school trained some 900 students, each for a period of six months, and by the end of 1946 there were at one time some 400 participants. Some of the teachers also came from among the camp inmates.'

Initially it had proved hard to encourage the young DPs to take the ORT courses in any significant numbers. The lack of materials available during the schools' early months added to the difficulties. An ORT report on vocational training in Belsen explains, 'Most of the young generation at Belsen had lost their school years in the Nazi camps. They had little education, few had parents to advise them, they were tired of forced labour and intoxicated with the freedom regained after liberation.'[36] ORT, who saw the need to encourage and rally the young was quick to remedy this situation. Under the leadership of Mack:

> They organised public meetings to discuss 'the future of the young generation', they made use of the local cinema for appeals to come to the school, they visited absentees in their lodgings and pleaded with the leaders of the Kibutzim and of the Jewish Committee not

to send to Camp work young people under 18 so that they might make use of an opportunity for training.[37]

Lavsky picks up on the feelings of apathy and the urgent need to exhort and encourage the DPs:

> Theoretically, there was every motive for people to live idly. The camp was separated from the German economy and dependent on British and Jewish welfare. There were many restraints on gainful employment, such as the lack of raw materials and the refusal to work with or for Germans ... no real incentive to work for a living, since basic needs were met through welfare.[38]

In Belsen the Central Committee of Liberated Jews took on the issue of education and made sure that all those under the age of 18 were in full time study. Aharon Megged explains:

> Since the number of children in the other DP camps and the local Jewish communities was too small to warrant establishing a separate school system with its own curriculum, the Belsen schools emerged as the only institutions equipped to provide an education adapted to the special needs of Jewish children.[39]

It is important to remember that in the early months of education and training in the DP camps, it was only the combination of the various welfare and social agencies working together that made any progress possible. The task of educating and training the DPs in Belsen and in the other DP camps across the American and British zones was so immense that only such a multi-agency approach would prove satisfactory. As described by Zeev Mankowitz:

> In the first half of 1946 the educational arrangements of *She'erith Hapleitah* went through an impressive period of growth and development. The pioneers of the early period were now joined by teachers who had arrived from Eastern Europe ... 'ORT' was critical in making vocational training possible, the Joint provided counsel and funding while many of the Palestinian emissaries were roped into educational work.[40]

Together, these groups forged ahead, overcoming the various obstacles and encouraging and supporting the survivors.

Although the school had only been established in Belsen in late 1945, by 1946 ORT was already making substantial headway. In 1946, 'ORT even introduced a program for dental technicians. An instructor was brought over from America for the sole purpose of directing the program.'[41] This instructor was Mr M. Greenman who proved extremely popular among his pupils. The dentist's laboratory was set up under the initiative of Dr Hadassa Rosensaft but it was under the tuition of Greenman that the school flourished. Soon after his arrival in Belsen, sixty students were enrolled on his programme and before long he was able to offer dental care to the entire Belsen population. By 1947 Greenman and his pupils had made over 750 sets of dentures.

ORT in Belsen was originally part of the Belsen high school to which all those under 18 were made to attend. However, 'in the summer of 1946, they were given the opportunity to move into four barracks in Camp No. 2 - with their own canteen'.[42] This move meant that ORT came under the auspices of the Central Committee for Liberated Jews.

Angelika Königseder and Juliane Wetzel write about ORT and its work in Belsen. They discuss its move within the camp and claim that ORT 'was therefore administered independently of the other educational facilities in the camp'. They continue to describe ORT's growth in Belsen and how this was made possible:

> With the assistance from the Joint and machines supplied by the Canadian Army, the school was able to upgrade its equipment and meet the standards of commercially operated vocational training programs. As a result of improving its organization and facilities, ORT expanded its programs to include courses in architecture, baking and cooking.[43]

The majority of students who took the ORT courses were aged between 17 and 25 and took anywhere between two and six months to complete each course. A report produced by American ORT in 1956 discussed the courses on offer and the amount of work the students were expected to complete: 'They were intensive however – as much as four to eight hours a day. Participants have described a sense of pulsating energy within the schools. The school often became the cultural, recreation and discussion center of the camp.'[44]

During the summer of 1946 Professor Jack Weingreen visited the DP camp at Belsen in order to assess the educational work being carried out. Weingreen wrote up his findings in a two-part report, the first of which is dated September 1946. The report covers all the educational activities in Belsen in which ORT played a major part. On the work of ORT Weingreen comments:

> The crafts for which the school caters are basic, namely, carpentry, tool-making and locksmith work, motor mechanics, electricity, tailoring, dressmaking, underwear making, cobbling and cap-making. There is also an efficient department of Dental-Mechanics which was established by ORT and which is a model of how a class should be operated.[45]

In the second section of Weingreen's report, dated 18 December 1946, he devotes a section to the 'ORT Trade School, Central Jewish Committee'. This starts by discussing the move of the ORT school and workshops to Camp II. Weingreen claims, 'though we have by no means reached the stage at which we can be satisfied, the school is displaying the potentialities of a controlled institution'.[46] Weingreen continues with a discussion of the Dental Mechanics course:

> The first six-monthly course in the ORT Dental Mechanics School has now been completed. It is amazing to see the results of this remarkable department, the founding and development of which is entirely due to the energy and initiative of the instructor Mr. Greenman. From very primitive and meagre beginnings he has succeeded in building up a modern, well-equipped and active laboratory, such as one expects to find in a progressive institution in a large city.[47]

By the time this report was produced, any apathy that had been present in the survivors in the immediate post-war months had all but vanished. As Weingreen explains, it was not a lack of interest in work that slowed things down but a lack of equipment with which to carry it out. Weingreen concludes:

> It is an entirely false assumption that our citizens are unwilling to work, but the lack of materials makes production impossible and the lack of amenities renders work profitless and frustrating. As an

example of their readiness to serve the camp community, one may quote the regular production of baby cots in the carpentry shop; they have already made scores of cots and production is limited only by the amount of wood available.[48]

On 28 December 1946, A.G. Kenchington, Chief of the PW and DP Division, wrote a report for the Control Office for Germany and Austria: Section G.I.B. on 'Jewish Vocational Training' which stands in opposition to Weingreen's report of 18 December 1946.[49] It claims: 'The Jews in Hohne certainly refuse to do any work which they can get done for them by the GERMANS'. Kenchington continues:

> Ceaseless efforts have been made first by the Mil.Gov. then by UNRRA and ORT / Organisation for Rehabilitation by Training / to initiate and encourage vocational training ... it is our opinion that requests by the Jewish Committee for vocational training are nothing more than propaganda to cover the refusal of the inhabitants of the camp to do any work whatsoever, except as a matter of personal enterprise on a profit making basis.[50]

Kenchington's report not only takes the opposite view to Weingreen but contradicts the mass of documentation produced by World ORT Union at the time. World ORT Union admitted that in some camps the courses were slow to gain momentum but there is no indication from any reports or correspondence that the DPs were lazy and ultimately disinterested as Kenchington claims. Kenchington's report concludes: 'The Jewish DPs are unwilling to work ... Hohne is reported by UNRRA as the dirtiest and worst maintained Assembly Centre in the Zone, although the installations – ex Wehrmacht Barrack buildings – are quite as good as anywhere else.'[51] This comment about Höhne/Belsen being the 'dirtiest and worst maintained' of the DP camps is offensive as it implies that it is the fault of the Jewish DPs that the camp was an unpleasant place to live. It was unpleasant due to the fact that too many people were crammed into military barracks, where there were poor hygiene facilities and often not enough food.

Contrary to Kenchington's remarks about the unwillingness of the Jewish DPs to work, it is extraordinary that, given the conditions in which these former concentration camp inmates where housed, any work was carried out at all. It is a testimony to their courage and willingness to face the future, and the dedication of the men and women on the ORT staff, that the classes were successful, that courses were completed and that graduations took place.

Josef Mack, director of the ORT in Belsen remained in the post until 6 February 1949. According to Königseder and Wetzel, Mack 'developed the so-called workshop system. Word of its success quickly spread beyond the limits of the camp and became a symbol in Belsen of the Jews' newly acquired self-esteem.'[52] They carry on to explain how:

> By mid July 1947, 250 drivers, 77 tailors, 150 dressmakers, 15 locksmiths, 12 carpenters, 60 dental technicians, 45 electricians, 80 corset seamstresses, and 15 lingerie makers had received their diplomas. In other words, approximately half of those enrolled in courses had successfully completed the ORT programs.[53]

During July 1947 the ORT graduates were able to display their skills at an exhibition of their work during the Second Congress of Liberated Jews. They had previously held an exhibition to mark the first anniversary of the school. The work exhibited during July 1947 was given a special mention in the correspondence of the JCRA. On 25 July 1947 Professor N. Bentwich wrote to Mr Leonard Cohen about the improvements in Belsen and what had struck him during his latest visit. Bentwich mentions 'The Exhibition of the Trade School, which showed very great resourcefulness'.[54]

Although the numbers attending the classes had increased dramatically, so much so that ORT had moved to their own buildings, the supply of machinery and equipment did not keep up with the demand of the pupils. In 1947 ORT wrote:

> The question of supplies was taken up by the Central Board and considerable quantities have since been sent to the school by a number of ORT Committees outside Germany, mobilised by the Central Board to bring their assistance to the Belsen Camp.[55]

The situation improved dramatically and soon it was possible to plan for the delivery of supplies months in advance due to the establishment of an ORT Central Supply Department in Munich.

It was after the supply office moved to Munich that additional courses were added to the curriculum in Belsen. Radio training was the latest innovation and during 1947 the Central Supply Department sent a fully equipped workshop for fifteen students to the camp. In addition: 'Even new textiles, a luxury unknown until then, were delivered to the needle work class in time for their examinations. Prior to that nothing but old clothing not fit for wear had to be cut up and used for making miniature samples.'[56]

The school in Belsen and the courses carried out there were so successful that many prominent people in ORT and the liberated Jewish community attended the ORT graduation ceremonies. In addition to the Belsen ORT staff and the newly graduated students, the ceremonies were attended by Mark J. Lester, the director of ORT in the British zone, Y. Baruchi, the head of the Jewish Agency in the British zone, and by Josef Rosensaft of the Committee of Liberated Jews.

In 1947 the ORT school in Belsen held a ceremony for two newly graduated students who were leaving for Palestine. They were two of ORT's best graduates in carpentry and machine tool making and in recognition of their skills they were awarded sets of tools which they could take with them to Palestine.

On Sunday 7 December 1947 the ORT school at Belsen celebrated its second anniversary. To mark this momentous occasion, ORT students put on an exhibition of their work which was opened by Mrs Mowshowitz. Various members of ORT gave speeches and the opening address was given by Dr Otto Dutch. Simon Bloomberg, the European director of the Jewish Relief Unit who attended these celebrations also spoke. He later recalled:

> On behalf of the JRU I said how closely we had been and were connected with ORT and I mentioned particularly the services in organising the school rendered by Professor Jack Weingreen. I also mentioned the various members of the organisation seconded to ORT at odd times and the material help given by J.R.U.[57]

While ORT's work in Belsen and the rest of the British zone flourished, important rehabilitation and educational work was also being carried out in the US zone. Throughout the latter half of 1946 several operational changes were made within ORT in the US zone. It was decided that ORT should initiate closer contact with the Central Committee of Liberated Jews and with UNRRA. It was hoped that this would forge better relations between all groups and lead to a 'normalization of the relations to the various Zionist groups among the refugees'.[58]

On 24 October 1946, an agreement was drawn up between ORT and the Central Committee of Liberated Jews in the US zone. This agreement announced that:

> To carry out the vocational training among Jews in the American zone, a committee will be created for vocational education and this Committee will be called 'Committee of ORT professional Schools' in co-operation with the Central Committee of Liberated Jews.[59]

This committee was to be comprised of six members, three from the members of Central Committee of Liberated Jews and three from ORT. The agreement stated that: 'The ORT Union undertakes to take care of these professional Schools for Jews in the American Zone and to furnish them with the necessary machines, tools, financial aid and literature for the proper functioning of the schools.'[60] Finally, the two bodies decided that: 'The Professional Schools in the American Zone will be called ORT Schools ... When the Jewish DPs leave Germany the ORT Union will be obliged to transfer the ORT Professional Schools together with the DPs.'[61]

Almost a year later, on 25 August 1947, Harry S. Messac wrote to Brigadier Thicknesse, Chief of the DP Division of the Control Committee for Germany (British Element), about the artisanal workshops in the US zone of occupation. Messac records:

> There are two kinds of cottage industry programs being conducted in the Jewish camps of the U.S. Zone Germany. The first is workshop training, primarily to accomplish rehabilitation. This training covers the fields of woodworking, carpentry, machine shop, automotive mechanics, tailoring and sewing ... The second is a clothing manufacturing project. This program employs about 1,000 Jewish DP tailors.[62]

In order to assess all the work that was taking place across the US zone, World ORT Union made site visits to all the DP camps. A visitor to the Stuttgart ORT school, recorded that

> The school classes are housed in ordinary dwelling rooms and are therefore much smaller than desirable ... The machine shop is

being extended from the basement of one apartment house to that of another, and this has been done by breaking through a two-foot masonry wall ... The general appearance of the shop is good. A fair amount of attention is given to records of pupils and preparation of work. The general program of instruction and utilisation of material follows the usual pattern.[63]

However, when it came to describing the lessons themselves, the report was not so favourable:

A rather fruitful lesson was being taught by a young German woman teacher. She was giving the technical information related to men's and women's clothing manufacture. The lesson was on cotton, its culture and uses. The drawing rooms were small and rather poorly lighted, but were usable. All the material for hat making comes from old hats. The photography course is being conducted in a kind of cubby-hole in the attic, hardly large enough to accommodate more than three or four people.[64]

It can be seen that much of this adverse comment was occasioned by lack of space and of materials and not related to the ability of the teachers or the attentiveness of the pupils.

Zelda Fuksman attended the ORT school in Stuttgart after she was smuggled into the US zone at the end of the war. She had spent the war hiding in forests in Poland and then later in Siberia. She recalls that the first contact she had with ORT was in Stuttgart where she 'started school and after school we attended sewing classes. We had no sewing machines so every stitch was done by hand. We were also taught the fine embroidery stitches.'[65] When asked how her fellow DPs viewed the ORT and the chance to study in Stuttgart she does not remember any feelings of apathy towards the courses. She recalls: 'I know that I loved learning whatever was taught. I was a good student and was hungry to learn. I was 11, 12, 13 years old in those days.'[66] She also fondly remembers the attitudes of the ORT staff who: 'treated the children with great kindness and patience of course depending on the behaviour and co-operation'.[67] When discussing how the courses helped the young and what they were able to gain from the experience, Fuksman claims, 'our spirits and self confidence was uplifted by our school, organisations and ORT ... I have learned that I can do just about anything. The wonderful sewing that I learned at ORT served me well throughout my life.'[68] Fuksman explains that although she did not use this skill in her professional life once she had emigrated to America, it 'developed in me a patience and desire to continue with many handcraft projects, such as needlepoint, crocheting, knitting, sewing'.[69] Fuksman summarises her time with ORT as being 'Useful and gave me a feeling of success and accomplishment'.[70]

In December 1947 World ORT Union celebrated two years work in the US zone of occupation. Soon evaluations and letters of praise were sent to the various ORT schools from a variety of sources. On 31 December 1947 Paul B. Edwards, Chief of Operations IRO US zone wrote a letter congratulating World ORT Union in the US zone on their second anniversary:

> May I offer my congratulations to you on the completion of two fruitful years of work in the U.S. zone. Your contributions to the rehabilitation of Displaced Persons cannot be measured in terms of numbers of students and schools alone. Beyond the content of courses given, the ORT school acts as a source of spiritual refreshment for all the people in the Assembly Centers.[71]

On 6 January 1948, Y. Levy of the Jewish Agency for Palestine in the US zone wrote to Jacob Oleiski echoing Edwards feeling about ORT's work. Levy wrote, 'your organisation, which gave thousands of our people the opportunity to receive vocational training that they may be able to live a productive future, has rendered a great and important service to our people.' He went on to say, 'We want particularly to note our great satisfaction that your plans for vocational training have been adjusted to the needs of emigration to Eretz-Israel.'[72]

A 1947 World ORT Union report explains how all ORT work in the US zone was divided into four districts, Munich, Stuttgart, Bamberg and Zeilsheim, with each area run by a district manager. By March 1947 there were 198 ORT facilities across these four districts operating in trade schools, training workshops and DP camps. The report explains how:

> Instruction is carried out in well-equipped institutions with a training period of 9 to 18 months, and directed by qualified teachers and instructors. Special attention must be called to the training workshops for motorcar mechanics in Munich, the school for

mechanical dentists there, and the locksmiths' workshops at Landsberg and Ainring, which are frequented by youthful aspirants of high merit in all respects.[73]

The work carried out by ORT in the Landsberg DP camp set the example for the rest of the zone. Once the DP system was fully established, education and schooling became a prominent part of daily life in the camps. Wyman claims:

> Soon the DP systems began expanding beyond the one room schoolhouse stage into a variety of levels and specializations. West German and Austrian education authorities gave them recognition. At the large Jewish camp at Landsberg, the systems ran from pre-school through college, with more than 700 high school students enrolled in training courses for carpenters, electricians, tinsmiths, auto mechanics, dress cutters, nurses, and other skilled occupations.[74]

In the March 1947 edition of the *ORT Economic Review* an article entitled 'The Spirit Will Rise' describes the work being carried out by ORT at Landsberg. It examines the courses on offer and assesses their popularity:

> Young people from all ends of the American Zone sought admission into these classes where, in spite of a heartrending shortage of instruments and supplies and an appalling lack of text books, products of amazing inventiveness, artistry and skill were produced. Enthusiasm, persistence, courage, and dauntless spirit overcame the hardships of cold, cramped class-rooms, uncomfortable benches, inadequate black-boards, and a pathetic lack of writing supplies.[75]

Elly Gotz was liberated from Dachau concentration camp on 25 April 1945 and later transferred to the DP camp at Landsberg. Gotz describes his early days in the camp:

> One day, around December 1945, I walked past a sign advertising a new ORT school opening for teaching Radio Mechanics. Curious, I walked in and sat down in the class. It was the very first day the

course was starting. A German lecturer came in (Mr. Albrecht) and began a general talk of how a radio works. I was fascinated! But I was planning to be a mechanical engineer, and this was electronics.[76]

Gotz continues to explain how he returned the following day and, as he was so interested, he enrolled on the course. He discusses the atmosphere in the class and how it captured the attention and imagination of the students. Gotz also recalls how the teachers inspired the pupils:

> Every day it got more interesting! Mr. Albrecht was a very good teacher, challenging us to discover some new details by ourselves ... After a few months of theory ... we began to build our own radio from scratch ... Slowly we each assembled our own chassis, mounted the parts and were looking forward to the happy moment when our receiver will jump to life and produce a sound.[77]

For some, the horrific experiences of the past few years would not fade and they found it almost impossible to face the present and future with anything other than despair. They could not shed the depression caused by the camps and the accompanying feelings of apathy in the immediate post-liberation months. Gotz describes one boy from his ORT class in Landsberg:

> We knew little about his history, but rumour had it that he had been through a particularly horrible set of experiences during the Holocaust. He was dour, was not friendly with anyone, although we tried to include him. If anyone touched his tools, he reacted with great anger. He never smiled. Now it so happened that his wireless receiver was the first in class to come on loud and clear! We all jumped to congratulate him. For the first time we saw a broad smile come on his face. We were so pleased to observe it! From that moment on he became part of our group, co-operative and friendly.[78]

This uplifting testimony highlights the patient and inspirational way in which the Landsberg ORT staff nurtured their pupils. It also supports World ORT Union's theory that the acquisition of a skill would add enormously to the self-confidence of the pupils on their courses. As Gotz claims: 'Knowing how to do something well has healing properties'.[79] Gotz concludes his testimony of his time in Landsberg by saying how: 'After 12 months of very energetic study I received my ORT diploma as a radio mechanic. All the while I took private lessons in mathematics and studied physics and a little chemistry on my own.'[80] On 23 July 1947, L.J. Walinksy, Director of the World ORT Union in the British and US zones of Occupation, wrote to A. Maegalith, the director of the ORT school in Landsberg, congratulating him on his work inside the camp.[81] The letter offered praise for the work being carried out at Landsberg saying that the standard of excellence achieved there should be the model for all schools in the US zone: 'As you know the fame of the ORT-Fachschule in Landsberg has spread far and wide wherever the name of ORT is known. I am personally very proud of the Landsberg Fachschule and of the job which you and your colleagues are doing there.'[82]

Dr Samuel Steinberg, who was responsible for ORT's work in the US zone, also wrote to the Director, Faculty of Landsberg Schools and Students on the 23 July:

> The high level of your vocational school, fashioned out of a jungle environment, demonstrates what the common man can achieve when he is given a chance for self-expression. Although displaced, you have found a place. Here is hoping that your minds and hearts will soon be given a chance to function as citizens and workers in the country of your choice.[83]

In November 1946, Dr David Lvovitch travelled to Austria to assess whether or not it would be possible to initiate ORT activities there. Harry Branton recorded in the ORT Illustrated Magazine, 'The Executive Committee, World ORT Union, was of course aware that at that time there were 45,000 Jews living in Austria and 35,000 of these were herded together in the DP camps in the U.S. zone of Austria.'[84] According to Rader, Lvovitch's visit had been prompted by requests made by UNRRA, the Special Advisor on Jewish Affairs to the US Army and the Viennese Jewish community to open similar programmes to those established in Germany. Rader claims: 'ORT responded immediately and centers of two types were opened: within the camps, as in Germany, and central schools in Vienna, Salzburg and Linz, for residents in nearby camps and DPs living outside the camps.'[85] In response to the request, World ORT Union extended its work to Austria at the end of 1946. The World ORT Union Annual Report for that year claims, 'when ORT took up its work in Austria, there were approximately 35,000 Jewish DPs in this country, 10,000 of whom were cared for by UNRRA and the rest by the U.S. Army.'[86]

In early 1947, Mrs Sylvia Margulies was given the job as Director of ORT in Austria and, together with technical director Eng. J. Steward, she coordinated all activities from their headquarters in Salzburg. According to a report produced by World ORT Union during the first quarter of 1947:

> Contrary to the development in Germany, ORT found in Austria no spontaneously created training workshops etc. Everything had to be planned and done from the very beginning. This fact, together with the lack of premises for training workshops, caused a delay in our work, but at the same time made for systematic procedure. The equipment for the various workshops was sent from Switzerland.[87]

Other differences existed between ORT in Austria and ORT in Germany. The World ORT Union Annual Report for August 1946–July 1947 notes that, unlike in Germany where ORT's work was carried out inside the DP camps, the training schools in Austria were on the whole moved out of the camps and into the cities. As most of the camps were on the outskirts of the cities the move was seemingly a minor one but it was of huge significance to the DPs who found themselves fully liberated at last.

In February 1947, the first ORT school in Austria was opened in Salzburg and in March a school was set up in Vienna. The Salzburg school consisted of six workshops and 200 students. The courses on offer were dressmaking, locksmithing, electro-installation, radio technics and carpentry. By the end of March a total of nine ORT workshops had been established. Harry Branton recalls, 'We started modestly with a central school in Salzburg which gradually created a fine reputation for itself and for ORT all over the country.'[88] Branton continues, 'Our work in Austria is respected by all organisations and has proved of great value in building up the self-confidence of the DPs and their appreciation of relief organisations.'[89]

The schools in Salzburg and Vienna were followed by the opening of a school in Linz in June 1947. The Linz school consisted of three workshops which offered dressmaking, millinery and electrical installation courses. It also had one vocational course in 'men's cutting out'.[90] All the courses based in Salzburg, Vienna and Linz ran for six to nine months. At this time ORT did not have its own premises and was allowed to operate out of existing Austrian trade schools. The two main trade schools in Vienna which 'hosted' ORT workshops and courses were the Vienna school for Radio Mechanics, and the Vienna Trade School for Dental Mechanics.

In July, Harry Branton took over as Director of ORT Austria when Mrs Margulies retired to the United States. Branton claimed that the ORT schools in Austria not only helped the DPs in terms of arming them with a skill and increasing their self-confidence, but he also believed that, 'ORT activities have also favourably impressed the Allied Forces and the native population thus they developed into an effective weapon in the fight against anti-Semitism.'[91] Once Branton took over as Director, ORT was quick to expand in Austria. By the end of 1947 in addition to the schools in Salzburg, Vienna and Linz, there were now schools in Hofgastein, Hallein, Bindermichl and Ebelsberg. The total number of pupils across these sites was 1,082. A total of 340 pupils now attended the Viennese school and the courses on offer there were auto-mechanics, radiotechnics, electro-engineering, dental mechanics, dress-making, lingerie making and cosmetics and hairdressing.[92] In 1948 ORT Austria expanded further, and by March 1948 there had been a total of 210 graduations. According to the 1948 Annual Report, 'At the present time, the Austrian ORT had 1,105 pupils in 7 training centers and 124 instructors engaged in the work. By the end of March, it is anticipated that 1,500 pupils will have enrolled.'[93]

In 1948, due to the changes in emigration and the creation of the state of Israel, Branton claimed:

> The great masses of Jewish people in the camps are going towards their real liberation, leaving the camps, emigrating to Israel or other countries of their choice. ORT Austria Mission has to face the same problems as our brothers in Germany and Italy. We shall do it with the same flexibility and the same success. We shall do our job as long as there are Jews in Austria.[94]

While post-war rehabilitation work was being carried out in Austria, substantial efforts to aid the Italian Jewish community were also being made. At the end of the war there were approximately 18,000 DPs in

Italy, of whom 9,000 were living in DP camps; the rest were scattered living in cities and villages. World ORT Union's work in Italy started later than in other countries; according to a report issued by ORT in 1947 this was because 'the fluidity of the Jewish DPs was greater here, and their patience even less than that of their ill-fated brothers in Germany and Austria'.[95]

According to the World ORT Union Annual Report for Italy, ORT Italy was divided into two clear sections: ORT-Rome and ORT-Northern Italy: 'The activity, initially concentrated particularly in the North where the major part of refugee camps were situated, between 1947 and 1950 progressively moved towards the centre.'[96] There were ORT training facilities situated in Milan, Rome, Grugliasco, Rivoli, Cremona and Grottaferrata. By early 1947 there were thirty-five trade schools, workshops and courses across these locations with a total of 876 pupils. Mr L Varrichione was the Chief of all DP Operations in Italy and he and his workers, according to ORT sources 'show great understanding for the work of ORT, and have a very helpful attitude'.[97] According to World ORT Union reports from 1947:

> after the first quarter of the present year, it could already be observed that the fact of such an energetic and firm beginning of systematic ORT activities had exercised an encouraging influence in all respects on large refugee masses who had been disappointed for so long, and that even here it had been possible to create a favourable atmosphere for the development of ORT institutions.[98]

The majority of ORT's work in Italy was directed towards those who were seeking entry to Palestine. ORT found itself working with DPs who wanted quick access to a skill which might facilitate their entry into Palestine and aid them in their new life there. At the end of the war, when masses of DPs were on the move, thousands of displaced adults and children were crossing the border into Italy and were converging on Milan. They had all been given the same address: 5 Via Unione, the address of the Jewish organisations in Italy and all that remained of the pre-war Jewish community.[99] According to ORT reports from 1947, 'The work of ORT in Italy deals almost exclusively with the DPs in the camps and towns, but extends, too, to emigrants, and includes in Rome also the care of Italian and Jewish, mostly orphaned, children.'[100]

In addition to the adult training and education being conducted by

ORT in Italy, there were ORT youth schools and workshops established in Avigliano and Selvino. At Selvino there was, 'one school for installers of electrical fittings with 25 pupils: one school for cabinet-makers with 20 pupils. In the same workshops for carpentry, a group of 20 adults are being trained as instructors for children's workshops.'[101]

By July 1947 there were forty-one ORT training schools with a total of 936 pupils. By November 1947 the number of pupils benefiting from ORT Italy had risen from 731 to 1,476 across fifty-eight institutions. During the period, July–November 1947, twenty-seven new ORT institutions were set up with 692 pupils. Between November 1947 and March 1948 a further eight ORT schools opened at: Lecco, Adriatico, Arona-Meina, Ivrea, Grottaferrata, Cinecitta, Bari and Barletta.

The World ORT Union Annual Report for Italy, December 1947–March 1948 addressed the topic of why ORT had been so successful in Italy. It concludes:

> The longer the ORT work is continued among the DPs, the stronger a relation arises between it and the DPs, and the greater their ambition becomes to continue their training until its successful conclusion. This is one of the most important causes for the favourable atmosphere for our work in Italy. Unfortunately, when we started our work there, this favourable circumstance had not yet made its appearance.[102]

Throughout the war, hundreds of Italian Jewish children had escaped deportation to ghettos and camps by hiding in convents and monasteries. After the war, Raffaele Cantoni, a prominent figure in the Italian pre-war Jewish community, began trying to locate these children. Cantoni worked closely with his assistant, Mathilda Cassin. In the weeks and months after the end of the war it became clear that this was a task too big for Cantoni and his staff to achieve alone so they called for assistance from the soldiers of the Solel Boneh Company of the Jewish Brigade. With the help of these soldiers, Cantoni began collecting children from the convents and monasteries and placing them in a boarding school overseen by Moshe Ze'iri, a member of the Solel Boneh.[103]

The collection of these surviving Jewish children was problematic. Due to their young age and the length of time they had been in hiding, more often than not the children had forgotten they were Jewish and had no recollection of their former lives. They wore black clothes and crucifixes and were highly suspicious of the Jewish adults who wanted to remove them. By July 1945 Cantoni and the Solel Boneh had collected so many children that they had to move up to the mountains to a village called Piazza Torre. Once based there, more children began to arrive, including the newly liberated children from the concentration camps. By this time Moshe Ze'iri and Mathilda Cassin were firmly established as the two house counsellors, working closely with all the children.

In the early weeks and months at Piazza Torre they became aware of both behavioural and linguistic problems amongst the children from the camps and convents. Those from the convents spoke Italian and could not understand those who had come from the camps who spoke Polish, Yiddish and Hungarian and who were in turn suspicious of the convent children. Both groups of children initially found it hard to communicate with the counsellors and teachers who had decided that in preparation for emigration to Palestine, Hebrew should be the house language. Nitza Sarner, the daughter of Moshe Ze'iri recalls: 'As far as possible everybody had to try and speak Hebrew. They had to learn in classes.'[104]

The community at Piazza Torre continued to grow as the Jewish brigade brought more and more children across the border from DP camps in Austria and Germany. As it expanded it became obvious that once again they needed to move in order to set up a proper home and educational centre. In response to this they moved further up the mountain to the village of Selvino where they occupied a large house called *Sciesopoli*. According to Aharon Megged, 'The house at Selvino came under the authority of the civilian administration in the regional capital of Bergamo; the administration had not yet been replaced, and the governor was a member of the Fascist Party.'[105] The community at Selvino expanded daily and soon included children 'from the camps, from the forests, from the convents where they had been hidden, speaking Polish, Yiddish, Hungarian, Romanian and Italian'.[106] Although these children were now safe, other problems continued, such as a shortage of food.

The lack of food at Selvino was a problem replicated for DPs all over Italy. The ORT annual report for August 1946–July 1947 recorded with sadness that, 'The fact, that in Cremona 2 good pupils of the ORT training workshops for cabinet-making left those to become street-sweepers, because they could earn a little money that way and thus appease their hunger, is not a unique case.'[107]

Moshe Ze'iri, who had lived in Palestine since 1932, ran Selvino like a Kibbutz with a strict set of seven house rules. These were as follows: 1. self-sufficiency – all work to be done by children and carers; no additional work staff; 2. shared responsibility; 3. common property – even stuff sent by relatives had to be shared amongst the children; 4. all adults to share work with children; 5. Hebrew to be house language; 6. no dwelling on the past – look to the future and to Israel; 7. importance of schooling/studies.

These rules had been put in place as many of the children routinely stole food from the kitchens and had difficulty interacting with other children and staff.

> There was a good deal of truculence and resentment during the first few weeks, particularly on the part of the older boys: towards the strict discipline; towards the requirement to get out of bed so early in the morning; towards the fact that they were not permitted to leave the grounds; towards the rationing of food.[108]

The future plan for all those children living in Selvino was emigration to Palestine. Megged writes: 'There was a profound longing to put an end to impermanence, to begin a new life, to put down roots.'[109] As very few certificates for legal emigration were making their way to the house they had to make plans for illegal emigration. Everything was geared towards a new life in Palestine and as Megged explains, 'the children lived vicariously through everything that went on in Palestine. Newspapers brought word, Brigade soldiers brought word.'[110]

Nitza Sarner describes the set-up at the house and the sleeping arrangements of the children:

> There were 2 enormous dormitories – one for girls and one for boys. Over 2 and a half years nearly 800 children passed through Selvino. We, the younger ones, had a separate room and my mother was our teacher. My parents had their own room right at the top of the house ... I slept with the children not with my parents, like in the Kibbutz.[111]

Education was an important part of life at Selvino and Ze'iri and the other counsellors saw to it that the children received a well-rounded schooling including practical trades and skills. In addition to Hebrew classes and other subjects, Nitza Sarner recalls:

Then there were all the ORT classes as well ... That time at the end of the war, there was a big DP camp in Milan and children kept coming. I think ORT came from the DP camp in Milan to the house ... There was metalwork, cobbling ... sewing (tailoring) and embroidering. The sewing classes were run by two sisters, one of them was a qualified teacher.[112]

Sarner explains how it was possible for ORT to set-up classes in the house:

At the end of the war lots of the organisations started to move in, in an official way. The Joint, the ORT – there were lots of workshops in the building. It was a huge building, sprawling. There was a cinema, a full-size cinema.[113]

In early 1948 while Moshe Ze'iri and ORT were working tirelessly at Selvino, the World ORT Union annual report recorded that, 'Of the 36,000 Jews in Italy, 11,000 live in Rome. The vast majority live from hand to mouth without the knowledge of any trade. Thus, the ORT program is of great significance.'[114] In the Rome area there were four ORT workshops and schools set up: the mechanical knitting school, the professional school, the workshops for shirt making, millinery and corsetry and the agricultural courses. There were also ORT activities taking place in three DP camps at this time, situated in Bari, Barletta and Trani.

Between 1946 and May 1948, several groups of children left Sciesopoli and the village of Selvino for Palestine through illegal channels of emigration. Sarner recalls how the younger group of children, of which she was a member, remained at Selvino until the establishment of the State of Israel. She stayed a few months longer: 'me and my mother stayed until December 1948. Israel was founded in May. The house shut down at the end of 1948.'[115]

NOTES

1. Elly Gotz, 'My Story', March 2007.
2. Mark Wyman, *DPs: Europe's Displaced Persons, 1945-1951* (Ithaca: Cornell University Press, 1989), p.150.
3. Ibid.
4. Ibid., p.151.
5. Ibid.
6. WL. Henriques Collection – Microfilm reel 5, document 5/5/16. Telegram to London from Belsen – UNRRA.

7. Hagit Lavsky, *New Beginnings: Holocaust Survivors in Bergen-Belsen and the British Zone in Germany, 1945-1950* (Detroit: Wayne State University Press, 2002), p.34.
8. Ibid.
9. *The Long Way Home*. Written and directed by Mark Jonathan Harris. WL video collection. Film no.1210.
10. Ibid.
11. Lavsky, *New Beginnings*., p.34.
12. TNA: FO 1052/73. 'Col. Robert Solomons - Jewish Advisor to Military Government, British Zone of Occupation, Report to Foreign Office, October 1948.'
13. Ibid.
14. Hagit Lavsky, 'A Community of Survivors: Bergen-Belsen as a Jewish Centre after 1945', in J. Reilly, D. Cesarani, T. Kushner and C. Richmond (eds), *Belsen in History and Memory* (London: Frank Cass, 1997), pp.171.
15. Jack Rader, *By the Skill of Their Hands* (Geneva: World ORT, 1970), pp.68-9.
16. Ibid., p.71.
17. WOA: d05a014. *Report on the ORT Activities August 1946-July 1947. Submitted to the meeting of the Central Board of the World ORT Union Paris, July 6th-7th 1947*, p.47.
18. Rader, *By the Skill of Their Hands*, p.64.
19. Ibid., p.65.
20. WOA, d07a007: *ORT - A Record of Ten Years - Rebuilding Jewish Economic Life* (New York: American ORT Federation, 1956), pp.4, 5.
21. TNA: FO 945/723, 'Jewish Advisory Committee' - 'Jewish DPs in Hohne Camp 1946-47'.
22. TNA: FO 1052/81 - 'Jews ORT Training Schools 1947-48'. Control Commission for Germany (British element).
23. This was opened in November 1945 and was run by Sadi Rurka from the JRU. It had a capacity for seventy orphans aged between 3-13 years. Information from Lavksy, *New Beginnings*.
24. This was opened at Celle in June 1945 and then moved to Belsen. It was operated by the JDC and had a capacity for up to eighty children aged between 2-6 years. Lavksy, *New Beginnings*.
25. This was opened at Celle in June 1945 and later moved to Belsen. The headmistress was Sela Leftowitch. At its height this school taught 300 pupils aged between 6-15 years. Lavsky, *New Beginnings*.
26. There were 200 students. Lavsky, *New Beginnings*.
27. This was opened in November 1945 under the leadership of Rabbi Zvi Meisels, 80-100 students. Lavsky, *New Beginnings*.
28. This was opened in December 1945. Headmistress Dr Helen Wrubel December 1945-April 1947. Dr Michael Lubliner April 1947-1949. Up to 130 students aged 15-22 years. Lavsky, *New Beginnings*.
29. This was opened during the summer of 1946 under the leadership of Rabbi Yehudah Leb Gerst for forty students. Lavsky, *New Beginnings*.
30. This was officially opened in January 1946 under the leadership of Josef Mack. It could train up to 250 students in rotation aged between 13-35 years. Lavsky, *New Beginnings*.
31. Opened in January 1946 under the leadership of Rafael Olevsky. Lavsky, *New Beginnings*.
32. These had 1,500 students in Belsen. Lavsky, *New Beginnings*.
33. Those youth movements active in Belsen included: Noham, Bethar, Hashomer, Hatza'ir, Bene Akiva, Noar Agudathi and Ezra. Lavksy, *New Beginnings*.
34. There is no specific information available about these.
35. Lavsky, *New Beginnings*, p.146.
36. WOA, d06a079: World ORT Union, *ORT Vocational School Bergen-Belsen, 1945-1947* (Geneva: World ORT Union, 1947), p.7.
37. Ibid., p.8.
38. Lavsky, *New Beginnings*, p.71.
39. Aharon Megged, *The Story of the Selvino Children - Journey to the Promised Land* (London: Vallentine Mitchell, 2002), p.183.
40. Zeev W. Mankowitz, *Life Between Memory and Hope - The Survivors of the Holocaust in Occupied Germany* (Cambridge: Cambridge University Press, 2002), p.135.
41. Königseder and Wetzel, *Waiting for Hope*, p.186.
42. Ibid.
43. Königseder and Wetzel, *Waiting for Hope*, p.141.
44. WOA, d07a007: *ORT - A Record of Ten Years - Rebuilding Jewish Economic Life*, pp.4, 5-6.

45. WL. Henriques Collection - Reel 14 - Jews in Germany: General. Report by Professor J. Weingreen, p.2.
46. Ibid., p.3.
47. Ibid., p.4.
48. Ibid., p.6.
49. TNA: FO 945/723, 'Jewish Vocational Training' - 'Jewish DPs in Hohne Camp 1946-47'.
50. Ibid., p.1.
51. Ibid., p.2.
52. Königseder and Wetzel, *Waiting for Hope*, p.121.
53. Ibid., p.122
54. WL. Henriques Collection - Reel 13 - *JRU Co-operation with Other Relief Organisations: Various Voluntary Groups - Prof. Norman Bentwich (Belsen)*, p.1.
55. *ORT Vocational School, Bergen-Belsen*, p.10.
56. Ibid., p.11.
57. WL. Henriques Collection - Reel 4 - *JCRA Organisation: Units in Germany, JRU Status Activities, 1946-50, Belsen*, p.1.
58. WOA, d07a150: *Partial Report: Illustrating the Expenditure incurred During the First Quarter of 1947*, p.14.
59. WOA, d07a151: *Agreement between ORT Union and the Central Committee of Liberated Jews in the American Zone in Germany*. 24 October 1946.
60. Ibid.
61. Ibid.
62. NA document: FO 945/723, 'Jewish Vocational Training - Jewish DPs in Hohne Camp 1946-47'.
63. WOA, d07a153: *Visit to ORT School Stuttgart, Friday, 19 September 1947*, pp.1-2.
64. Ibid., p.2.
65. Zelda Fuksman, interview with Sarah Kavanaugh, 27 January 2006.
66. Ibid.
67. Ibid.
68. Ibid.
69. Ibid.
70. Ibid.
71. WOA, d04a018: 'ORT US Zone Germany 1945-1947', p.8.
72. Ibid., p.10.
73. WOA, d07a150: *Partial Report: Illustrating the Expenditure incurred During the First Quarter of 1947*, p.14.
74. Wyman, *DPs: Europe's Displaced Persons*, p.101.
75. WOA, d05a092: A.C. Glassgold, 'The Spirit Will Rise: The Miracle of Landsberg', in *ORT Economic Review, March 1947*, pp.17-18.
76. Gotz, 'My Story'.
77. Ibid.
78. Ibid.
79. Ibid.
80. Ibid.
81. WL YIVO collection. Reel 15, *2 Years of ORT in Landsberg*, p.1. 23 July 1947. Walinksy to Maegalith.
82. Ibid.
83. Ibid.
84. *ORT Illustrated Magazine*, December 1948, no.10. WL.
85. Rader, *By the Skill of Their Hands*, p.68.
86. WOA, d05a014: *Report on the ORT Activities August 1946-July 1947. Submitted to the meeting of the Central Board of the World ORT Union Paris, July 6th-7th 1947*, p.51.
87. WOA, d07a150: *Partial Report: Illustrating the Expenditure incurred During the First Quarter of 1947*, p.15.
88. 'Report to the Central Board Meeting in Paris on July 11-13, 1948 on World ORT Union in Austria.' Speech made by Mr. Harry Branton. *ORT Illustrated Magazine*, August-September 1948, No.6-7. From YIVO collection at the WL.
89. Ibid.
90. WOA, d07a150: *Report on the ORT Activities August 1946-July 1947*, pp.51-2.
91. 'Report to the Central Board Meeting in Paris on July 11-15, 1948 on World ORT Union in

Austria'.
92. WOA, d05a015: *Report on the ORT Activities July-November 1947. Submitted to the meeting of the Executive Board of the World ORT Union Zurich, November 22nd-23rd 1947*, p.60.
93. WOA, d05a016: *Report on the ORT Activities December 1947-March 1948. Submitted to the meeting of the Executive of the World ORT Union Paris, March 6th-7th 1948*, p.56.
94. WL YIVO Collection: 'Report to the Central Board Meeting in Paris on July 11-13, 1948 on World ORT Union in Austria.'
95. WOA, d07a150: *Partial Report: Illustrating the Expenditure incurred During the First Quarter of 1947*, p.16.
96. 'ORT in Italy', in *ORT 1880-1980* (Rome: Carucci editore Roma, 1980), p.145.
97. WOA, d07a150: *Partial Report: Illustrating the Expenditure incurred During the First Quarter of 1947*, p.16.
98. Ibid., p.17.
99. For a description of this see Aharon Megged, *The Story of the Selvino Children - Journey to the Promised Land* (London: Vallentine Mitchell, 2002), pp.1-34.
100. WOA, d07a150: *Partial Report: Illustrating the Expenditure incurred During the First Quarter of 1947*, p.18.
101. Ibid., p.17.
102. WOA, d05a016: *Report on the ORT Activities December 1947-March 1948*, p.57.
103. For a full biography of Moshe Ze'iri see Megged, *Selvino Children*, pp.12-17.
104. Nitza Sarner interview with Sarah Kavanaugh, 13 March 2007.
105. Megged, *Selvino Children*, p.40.
106. Ibid., p.42.
107. WOA, d05a014: *Report on the ORT Activities August 1946-July 1947*, p.58.
108. Megged, *Selvino Children*, p.58.
109. Ibid., p.88.
110. Ibid., p.109.
111. Sarner interview with Kavanaugh.
112. Ibid.
113. Ibid.
114. WOA, d07a146: Henry Field, *The History of ORT: Organisation for Rehabilitation through Training 1880-1949* (Washington, DC: unpublished, 1949), p.126.
115. Sarner interview with Kavanaugh.

The End of the DP Camps, Israel and Emigration

> Everybody demands skilled workers. A skill is still the best passport to any country that a Displaced Person can have.[1]

Rebuilding Jewish Economic Life, a report produced by American ORT highlights how the lack of emigration possibilities available to those still residing in the DP camps in the late 1940s added to the negative feelings they were experiencing:

> Delay in opening channels of emigration produced a mood of desperation. Three years after the allied armies had overthrown Nazi rule and the barbed wire fences and searchlights had been removed, many of the inmates remained in the same camps. Conditions in the camps were bad enough. But the enervating effects of idleness and waiting worked a terrible attrition of the spirit.[2]

World ORT Union worked hard to combat these feelings of resentment and apathy. In addition to the training they offered in the camps, World ORT Union did all it could to secure emigration visas for its pupils. In fact ORT certificates were viewed favourably by most of the countries in which the survivors wished to settle. American ORT claimed that, 'An ORT diploma was accepted by many governments as a document indicating trade qualification and became known as a "passport to freedom", helping thousands to meet visa requirements.'[3]

Prior to discussing immigration to Palestine and later to Israel, it is important to examine the history of the creation of the State of Israel. On the eve of the Second World War the British Government had published a White Paper on the future of Palestine which was then under British rule by virtue of a Mandate from the League of Nations that included responsibility for the development of a Jewish National Home in line with the promise made to the Jews in the Balfour Declaration of 1917. However, Palestinian Arabs resented the pledge to create a Jewish homeland, fearing the emergence of a Jewish state on their soil, and resisted Jewish immigration. The Mandate proved a headache for the British, punctuated by riots and rebellions from the 1920s to the 1940s. The 1939 White Paper attempted to resolve the situation once and for all. It limited the land that Jews could purchase and settle on and restricted the rate of Jewish immigration to 1,500 per month for five years up to a total of 75,000. At the end of that period the people of Palestine, which due to the balance of the population inevitably meant the Palestinian Arab majority, would decide on the future of the territory. In effect this decreed a state with a permanent Jewish minority because the Arabs would control immigration. During the war the British government, now led by Winston Churchill who was a long time supporter of Zionism, moved away from the White Paper policy and towards the creation of a Jewish state in part of Palestine. The British Labour Party seemed very much in favour of this. However, soon after it was elected to power in July 1945 the new Labour Government declared that it would maintain the White Paper pending a permanent solution to the dilemma of Palestine. This policy came under severe pressure from Jews in the United States who wanted to see the gates of Palestine opened for the survivors of Nazi persecution. President Harry S. Truman who had sent Earl G. Harrison to inspect the DP camps, backed Harrison's recommendation that 100,000 be allowed to emigrate immediately to relieve pressure on the camps.

Even when the DP camps were overflowing and Zionist groups were gaining momentum both inside and outside the camps, the British government refused to change its policy towards the DPs, insisting there was no link between the situation in the camps and events in Palestine. Joanne Reilly sees this as a notable failure on the part of the British: 'Briefly, the British were constantly torn between the commitment of the Balfour Declaration in 1917 to establish a Jewish National Home in Palestine and the protection of British interests in the Middle East.'[4]

Throughout 1946, Zionist groups became active inside several of the DP camps, mainly across the British zone of occupation. These groups were particularly prominent in the Belsen DP camp where they taught Zionism and Judaism and instilled in the DPs a strong desire to move to Palestine. This wish to emigrate to Palestine was reflected in a poll carried out in DP camps in Germany in 1947. Out of the 19,000 Jewish DPs polled, 97 per cent were in favour of settling in Palestine.

The British Government tried to placate the Arab and Muslim world which was upset by the recommendation made by the Harrison Report that 100,000 DPs be allowed to emigrate. However, the British believed that they could not solve the problem themselves and tried to get American cooperation by setting up an Anglo-American Committee of inquiry. They hoped it would suggest a policy that would allow Britain to remain in Palestine where the Army had bases that were considered essential to the strategic position of the British Empire. Meanwhile, the Jews of Palestine commenced an underground war against the British. It was initially led by the Hagana, the semi-official Jewish defence force in Palestine. But more radical groups that had been attacking the British since the late 1930s quickly expanded the scope and ferocity of the insurgency. They were the Irgun Zvai Leumi (the Irgun) and Lohamei Herut Israel, (Lehi, also known as the Stern Gang). The Anglo-American Committee issued its report in April 1946. While it was equivocal about a long-term settlement, it called for 100,000 Jewish DPs to be allowed into Palestine. The British Government could not accept this and while the diplomats wrangled the terrorist campaign reached new heights of viciousness.

While resistance in Palestine was taking shape, Hagana, the Jewish paramilitary organisation, was also stepping up its activities in Germany. They were responsible for bringing survivors from eastern Europe into Germany and from there to sea ports in Italy and then on to Palestine. Groups of former Jewish partisans and Holocaust survivors, together with the Jewish Brigade, formed by the British Army in 1944, started to help Jewish DPs cross borders and zones of occupation prior to escaping Europe. This process was known as the *Bricha,* meaning flight.[5] According to Yehuda Bauer:

> The most important thing to remember about the Bricha is, I think, that even more than the survivors' organisations in the DP countries, it was founded and organised by survivors, and not outside

helpers. In this case it was a small group of partisans and fighters ... In February 1945, they met in Lublin with the survivors of the ghetto rebellions, and founded Bricha, to smuggle their followers into Romania on their way to Palestine.[6]

The illegal immigration of Jews into Palestine, *Aliyah Bet,* was also aided by the *Mosad le-Aliyah Bet* formed by the Jewish leadership in Palestine. Often the ships fleeing mainland Europe were intercepted by the British navy and the Jewish passengers were sent to internment camps in Palestine and later in Cyprus. Bauer explains the motivation behind the illegal immigration, 'Aliyah Bet was a result of DP pressure, and combined with the burning desire of the Palestinian leadership to get as many Jews into Palestine as possible in order to intensify their struggle for a Jewish state.'[7] Bauer claims that the total number of immigrants between May 1945 and May 1948 reached 69,000.[8]

In Europe, the Jewish Brigade were helped by other concerned individuals such as US Army Chaplain Herbert Friedman. Friedman recalls how he was responsible for bribing border guards between the German zones of occupation with cigarettes – one carton of cigarettes per Jewish DP smuggled across the border. The cost of each carton was $150 and each night he would hand over up to $45,000 in cigarettes, guaranteeing that 300 DPs crossed the border each night.[9]

Those attempting the journey to Palestine endured terrible conditions as they were forced to trudge for miles over snow covered mountains often carrying children and babies. Oleiski recorded that illegal immigration 'involved such difficulties and suffering that only young idealists could withstand them'.[10]

Once the DPs and other refugees had crossed into the British and US zones of Germany they headed to Italy where they were packed onto ships, which were often old cargo ships and river cruisers, which those organising the Bricha had been able to procure. Out of the sixty-three ships that travelled illegally to Palestine between 1945-48, only six arrived undetected by the British. All those ships which were intercepted were turned back to Europe, although later the British established detention camps in Cyprus where the DPs were interned.[11] One such ship was the Exodus.[12] It was stopped by the British en route to Palestine on 17 July 1947 while carrying 4,515 Jewish DPs. It resisted arrest and was attacked by the British during which three people were killed and many injured.

During the autumn of 1946 David Ben Gurion, Chairman of the Jewish Agency for Palestine, visited several DP camps in Germany. Friedman was tasked with escorting him round the camps. Ben Gurion spoke to the assembled crowds at both the Belsen and Zeilsheim DP camps announcing, 'I come to you with empty pockets – I have no certificates to give you. Therefore I have to ask you for patience and hope.'[13]

Between April 1946 and February 1947, the British attempted by themselves to find a solution to the Palestine question that would preserve their presence there, in the wider Middle East, and so maintain their global strategic position. They attempted to bring the Jews and the Arabs together in a conference that met periodically in London between September 1946 and January 1947, floating various ideas that included local autonomy and federated areas under overall British rule. None of these solutions were acceptable to the Arabs or the Jews. In despair, in February 1947 the British Government resolved to hand Palestine back to the United Nations, the successor organisation to the League of Nations. The UN sent a special commission to find a solution. It investigated between May and August 1947, during which time the terrorist war against the British rumbled on and illegal emigrants tried to run the blockade that the British maintained in order to preserve the status quo until the UN made its decision. Eventually a majority of the commission proposed the partition of Palestine. In November 1947 the UN General Assembly voted to accept the report and so create a Jewish and an Arab state in the territory of Palestine.

The British announced that they would pull out of Palestine by May 1948 and began to withdraw their forces. Communal warfare now raged between Jews and Arabs, but the British Army did little except preserve the 'status quo' and the Royal Navy continued to prevent 'illegal immigration'. In May, the Jewish Agency decided to declare the independence of the Jewish state so that it could at last take control of its own destiny and create the conditions for free Jewish immigration. Within minutes of the declaration of independence in Tel Aviv, President Truman announced US recognition of the new state, against the urgings of his own State Department. This made the USA the first to give recognition to the state and fulfilled Truman's long held humanitarian wish to see the DPs leave the camps for a better life elsewhere.

The declaration of the state of Israel opened the doors to those who had been waiting to emigrate for so long. Soon those who had been refused entry and interned on Cyprus were allowed into Israel to start new lives there. Leonard Dinnerstein claims, 'with the establishment of Israel in 1948, a safety-valve opened up, and those Jews who could not go elsewhere wound up in the promised land'.[14]

One woman who had recently arrived in Palestine from the DP camps recalls: 'When I heard the wonderful news announced on the radio I became for a short while speechless.'[15] Rifka Muscovitz Glatz, who was born in Hungary in 1937, remembers the moment when the state of Israel was declared:

> I remember when Israel was declared a free state. We were sleeping ... I was 11 years old ... we were awakened all to come out and dance, and everybody was very happy. It took me time from being awakened in the middle of the night to understand the consequences and the ramifications of this news.[16]

The creation of the state of Israel also helped solve a problem with regard to the emigration of certain groups of DPs. Since the end of the war there had been a continuous problem with resettling the elderly and the disabled as no one wanted to take them. Wyman writes that: 'Only Israel drew no line on age or physical condition.'[17]

In the immediate post-war years emigration opportunities remained extremely limited for Jewish DPs:

> Resettlement opportunities developed slowly, excruciatingly slowly. In the United States, where a poll found that a majority wished to see European immigration either reduced or eliminated, ethnic and religious groups were silent on the issue for many months.[18]

Gradually the situation started to change. Wyman explains how quotas on immigration started to ease and countries began to look more favourably on the non-Jewish DPs as possible immigrants. In Autumn 1946, Belgium offered places to 20,000 Balts and their families to come and work as coal miners. Britain was next offering places to 86,000 DPs. Wyman claims:

> It was the earlier experience with foreign soldiers, however, as well as with refugees during the war, that prepared the way for welcoming DPs. The British found that the 115,000 Polish army veterans who elected to join the 'Polish Resettlement Corps' and stay in Britain after 1945 were a benefit, not a problem.[19]

Wyman continues, 'The eyes of Labour Government planners soon turned to the regular DPs languishing in camps across Germany, Austria, and Italy ... Then with "Operation Westward Ho" in 1947, Britain set a goal of up to 100,000 DPs and recruited 79,000 by mid-1948.'[20]

During 1947 Canada also began to consider DPs as possible immigrants but this decision had been reached more out of a need for labour rather than as a humanitarian act. Up until 1948 Canada had refused to take any Jewish DPs at all.

It is important at this point to examine how World ORT Union was viewed by the immigration authorities and what they did to aid those seeking emigration to Palestine. While the emigration possibilities were limited for the majority of the DPs it is certain that the acquisition of a trade proved beneficial. Yehuda Bauer claims: 'nobody wanted to take Jewish tailors who had not worked at their trade in any case for a number of years',[21] demonstrating that those who had an ORT certificate and a newly acquired and practiced trade would be in an advantageous position. Norman Frajman who took an ORT photography course in the Bamberg DP camp claims, 'The certificate of my graduation from the course was looked at favourably by the American Consulate prior to being issued a visa.'[22] In 1948, Dr William Haber, the Special Advisor on Jewish Affairs to General Clay in the US zone, declared, 'Immigration possibilities exist for overseas countries, but only to the extent that trained people can be sent there'.[23]

From 1947 onwards, immigration into America eased slightly, although it continued to discriminate against Jewish DPs. The situation for the Jews did not change until 1950. On 1 April a US bill announced that 400,000 DPs would be allowed entry into the United States over the next four years in addition to the immigration quotes already decided upon. Whereas the British had refused to identify any relationship between DPs and the situation in Palestine, Reilly explains: 'The Americans saw clearly the link between the Palestine question and the Jewish DP problem in Europe. One offered the solution to the other.' Dinnerstein explains how, in response to mounting pressure, 'President Truman, first in January 1947, and again in July, called upon Congress to produce suitable legislation to aid displaced persons'.[24]

During the autumn of 1947 the House of Representatives and Senate both sent fact finding committees to Europe to tour the DP camps as they were still wary of passing any bill that would prove too unpopular at home. Once their tour was completed the House committee reported that, 'If the Jewish facet of the problem could be cleared up, the solution of the remainder of the problem could be facilitated. The opening of Palestine to the resettlement of Jewish displaced persons would break the logjam'.[25] In order to explore and exhaust all possibilities surrounding the emigration of DPs Truman set up the Displaced Persons Commission in August 1948. Up until 1948, America had only admitted 40,000 DPs in less than three years. But even after US quotas expanded, difficulties remained. There are countless reports of the gruelling immigration process. Wyman describes how,

> One DP was asked whether he would be willing to join the U.S. Army. He said he would. Then the immigration officer asked, 'If, while in the Army, you had a chance to capture Stalin, what would be the worst punishment you could give him?' The DP shot back: 'I'd bring him here to Funk Kaserne and make him go through processing for emigration to the States'.[26]

Although the immigration process was lengthy and difficult, it did not detract from the feelings of joy and relief experienced by the newly arrived immigrants. One new arrival in America remembers how, 'nobody told stories about the past although everyone had a story to tell. There was the expectation of new things in the air.'[27] He continues to explain how, due to the fact he had nothing left in Europe, he felt as if he was starting a whole new life:

> I felt completely at home the first day. I had left nothing on the other side but misery, tragedy and horror. It was like emerging from the ashes like a phoenix with this exhilarating feeling of freedom. The tragedy was in me and would stay with me but for the moment this was my re-birth. I felt like a hunchback with the hunch suddenly removed who can straighten up and walk like a man.[28]

The creation of the state of Israel and the closure of the DP camps were closely related. According to Königseder and Wetzel, 'After the establishment of the state of Israel, ORT's programs, as well as other aspects of life in the Jewish DP camps, had to be reevaluated in light of the fledgling Jewish state's needs.'[29] This is an important statement as it can be argued that the creation of the state of Israel marked a turning point in the history of World ORT Union. Shapiro also discussed this link claiming:

The establishment of the State of Israel in 1948 and, to a lesser extent, the U.S. Displaced Persons Act of 1948, provided new outlets for emigration and resettlement. At the beginning of 1949, only some 50,000 persons remained in the camps; three years later; in 1952, there remained a hard core of 15,000.[30]

From the moment the new state of Israel was declared, the focus of World ORT Union's work would shift from rehabilitation towards immigration. However, although the focus did shift towards Israel, according to the minutes of a meeting held in Paris during November 1948, preferential treatment could not be given to those seeking entry to Israel over those seeking entry to other countries of settlement. The minutes read, 'Keen controversy exists as to whether Jewish organisations supported by Jewish funds have the right to assist in the individual resettlement of a person who for some reason of his own decides to emigrate to a land other than Israel.'[31] It concludes however that: 'Those of us whose mandate it is to render all possible assistance to every displaced and refugee Jew should not be drawn into ideological considerations.'[32]

In the report of her tour of the DP camps during 1949, Rose Henriques Chairman of the German Department of the Jewish Committee for Relief Abroad wrote about how the work of ORT remained vital:

> ORT and Belsen are synonymous and the thousands of persons, young and old, who have to thank the ORT School at Belsen for opening to them the gates of a trade will fully realise, now that so many of them are already emigrated, how valuable a part of their future is the training they got in these grim surroundings.[33]

Having looked at ORT's work in Belsen, Henriques discusses ORT's work in Germany on a broader level:

> As far as ORT in Germany is concerned, I can only say I am most deeply impressed by the magnificent work that is being done. The fact that an ORT diploma is a recognised guarantee of the holders' ability, means that the individual goes to his or her new life with a very real asset to back up the precious and newly-won passport.[34]

DPs in Austria and Germany were by no means oblivious to the political tensions and upheavals in Europe and the Middle East during 1947 and early 1948. Due to this they became aware of how an ORT certificate could help them during their emigration.

With the creation of the state of Israel and a relaxing of the US immigration quotas came a mass feeling of relief in the DP camps. Wyman describes how the feelings of depression and uselessness were turned into those of anticipation and hope. He continues to explain how this led to: 'a new concern for vocational training, for language classes, for any classes'.[35] Although emigration conditions had eased according to Wyman, 'But many could not leave. When the International Refugee Organisation took its final census on 1 January 1952, it found 177,000 DPs still on the rolls, less than half of whom were employed in the German or Austrian economy.'[36]

During 1947 and 1948 the DP camp population in Germany was in constant movement as some camps were closed and other more temporary ones were established. An example of this can be seen in the Germany section of the World ORT Union Annual Report from 1 July–31 October 1948. The report describes how, 'the American Government decided to evacuate all D.P.'s from Berlin to the U.S. zone of Germany, the two ORT schools there had to be closed. But soon afterwards a new ORT school was formed for free-living Jews of Berlin.'[37] The period covered by this annual report, July–October 1948, shows that there were seven areas remaining in the US zone where ORT schools were operating. In the British zone the ORT schools at Neustadt/Holstein, Ahlem Farm, Emden and Sengwarden were all closed down when the Berlin schools were shut. The British zone still had 650 students on the ORT registers compared to 6,000 in the US zone and 1,050 in Austria. The ORT schools in these areas were, by this time, divided into four different categories: first, *Fachmitteschulen*/special schools, which, 'provide a happy combination of the teaching of general subjects (languages, physics, chemistry, history, etc.), in the mornings, and training in technical skills in the afternoons';[38] secondly, rehabilitation centres for those suffering from TB; thirdly, schools for disabled people and invalids; and fourthly, 'Free-living Jews'/those living in the cities who were keen to register on a course.

From 1 October 1948, a World ORT Union monthly journal, *The ORT Idea* was issued from Munich. The first edition announced:

> There are at the moment approximately 75,000 Jewish DP's, [and]

30,000 free-living Jews in the US zone of Germany. There are in the British zone of Germany and Berlin, about 5,000 Jewish DP's and 10,000 free-living Jews the latter being concentrated mainly in Berlin, Hamburg and Hannover. Austria has about 10,000 Jewish DP's and 2,000 free living Jews.[42]

While 1947 had marked a year of growth for ORT in both Germany and Austria, 1948 proved more complex. The first six months were dedicated to consolidating the previous year's work while the second half of the year focused on emigration to Israel. Statistics collected for the World ORT Union Annual Reports from 1948 show that one out of every four DPs received some training from ORT and that half of all DPs who received some kind of vocational training received it from ORT.

The work of World ORT Union gained far-reaching appreciation. The Sub-committee of the Committee on Foreign Affairs of the 80th US Congress wrote a report on the success of ORT's work in Germany, Austria and Italy during the late 1940s. It concluded, 'The ORT program is very effective, while such a program for non-Jewish children is almost completely lacking. ORT has done the best job of vocational training in the Displaced Persons' camps.'[40]

The Belsen DP camp which had been so prominent during the years 1945–48 had all but closed by 1950. The last remaining DPs left in August 1951. The majority of the Belsen DPs emigrated to Israel. Landsberg, which like Belsen had been instrumental in the rehabilitation of Holocaust survivors, closed on 15 October 1950. When discussing the final weeks of the Belsen camp and the feelings of those who spent their post-war years there, Reilly concludes:

> A myriad of feelings and experiences were associated with it, and almost always they involved sorrow, loneliness and anxiety. Furthermore, the notion of liberation as providing 'a neat ending' to the Jewish suffering of the wartime years is simplistic and misleading: the very length of the Belsen DP camp's existence is evidence enough of that.[41]

Wyman discusses the final months of the DP camps and claims, 'Toward the closing of the DP camps, educational enterprises eventually became a matter for the local communities' leadership. The JRU and

ORT especially aimed at helping the communities develop educational systems of their own.'[42] This is an important point as it shows that ORT was responsible for transferring its courses prior to leaving certain areas.

Statistics on the number of people helped by World ORT Union inside the DP camps varies according to whether you count all those who registered on courses, those who completed them or only those who graduated from an ORT course and received a certificate. Shapiro records the figure of between 40,000–45,000 trainees. He claims this is the number who received, 'systematic training' – those who regularly attended a course and graduated from it. Rader, on the other hand, gives a figure of closer to 80,000 which incorporates all those who attended an ORT course however briefly. J. Donald Kingsley, Director General of the IRO who wrote to Syngalowski on 31 October 1951, claimed that World ORT Union was responsible for training, 'approximately 12,000 students at one time'.[43]

1951 marks a turning point in the history of the DP camps as a large proportion of the remaining DPs left the camps for Australia, Canada, the United States and Israel. Shapiro describes what was left of the camp system during the early 1950s:

> During the 1950s, the ORT school in Hamburg, in the British zone, closed, as did the schools in Frankfurt, Furth, Stuttgart, Wiesbaden, and Passen in the American zone. While the DP problem had, in the main, been solved by 1951, there was still one camp, Föhrenwald, in Bavaria, that was not closed until 1951.[44]

On 1 December 1951, Föhrenwald DP camp was handed over to the German authorities, although it remained open until 1957. Between 1951 and 1957 it functioned as a camp for Jews who had nowhere to go. ORT remained active in Föhrenwald until 1956.

In Austria ORT schools were also closing down during the late 1940s and by the end of 1950 there were only two ORT projects still running with a total of 280 pupils. These two schools were situated in Vienna and Hallein.

In Italy, unlike in Germany and Austria, ORT courses and schools not only continued to flourish but actually expanded. They took on a new importance in the post-DP era and became part of the educational establishment. According to Shapiro:

The new five-year *Lycee Scientifico* and the Business and Language Schools in Rome and Milan are considered an important part of the Jewish school system, providing both general and Jewish education. ORT-Italy also has assisted the Jewish communities of Venice, Genoa, and Florence with Hebrew teaching.[45]

As various ORT courses and schools closed in Italy, attempts were made to transfer schools and projects en masse to Israel. An example of this is the transfer of Italian pilots and pilot training to Israel. ORT in Italy was responsible for providing Israel with its first pilot school. The number of pilots trained by ORT Italy between July and November 1948 was 3,117.

Once the majority of DPs had left the camps in Italy, the Italian authorities began to request that ORT give up their premises, most of which were located in the north of the country, and move south. The World ORT annual report for 1948 explains that this proved disruptive: 'Simultaneously with the transfer of the numerous DP camps to the South came, in the course of the whole summer, the determined effort for a speedily organised emigration to Israel.'[46] As a result of these changes, the majority of Jewish DPs in Italy were now concentrated in three southern DP camps based at Trani, Bari and Barletta. The total number of pupils registered for the academic year 1949/50 was 1,379; for the following year this figure rose to 1,542.

On 27 June 1948 a conference organised by the co-chairmen of World ORT Union, Dr Lvovitch and Dr Syngalowski, was held in Germany. Professor William Haber the Special Advisor on Jewish Affairs, Samuel Haber Director of the JDC and representatives of the IRO were also in attendance. Oleiski recorded that, 'All participants at the Conference realized that many schools would soon be closed because of the gradual decline in the number of students ... many of the students were making preparations for emigration to America.'[47] Not long after the conference concluded, the ORT headquarters in Munich began the transfer of ORT equipment from Germany to Israel. The ORT office in Munich was closed in 1957 after the Föhrenwald DP camp was disbanded. According to Oleiski:

> With the liquidation of the last camp, ORT's historic mission for survivors of the Holocaust came to an end. For five years. ORT had performed the tremendous task of giving vocational training

and the hope of a new life to the Jewish refugees in Germany, a work which will forever be a shining light in the history of ORT.[48]

The closure of the last DP camp meant that all responsibility for DPs still remaining in Germany and Austria now passed to the German and Austrian authorities. According to Wyman, 'Those remaining in West Germany were guaranteed legal equality with Germans, except voting rights, and citizenship could be granted after five years.'[49]

On 11 July 1948, the Central Board of the World ORT Union met in Paris. The Central Board declared that it welcomed

> the new State of Israel and gives assurance of its full support for the building up of Israel's skilled labor force ... the Central Board affirms its readiness to negotiate with the Israeli Government the transfer of ORT DP schools and further working in Israel and confirms the decision of the Interim Committee that Dr. Syngalowksi should proceed to Israel as soon as possible.[50]

Dr Syngalowski left Venice for Tel Aviv on 1 November 1948 on a fact finding mission to establish how ORT could transfer its courses and equipment to the new state.

The creation of the state of Israel and the subsequent immigration of the DPs combined with the closure of the DP camps marked a turning point in the history of World ORT Union. As more and more groups of DPs started to arrive in Israel, ORT followed closely behind shifting the focus of its work from Europe to the new state. In a publication produced by American ORT Federation, this process is described: 'The agreement with UNRRA and the Central Committee of Liberated Jews had specified that school equipment would follow the DPs to their new home. Large quantities began to arrive in Israel during 1949.'[51] According to Shapiro, ORT had

> been present in Palestine, not as a functioning organization but through its many alumni. Graduates of ORT schools in Poland, Rumania, and Lithuania, had gone there on Aliyah and were among the builders, both in the kibbutzim and the private sector, of the State of Israel.[52]

An important World ORT Union meeting regarding the future of the organisation had taken place in August 1948 between a manager from Geneva, Dr Jehuda Beham, President of the ORT Tool Supply Corporation for Palestine Ltd., and Mr Shlomo Jaffe, Tel Aviv, member of the Council of the ORT Tool Supply Corporation. The minutes of the World ORT Union Administrative Committee held in Paris on 10 November 1948 record:

> The two Israeli delegates made a complete report on the present situation in Israel, vocational training needs and the situation with regard to the supply of artisans and kibbutzim with machines and tools on credit. In the course of the ensuing debates which lasted all week the possibilities of ORT activities in Israel were examined and preparations for beginning of ORT's work discussed.[53]

Between June and October 1949, the following machinery and tools were transferred from Germany to Israel: '10 Universal wood working machines, 10 Dubied knitting machines, 10 knitting machines of Swedish manufacture, 10 lathes, 100 sewing machines.'[54] In addition to the meeting held on the transfer of individuals and tools, preparations were made for transferring entire schools from Germany, Austria and Italy. It was decided however that this could not start until Dr Syngolowski had returned from his trip to Israel in November 1948.

Two conferences were held by the World ORT Union in Geneva on the subject of the transfer of the European schools to Israel. These were organised by Dr Lvovitch and Dr Syngalowksi and in addition to them, they were attended by Dr O. Dutch, Director for Germany and Austria, Mr A. Saolun, Chief of Supply and Transport for Germany and Austria and Mrs D. Greene, Director of the American zone of Germany.

Between the years 1948 and 1949, 341,000 immigrants arrived in Israel to start new lives there: 'Within a period of two years, the Jewish population – which numbered 650,000 persons at the inception of the State, absorbed the influx of immigrants and the population jumped more than 50%.'[55]

According to a Foreign Office document sent from the Chancery to the British Embassy in Tel Aviv on 2 August 1955:

> At the end of 1948, ORT extended its activities to Israel and transferred here a number of schools, complete with equipment. Training centres have now been established in some of the main

towns and larger agricultural settlements and plans have been laid for a further extension of its activities in Israel.[56]

The document also commented on the quality of this early training on offer from ORT in Israel saying: 'The Ambassador has visited some of them and was much impressed by the excellence of the training given and by the spirit and manners of the pupils.'[57]

The following epilogue describes how those who emigrated to Israel and other countries of settlement viewed their new lives and how they looked back on their time with ORT. What are their lasting memories of the DP camps and how does World ORT Union fit into them? According to Wyman:

> the DP story is one of mixed results and mixed endings, and the contrasts did not stop when some refugees boarded ships and planes for distant lands. Within his own memory, each DP can search and find great joy and great pain as images of those years come into view.[58]

NOTES

1. David Lvovitch in speech given to the Women's ORT-OZE in South Africa. 1947. In WOA, d07a148: *ORT-OZE 1947 Caravan*. ORT Johannesburg 1947, p.23.
2. WOA, d07a007: *ORT – A Record of Ten Years – Rebuilding Jewish Economic Life* (New York: American ORT Federation, 1956), p.4.
3. Ibid.
4. Joanne Reilly, *Belsen, the Liberation of a Concentration Camp* (London: Routledge, 1998), p.86.
5. For more on the Bricha see Yehuda Bauer, *Flight and Rescue: Brichah* (New York: Random House, 1970).
6. Yehuda Bauer, 'The DP Legacy', in Menachem Z. Rosensaft (ed.), *Life Reborn, Jewish Displaced Persons 1945-1951. Conference Proceedings* (14-17 January 2000) (Washington DC: United States Holocaust Memorial Museum, 2001), p.29.
7. Ibid., p.32.
8. For more on the illegal emigration of Jews to Palestine see, Ze'ev Venia Hadari, *Second Exodus: the Full Story of Jewish Illegal Immigration to Palestine, 1945-1948* (London: Vallentine Mitchell, 1991); Ze'ev Venia Hadari and Ze'ev Tsahor, *Voyage to Freedom: an Episode in the Illegal Immigration to Palestine* (London: Vallentine Mitchell, 1985); Dalia Offer, *Escaping the Holocaust: Illegal Immigration to the Land of Israel, 1939-1944* (New York: Oxford University Press, 1990).
9. WL: *The Long Way Home*. Written and directed by Mark Jonathan Harris. WL video collection. Film no.1210.
10. I. Posner (ed.), *Jacob Oleiski, A Man's Work* (Israel: ORT Israel, 1986), p.66.
11. For more on internment in Cyprus, see Morris Laub, *Last Barrier to Freedom: Internment of Jewish Holocaust Survivors on Cyprus: 1946-1949* (California: Judah L. Magnus Museum, 1985).
12. For more on the Exodus see Peter Abolson, 'The Exodus Affair: Hamburg 1947', *Journal of Holocaust Education*, 6, 3 (Winter 1997), pp.65-79; Ruth Gruber, *Exodus 1947: The Ship that Launched a Nation. Destination Palestine: the Story of the Hagannah Ship Exodus 1947* (New

York: Times Books, 1999); Aviva Halamish and Ora Cummings, *The Exodus Affair: Holocaust Survivors and the Struggle for Palestine* (London: Vallentine Mitchell, 1998).
13. WL: *The Long Way Home*.
14. Ibid.
15. Ibid.
16. USHMM testimony on creation of the state of Israel.
17. Mark Wyman, *DPs: Europe's Displaced Persons, 1945-1951* (Ithaca, NY: Cornell University Press, 1989), p.203.
18. Ibid., p.185.
19. Ibid., p.189.
20. Ibid.
21. Bauer, 'The DP Legacy', p.32.
22. Frajman, interview with Kavanaugh.
23. Jack Rader, *By the Skill of Their Hands* (Geneva: World ORT, 1970), p.70.
24. Leonard Dinnerstein, 'The United States and the Displaced Persons'. Taken from *She'erit Hapletah, 1944-1948 Rehabilitation and Political Struggle. Proceedings of the Sixth Yad Vashem International Conference* (Jerusalem: Yad Vashem, 1985.), pp.357-8.
25. Ibid., p.359.
26. Wyman, *Europe's Displaced Persons*, p.198.
27. WL: *The Long Way Home*.
28. Ibid.
29. Angelika Königseder and Juliane Wetzel, *Waiting for Hope: Jewish Displaced Persons in Post-World War II Germany* (Illinois: Northwestern University Press, 2001), pp.95-166.
30. Leon Shapiro, *The History of ORT: A Jewish Movement for Social Change* (New York: Schocken Books, 1980), p.245.
31. WOA, d07a004: *Immigration - Emigration. Paris Conference November 1948*, p.8.
32. Ibid.
33. WL. Henriques Collection: Rose Henriques, - Reel 5-2/10/67, *Impressions of Some ORT Schools in Germany, 4.01.49*, p.2.
34. Ibid.
35. Wyman, *Europe's Displaced Persons*, p.179.
36. Ibid., p.202.
37. WOA, d05a018: *Report on ORT Activities July 1-October 31, 1948. Submitted to the meeting of the Executive of the World ORT Union Paris, November 18th-19th* 1948, p.81.
38. Ibid., p.84.
39. WL YIVO Collection, Reel 15-10, *The ORT Idea No. 1*. 1 October 1948, p.7.
40. WL YIVO Collection, Reel 17, 2, *The Sub-committee of the Committee on Foreign Affairs of the 80th US Congress*, p.1.
41. Reilly, *Belsen*, p.117.
42. Wyman, *Europe's Displaced Persons*, p.187.
43. Shapiro, *The History of ORT*, p.245.
44. Ibid., p.287.
45. Ibid., p.289.
46. *Report on ORT Activities July 1-October 31, 1948*, p.89.
47. Posner, *Jacob Oleiski*, p.68.
48. Ibid., p.69.
49. Wyman, *Europe's Displaced Persons*, p.204.
50. WOA, d05a018: *Report on ORT Activities July 1-October 31, 1948*, p.6.
51. *ORT - A Record of Ten Years - Rebuilding Jewish Economic* Life (American ORT Federation, New York: 1956). p.4. World ORT Archive: d07a007, p.6.
52. Shapiro, *The History of ORT*, p.328.
53. WOA, d05a018: *Report on ORT Activities July 1-October 31, 1948*, p.48.
54. Ibid., p.47.
55. Posner, *Jacob Oleiski*, p.70.
56. TNA FO 371/115929 - 'World Association for vocational training among Jewish Centres in the Diaspora (ORT) founded in 1880.'
57. Ibid.
58. Wyman, *Europe's Displaced Persons*, p.206.

Conclusion

ORT saved my life.[1]

This book has examined the work of ORT from its origins in Russia in 1880 up until the foundation of the state of Israel in 1948 and beyond. It has focused on the work of World ORT Union prior to the Second World War in Berlin and later, inside the ghettos of eastern Europe during the war. It has also highlighted the work of World ORT Union during the post-war period in Germany inside the DP camps across the British and American zones of occupation in addition to shedding light on some of the work which took place in Austria and Italy in the post-war years.

Prior to the outbreak of the Second World War, under the shadow of the Nazi Party, ORT Germany facilitated the transfer of the Berlin school to the United Kingdom where it established the Leeds school. This was a lifesaving mission and one that was not only responsible for saving the lives of the Berlin boys and teachers who travelled to Leeds but one that would benefit and enrich British ORT for years to come.

In the ghettos of eastern Europe during the Holocaust ORT did much to aid the starving and destitute Jewish populations. Wherever possible they gave food and shelter to those who sought it and they fought hard to obtain exemption from deportation for those fortunate enough to find a place within their workshops. In several cases they were able to save the lives of their pupils and staff, although most were killed. While the majority of the ORT staff from the ghettos died in the concentration and death camps, including Jashunsky head of ORT in the Warsaw Ghetto, some, like Jacob Oleiski from Kovno, went on to shape the character of World ORT Union's rehabilitation work after the war.

It was Oleiski's strength and ingenuity that guided the post-war organisation inside the DP camps and helped to make World ORT Union the leading force in the rehabilitation of Holocaust survivors.

World ORT Union's post-war work was crucial in the rehabilitation of thousands of Holocaust survivors. It was instrumental in equipping them with the skills they needed in order to forge their new lives and with helping them to come to terms with what they had lost. The presence of ORT inside the DP camps made the immediate post-war months and years bearable. The importance of the provision of long-term stimulation for those housed in the DP camps cannot be underestimated. It was the diligence and initiative of the ORT workers that was responsible for instilling self-worth and purpose back into the lives of the survivors.

World ORT Union was so successful in the field of rehabilitation primarily because it was able to help survivors address their painful past while helping them towards a positive and active future. The ORT schools enabled the survivors to view their future not only with trepidation, but with hope. This hope sprang from the realisation that their ORT certificate would aid them to settle in a new country armed with a fresh skill. The acquisition of this skill would not only help them through the immigration process but also enable them to find jobs.

In the sphere of post-war rehabilitation work World ORT Union was not alone. However, to the extent that it managed to rehabilitate the survivors, it was ahead of many of the other relief groups that operated at the time.

Zelda Fuksman claims that the courses taught by ORT equipped the pupils with more than their chosen skill. Through the acquisition of the new skill the pupils became rejuvenated:

> I have learned that I can do just about anything. The wonderful sewing that I learned at ORT served me well throughout my life ... I did not continue with a sewing job, but continued with education in the USA and did other work, but the fine sewing, has developed in me a patience and desire to continue with many handcraft projects, such as needlepoint, crocheting, knitting, sewing.[2]

In conclusion she claims that ORT was 'useful and gave me a feeling of success and accomplishment'.[3]

It was not only the ORT pupils who were stimulated by the courses. The teachers were also instilled with new feelings of accomplishment.

William Tannenzapf remembers how, 'I felt useful and enjoyed administration as well as teaching. I used my teaching skills again for ORT when we arrived in Montreal in evening and week-end courses.'[4] When describing the courses he taught inside the DP camps, Tannenzapf concludes: 'I think the courses were enormously useful. Many students who came to Canada with a foundation from ORT went on to lead successful lives here.'[5]

Elly Gotz who graduated from the Landsberg ORT course in radio mechanics describes how important ORT has been for him during his life, both as a DP in Germany and after emigrating to Canada. Gotz claims: 'My knowledge of how important it is to learn a skill prompted me to urge my son to learn a trade'.[6] He concludes, 'ORT has, through 126 years of its existence, created a happier people, given untold humans a solid, permanent base of joy in life. I know it did it for me.'[7]

It is the testimony of Elly Gotz and countless others who took the ORT courses that shed light on the important work carried out by ORT inside the DP camps at the end of the Second World War. It is their experiences and voices that considerably add to our understanding of the immediate post-war period and highlight this significant part of the history of World ORT Union.

NOTES

1. James interview with Kavanaugh.
2. Fuksman interview with Kavanaugh.
3. Ibid.
4. Tannenzapf interview with Kavanaugh.
5. Ibid.
6. Gotz, 'My Story'.
7. Ibid.

Bibliography

PRIMARY SOURCES

Unpublished – By Archive

World ORT Archive, London, UK (WOA)

WOA, d00a010c: N. Scharf, ed. *Between the Two Wars: (1919-1939) II. The Thirties B* (Geneva: World ORT Union, 1979-80).

WOA: d00a010c. N. Scharf, 'The Progress of our Work and our new institutions in Eastern and Central Europe'. In *Between the Two Wars, 1919-1939, II The Thirties B.*

WOA: d00a014c. Vladimir Akivisson, 'ORT's Work in the French Internment Camps', in Norah N. Scharf (ed.), *The Fateful Years 1938-43* (Geneva: World ORT Union, 1979-80), pp.57-63.

WOA: d00a014c. Rachel Gourman, 'ORT's Activities in Nazi Dominated Europe', in Norah N. Scharf (ed.), *The Fateful Years 1938-43* (Geneva: World ORT Union, 1979-80).

WOA: d00a0133. Norah N. Scharf, *From Despair to Hope*, 1933-1960 (Geneva: World ORT Union, 1979-80).

WOA: d02a001b. M. Rechenberg, *ORT Shanghai: Activities for the Years 1947-1948* (Shanghai, 1949).

WOA: d04a010. H.W. Futter, *Memories of ORT Old Boys*, 30 September 1966.

WOA: d04a018. 'ORT US Zone Germany 1945-1947.'

WOA: d05a014. *Report on the ORT Activities August 1946-July 1947. Submitted to the meeting of the Central Board of the World ORT Union Paris, July 6th-7th 1947.*

WOA: d05a015. *Report on the ORT Activities July-November 1947.*

Submitted to the meeting of the Executive of the World ORT Union Zurich, November 22nd-23rd 1947.

WOA: d05a016. *Report on the ORT Activities December 1947-March 1948. Submitted to the meeting of the Executive of the World ORT Union Paris, March 6th-7th 1948.*

WOA: d05a018. *Report on ORT Activities July 1-October 31, 1948. Submitted to the meeting of the Executive of the World ORT Union Paris, November 18th-19th 1948.*

WOA: d05a022. *The Work of the O.R.T. in Europe - January-May 31, 1946 - Report presented to the members of the Executive Committee of the ORT Union at the meeting called in Paris June 2-4, 1946.*

WOA: d05a085. Sussia Goldman, *Ten Years of Reconstruction Work - ORT Activities 1945-55.* c.1955.

WOA: d05a088. David Lvovitch, 'L.M. Bramson and World ORT", in *ORT Economic Review, November 1944,* Vol.4, No.2.

WOA: d05a089. Solomon F. Bloom, 'ORT - Fifty Years of Jewish Relief in Eastern Europe', in *ORT Economic Review, December 1945,* Vol.5, No.2 (New York: American ORT Federation, 1945).

WOA: d05a089. Vladimir Grossman, 'First Aid and Personal Rehabilitation for Displaced Persons', in *ORT Economic Review, December 1945* (New York: American ORT Federation, 1945).

WOA: d05a091. Dr David Lvovitch, *ORT Economic Review, Sept-Dec 1946* (New York: American ORT Federation, 1946).

WOA: d05a092. A.C. Glassgold, 'The Spirit Will Rise: The Miracle of Landsberg', in *ORT Economic Review March 1947* (NYC, USA: American ORT Federation).

WOA: d05a093. Franklin J. Keller, 'Miracle of ORT Among the DPs', in *ORT Economic Review, June-September 1948* (New York: American ORT Federation, 1948).

WOA: d06a079. World ORT Union, *ORT Vocational School Bergen-Belsen, 1945-1947.* (Geneva: World ORT Union, 1947).

WOA: d07a001a. Mark Wischnitzer, *The World ORT Union and the American ORT Federation: A Study Made under the Auspices of the Budget Research Committee* (New York: Council of Jewish Federations and Welfare Funds, Inc., July 1943).

WOA: d07a004. *Immigration - Emigration. Paris Conference November 1948.*

WOA: d07a006. Proposed deployment of JCRA Personnel in British Zone. Letter from Leonard Cohen, Vice-Chairman of JCRA to Mr

Rhatigan, Deputy Director General of UNRRA, 2 October 1945.

WOA: d07a007: *ORT - A Record of Ten Years - Rebuilding Jewish Economic Life*. Forward by William Haber, President of the American ORT Federation (New York: American ORT Federation, 1956).

WOA: d07a008. William Graetz, 'ORT's Work in Germany', in N. Scharf (ed.), *Material and Memoirs Chapters for the History of ORT* (Geneva: World ORT Union, 1955).

WOA: d07a009. Rachel Gourman, 'In the Ghetto of Warsaw: ORT under the German Occupation', in N. Scharf (ed.), *Material and Memoirs Chapters for the History of ORT* (Geneva: World ORT Union, 1955).

WOA: d07a146. Henry Field, *The History of ORT: Organisation for Rehabilitation through Training 1880-1949* (Washington DC: unpublished, 1949).

WOA: d07a148. David Lvovitch in speech given to the women's ORT-OZE in South Africa. 1947. In *ORT-OZE 1947 Caravan*. ORT Johannesburg 1947.

WOA: d07a149. *The Problem of Vocational Adaptation of the Refugees - Memorandum submitted to The International Refugees' Conference at Evian-Les-Bains, by the Central Executive of the 'ORT'*. (Paris, 2 July 1938).

WOA: d07a150. *Partial Report: Illustrating the Expenditure incurred During the First Quarter of 1947*.

WOA: d07a151. *Agreement between ORT Union and the Central Committee of Liberated Jews in the American Zone in Germany*. 24 October 1946.

WOA: d07a153. *Report on Visit to ORT School Stuttgart, Friday, 19 September 1947*.

WOA: d07a154. Col. J.H. Levey, *Regulations of the Leeds ORT Technical and Engineering School*, 27 November 1939.

WOA: d07a166. Joseph Heller, *Joseph Heller Comments on ORT Berlin Photo Album*, 24 August 1999.

WOA: d07a169. Reference for Heinz Jacobius [Henry James] from Col. Levey and F. Heilborn, 18 August 1941.

WOA: d07a173. Christine Stutz interview with Lou Raphaelson, *Saved by ORT*, Fall 1998.

WOA: DC/0109. *The Financing of the Work of the ORT Union in 1939 (Expose and Budget Forecast)* (World ORT Union, 1939).

The National Archives, London, UK (TNA)

TNA: FO 371/115929, 'World Association for vocational training among Jewish Centres in the Diaspora (ORT) founded in 1880'.
TNA: FO 945/723, 'Jewish Advisory Committee' - 'Jewish DPs in Hohne Camp 1946-47'.
TNA: FO 945/723, 'Jewish Vocational Training - Jewish DPs in Hohne Camp 1946-47'.
TNA: FO 1049/195/107: CCG to WO 6 September 1945.
TNA: FO 1052/73. 'Col. Robert Solomons - 'Jewish Advisor to Military Government, British Zone of Occupation, Report to Foreign Office, October 1948'.
TNA: FO 1052/81, 'Jews ORT Training Schools 1947-48'.
TNA: FO 1052/283, 'Report on "Jewish Congress" at Hohne Camp'.
TNA: FO 1052/283, pt 2b, 'Report on "Jewish Congress" at Hohne Camp'.

Wiener Library, London, UK (WL)

Wiener Library Bulletin, 'Reconstruction - the Work of ORT', Vol.3, No.2 (March 1949).
WL: 4014, unpublished memoir - Henry Lippmann.
WL: 644/1, Kitchener Camp.
WL: OSP921, Elaine Bentley, 'Reception in the United Kingdom of Jewish refugees with special emphasis on the role of the Kitchener Camp, 1938-1939' (Doctoral Thesis. Polytechnic of Central London, 1989).
WL: YIVO Collection. Reel 15, *2 Years of ORT in Landsberg*, p.1. 23 July 1947
WL: *ORT Illustrated Magazine*, December 1948, no.10.
WL: YIVO Collection. 'Report to the Central Board Meeting in Paris on July 11-13, 1948 on World ORT Union in Austria.' Speech made by Mr. Harry Branton. *ORT Illustrated Magazine*, August-September 1948, No.6-7.
WL: YIVO Collection, Reel 15-10, *The ORT Idea No. 1*. 1 October 1948.
WL: YIVO Collection, Reel 17, 2, *The Sub-committee of the Committee on Foreign Affairs of the 80th US Congress.*

Henriques Collection (HC)

WL: HC, Microfilm Reel 1: HA1 1/7.

WL: HC, Microfilm Reel 1: 1-HA2/2/5/B.
WL: HC, Microfilm Reel 5: 5/5/16.
WL: HC, Microfilm Reel 14: 2.
WL: HC Microfilm Reel 13: *JRU Co-operation with Other Relief Organisations: Various Voluntary Groups – Prof. Norman Bentwich (Belsen).*
WL: HC Microfilm Reel 4: *JCRA Organisation: Units in Germany, JRU Status Activities, 1946–50, Belsen.*
WL: HC Microfilm Reel: 5-2/10/67, *Rose Henriques, Impressions of Some ORT Schools in Germany, 4.01.49.*

United States Holocaust Memorial Museum (USHMM)

USHMM: Oral History Archive, testimony: RG – 50.106.07, Ernst Kolben.
USHMM: Testimony of Harold Herbst. Personal Histories Collection – Liberation.
USHMM: Testimony of Lieutenant-Colonel R.I.G. Taylor. Personal Histories Collection – Liberation.
USHMM: Testimony of Alan Zimm. Personal Histories Collection – Liberation.

US Library of Congress

George C. Marshall, USA Congressional Record, 30 June 1947.

Fortunoff Video Archive for Holocaust Testimonies (HVT)

HVT: 1219: Testimony of Col. Edmund M. Fortunoff Video Archive for Holocaust Testimonies, Yale University, USA.

Interviews by the Author

Max Abraham – London: Interviewee's Home – March 2007.
Norman Frajman – Via Email – January 2006.
Zelda Fuksman – Via Email – January 2006.
Hans Futter – London: Interviewee's Home – March 2007.
Elly Gotz – 'My Story of how ORT influenced my life' – Via Email – March 2007.
Henry James – Via Telephone – February 2007.
Nitza Sarner – London: Interviewee's Home – March 2007.
William Tannenzapf – Via Email – December 2005.

Published

Document Collections

Arad, Yitzhak, Yisrael Gutman and Abraham Margaliot (eds), *Documents on the Holocaust – Selected Sources on the Destruction of the Jews of Germany and Austria, Poland and the Soviet Union* (Jerusalem: Yad Vashem, 1981).

Noakes, J. and G. Pridham (eds), *Nazism 1919-1945. Volume 1. The Rise of Power 1919-1934* (Exeter: University of Exeter Press, 1998).

Noakes, J. and G. Pridham (eds), *Nazism 1919-1945. Volume 2. State, Economy and Society* (Exeter: University of Exeter Press, 1998).

Noakes, J. and G. Pridham (eds), *Nazism 1919-1945. Volume 3. Foreign Policy, War and Racial Extermination* (Exeter: University of Exeter Press, 1998).

Diaries and Memoirs

Elkes, Joel, *Values, Beliefs and Survival: Dr. Elkanan Elkes and the Kovno Ghetto: A Memoir* (London: Vale, 1997).

Greene, Joshua and Shiva Kumar (eds), *Witness – Voices from the Holocaust* (New York: Free Press, 2000).

Klemperer, Victor, *I Shall Bear Witness – The Diaries of Victor Klemperer 1933-41* (London: Weidenfeld and Nicolson, 1998).

Klemperer, Victor, *To the Bitter End – The Diaries of Victor Klemperer 1942-45* (London: Weidenfeld and Nicolson, 1999).

Levi, Primo, *The Drowned and the Saved* (London: Abacus, 1989).

Schiff, Vera, *Theresienstadt, the town the Nazis Gave to the Jews* (Toronto: Lugus, 1998).

Videos

David. Directed by Peter Lillienthal. (Germany: Kino on Video, 1987).

The Long Way Home. Written and directed by Mark Jonathan Harris. WL video collection. Film no.1210.

Online Resources

Bergen-Belsen and Theresienstadt Lists: www.jewishgen.org/yizkor

Fortunoff Video Archive – Yale University: www.library.yale.edu/testimonies

Imperial War Museum: www.iwm.org
Shoah Foundation: www.vhf.org
United States Holocaust Memorial Museum, Archives: www.ushmm.org/research

SECONDARY SOURCES

Books

Aschheim, Steven E., *Culture and Catastrophe: German and Jewish Confrontations with National Socialism and other Crises* (London: Macmillan, 1996).
Avineri, Shlomo, *The Making of Modern Zionism* (New York: Basic Books, 1981).
Baker, Leonard, *Days of Sorrow and Pain – Leo Baeck and The Berlin Jews* (Oxford: Oxford University Press, 1978).
Bankier, David (ed), *Probing the Depths of German Anti-Semitism – German Society and the Persecution of the Jews, 1933–1941* (New York: Berghahn Books, 2000).
Barkai, Avraham, *From Boycott to Annihilation – the Economic Struggle of German Jews 1933–1943* (New England: Brandeis University Press, 1989).
Bartov, Omer, *Murder in Our Midst: the Holocaust, Industrial Killing and Representation* (Oxford: Oxford University Press, 1995).
Bauer, Yehuda, *Flight and Rescue: Brichah* (New York: Random House, 1970).
——, *American Jewry and the Holocaust: the American Jewish Joint Distribution Committee, 1939–1945* (Jerusalem: Hebrew University of Jerusalem, 1981).
——, *Jews for Sale? Nazi-Jewish Negotiations, 1933–1945* (New Haven, CT: Yale University Press, 1994).
Baumel, Judith Tydor, *Kibbutz Buchenwald. Survivors and Pioneers* (New Brunswick, NJ: Rutgers University Press, 1997).
——, *Double Jeopardy. Gender and the Holocaust* (London: Vallentine Mitchell, 1998).
Ben-Sasson, H.H. (ed.), *A History of the Jewish People* (Massachusetts: Harvard University Press, 1976).
Birnbaum, Pierre and Ira Katznelson (eds), *Paths of Emancipation – Jews, States and Citizenship* (Princeton, NJ: Princeton University Press, 1995).

Bourke, Eoin, *The Austrian Anschluss in History and Literature* (Galway: Arlen House, 2000).

Brenner, Michael, *After the Holocaust. Rebuilding Jewish Lives in Postwar Germany* (Princeton, NJ: Princeton University Press, 1997).

Browning, Christopher R., *Nazi Policy, Jewish Workers, German Killers* (Cambridge: Cambridge University Press, 2000).

Bullivant, Keith, *Culture and Society in the Weimar Republic* (Manchester: Manchester University Press, 1977).

Burleigh, Michael, *The Third Reich - A New History* (London: Macmillan, 2000).

Burleigh, M. and W. Wippermann, *The Racial State: Germany 1933-1945* (Cambridge: Cambridge University Press, 1991).

Cesarani, David, *The Final Solution: Origins and Implementation* (London: Routledge, 1996).

Cohn, David, *British ORT Report*, Edition 4 (London: British ORT, 2001).

Cohn-Sherbok, Dan, *Anti-Semitism* (Stroud: Sutton Publishing, 2002).

Collier, Richard, *Bridge across the Sky: the Berlin Blockade and Airlift, 1948-1949* (London: Macmillan, 1978).

Colodner, Solomon, *Jewish Education in Germany Under the Nazis* (New York: Jewish Education Committee Press, 1964).

Corni, Gustavo, *Hitler's Ghettos - Voices from a Beleaguered Society 1939-1944* (London: Arnold, 2003).

Dawidowicz, Lucy, *The War Against the Jews 1933-1945* (London: Penguin, 1990).

Davies, Peter, *France and the Second World War: Occupation, Collaboration and Resistance* (London: Routledge, 2001).

Dowling, Maria, *Czechoslovakia* (London: Arnold, 2002).

Edelheit, Abraham J. and Edelheit Hershel (eds), *History of the Holocaust - A Handbook and Dictionary* (Boulder, CO and Oxford: Westview Press, 1994).

Essner, Cornelia, *Die Nürnberger Gesetze oder Die Verwaltung des Rassenwahns, 1939-1945* (The Nuremberg Laws and the Management of Racial War 1939-1945) (München: Schöningh, 2002).

Falbaum, Berl, *Shanghai Remembered: Stories of Jews who Escaped to Shanghai from Nazi Europe* (Michigan: Momentum Books, 2005).

Fischer, Klaus P., *The History of an Obsession - German Judeophobia and the Holocaust* (London: Constable, 1998).

Friedlander, Albert H., *Leo Baeck, Teacher of Theresienstadt* (New York: The Overlook Press, 1968).

—, *Leo Baeck – Leben und Lehre* (Leo Baeck – Life and Teachings) (Munich: Kaiser Taschenbücher, 1990).

Friedländer, Saul, *Nazi Germany and the Jews: The Years of Persecution 1933–39* (London: Phoenix, 1998).

Friedländer, Saul (ed.), *Probing the Limits of Representation: Nazism and the Final Solution* (Massachusetts: Harvard University Press, 1992).

Gay, Ruth, *The Jews of Germany* (New Haven, CT and London: Yale University Press, 1992).

—, *Safe Amongst Germans. Liberated Jews After WW2* (New Haven, CT: Yale University Press, 2002).

Geller, Jay Howard, *Jews in Post-Holocaust Germany 1945–1953* (Cambridge: Cambridge University Press, 2005).

Gill, Alan, *Interrupted Journeys – Young Refugees From Hitler's Reich* (Pymble, NSW: Simon and Schuster, 2004).

Graml, H., *Antisemitism in the Third Reich* (Oxford: Blackwell, 1992).

Greenspan, Henry, *On Listening to Holocaust Survivors – Recounting and Life History* (Connecticut: Praeger Publishers, 1998).

Gregor, Neil, *Nazism* (Oxford: Oxford University Press, 2000).

Grobman, Alex, *Rekindling the Flame* (Detroit, MI: Wayne State University Press, 1993).

Gruber, Ruth, *Exodus 1947: The Ship that Launched a Nation. Destination Palestine: the Story of the Hagannah Ship Exodus 1947* (New York: Times Books, 1999).

Gutman, Israel, *The Warsaw Ghetto Uprising* (Boston: Houghton Mifflin, 1994).

Hadari, Ze'ev Venia, *Second Exodus: the Full Story of Jewish Illegal Immigration to Palestine, 1945–1948* (London: Vallentine Mitchell, 1991).

Hadari, Ze'ev Venia and Ze'ev Tsahor, *Voyage to Freedom: an Episode in the Illegal Immigration to Palestine* (London: Vallentine Mitchell, 1985).

Halamish, Aviva and Cummings, Ora, *The Exodus Affair: Holocaust Survivors and the Struggle for Palestine* (London: Vallentine Mitchell, 1998).

Handlin, Oscar, *A Continuing Task: the American Jewish Joint Distribution Committee, 1914–1964* (New York: Random House, 1994).

Haydock, Michael D., *City Under Seige: the Berlin Blockade and Airlift, 1948-1949* (London: Brassey, 1999).

Hecht, Ingeborg, *Invisible Walls - To Remember is to Heal - Encounter Between Victims of the Nuremberg Laws* (Illinois: Northwestern University Press, 1984).

Heymont, Irving, *Among the Survivors of the Holocaust - 1945. The Landsberg DP Camp Letters of Major Irving Heymont, United States Army* (Cincinnati: American Jewish Archives, 1982).

Hilberg, Raul, *The Destruction of the European Jews* (Chicago: Quadrangle, 1961).

Hilliard, R.L., *Surviving the Americans.* (New York: 1997).

International Refugee Organisation, *IRO: what it is, what it does, how it works* (Geneva: IRO, 1949).

—, *Constitution of the IRO* (London: HM Stationery Office, 1950).

Jackson, Julian, *France: the Dark Years, 1940-1944* (Oxford: Oxford University Press, 2001).

Kershaw, Ian, *Hitler: 1889-1936: Hubris* (London: Allen Lane, 1998).

—, *Hitler: 1936-1945: Nemesis* (London: Allen Lane, 2000).

Klemme, Marvin, *The Inside Story of UNRRA: An Experience in Internationalism: A first hand report on the Displaced People of Europe* (Washginton, DC: Lifetime Editions, 1949).

Knox Doherty, Muriel, *Letters from Belsen, 1945: An Australian Nurse's Experiences with the Survivors of War* (Australia: Allen and Unwin, 2000).

Kolinsky, Eva, *After the Holocaust Jewish Survivors in Germany after 1945* (London: Pimlico, 2004).

Königseder, Angelika and Juliane Wetzel, *Waiting for Hope: Jewish Displaced Persons in Post-World War 11 Germany* (Illinois: Northwestern University Press, 2001).

Kushner, Tony, *The Holocaust and the Liberal Imagination* (Oxford: Blackwell, 1995).

Landau, Elaine, *The Warsaw Ghetto Uprising* (New York: New Discovery Books, 1992).

Lang, Berel, *Writing and the Holocaust* (New York: Holmes and Meier, 1988).

Laub, Morris, *Last Barrier to Freedom: Internment of Jewish Holocaust Survivors on Cyprus: 1946-1949* (California: Judah L. Magnus Museum, 1985).

Lavsky, Hagit, *New Beginnings: Holocaust Survivors in Bergen-Belsen* and the *British Zone in Germany, 1945-1950.* (Detroit: Wayne State University Press, 2002).

Lawrence Miller, Richard, *Nazi Justiz - Law of the Holocaust* (Westpoint, CT: Praeger, 1995).

Lindemann, Albert S., *Essau's Tears - Modern Anti-Semitism and the Rise of the Jews* (Cambridge: Cambridge University Press, 1997).

Makarova, Elena, Sergei Makarov and Victor Kuperman, *University over the Abyss: The Story behind 489 Lectures and 2309 Lecturers in K2 Theresienstadt 1942-1944* (Jerusalem: Verba, 2000).

Mankowitz, Zeev, *Life Between Memory and Hope. The Survivors of the Holocaust in Occupied Germany* (Cambridge: Cambridge University Press, 2002).

Megged, Aharon, *The Story of the Selvino Children - Journey to the Promised Land* (London: Vallentine Mitchell, 2002).

Meyer, Michael (ed.), *German-Jewish History in Modern Times: Volume 3. Integration in Dispute 1871-1918* (New York: Columbia University Press, 1997).

——, *German-Jewish History in Modern Times: Volume 4. Renewal and Destruction 1918-1945* (New York: Columbia University Press, 1997).

Neipris, Joseph and Ralph Dolgoff, *The American Jewish Joint Distribution Committee and its Contribution to Social Work Education* (Jerusalem: JDC Israel, 1992).

Nicosia, Francis R., *The Third Reich and the Palestine Question* (London: I.B. Tauris and Co. Ltd, 1985).

Niewyk, Donald, *Socialist, Anti-Semite and Jew: German Social Democracy Confronts the Problems of Anti-Semitism 1918-1933* (Baton Rouge, LA: Louisiana State University Press, 1971).

Niewyk, Donald L. *The Jews in Weimar Germany* (Baton Rouge, LA and London: Louisiana State University Press, 1980).

Offer, Dalia, *Escaping the Holocaust: Illegal Immigration to the Land of Israel, 1939-1944* (New York: Oxford University Press, 1990).

Pearl, Cyril, *The Dunera Scandal: Deported by Mistake* (London: Angus and Robertson, 1983).

Peck, Abraham J., *American Jewish Archives, Cincinnati: the Papers of the World Jewish Congress 1945-1950: Liberation and the Saving Remnant* (London: Garland, 1990).

Pettiss, Susan, *After the Shooting Stopped: The Memoir of an UNRRA Welfare Worker Germany 1945-1947* (London: Trafford Publishing, 2004).

Posner, I. (ed.), *Jacob Oleiski, A Man's Work* (Israel: ORT Israel, 1986).
Pulzer, Peter, 'The Response to Antisemitism', in Michael Meyer (ed.), *German-Jewish History in Modern Times: Volume 3. Integration in Dispute 1871–1918* (New York: Columbia University Press, 1997).
Rader, Jack, *By the Skill of Their Hands* (Geneva: World ORT, 1970).
Reilly, Joanne, *Belsen, the Liberation of a Concentration Camp* (London: Routledge, 1998).
Reilly, J., D. Cesarani, T. Kushner and C. Richmond (eds), *Belsen in History and Memory* (London: Frank Cass, 1997).
Rosensaft, Menachem Z. (ed.), *Life Reborn, Jewish Displaced Persons 1945–1951. Conference Proceedings* (Washington DC: United States Holocaust Memorial Museum, 2001).
Ross, James R., *Escape to Shanghai: A Jewish Community in China* (New York: Free Press, 1994).
Rovit, R. and A. Goldfarb (eds), *Theatrical Performances during the Holocaust: Texts, Documents, Memoirs* (Baltimore, MD: John Hopkins University Press, 1999).
Ryan, Donna F., *The Holocaust and the Jews of Marseilles: the Enforcement of anti-Semitic Policies in Vichy France* (Urbana, IL: University of Illinois Press, 1996).
Schiff, Vera, *Theresienstadt, the Town the Nazis gave to the Jews* (Toronto: Lugus, 1998).
Schorsch, Ismar, *Jewish Reactions to German Anti-Semitism, 1870–1914* (Philadelphia: Jewish Publication Society of America, 1972).
Schuschnigg, Kurt von and Richard Barry, *The Brutal Takeover: The Austrian ex-Chancellor's Account of the Anschluss of Austria by Hitler* (London: Weidenfeld and Nicholson, 1971).
Schwarz, Leo W., *The Redeemers: a Saga of the Years 1945–1952* (New York: Straus and Young Farrar, 1953).
Schwertfeger, Ruth, *Women of Theresienstadt – Voices from a Concentration Camp* (New York: Berg, 1989).
Sereny, Gitta, *The German Trauma: Experiences and Reflections 1938–2000* (London: Penguin, 2000).
Shapiro, Leon, *The History of ORT: A Jewish Movement for Social Change* (New York: Schocken Books, 1980).
Shephard, Ben, *After Daybreak – The Liberation of Belsen, 1945* (London: Jonathan Cape, 2005).

Theresienstädter Gedenkbuch: die Opfer der Judentransporte aus Deutschland nach Theresienstadt 1942-1945 (Theresienstadt Memorial Book) (Prague: Institut Theresienstadter Initiativ, 2000).

Tobias, Sigmund and Michael Berenbaum, *Strange Haven: A Jewish Childhood in Wartime Shanghai* (Urbana, IL: University of Illinois Press, 1999).

Tory, Avraham, *Surviving the Holocaust - The Kovno Ghetto Diary.* Introduction by Martin Gilbert (London: Pimlico, 1991).

Trunk, Isaiah, *Judenrat - The Jewish Councils in Eastern Europe Under the Nazi Occupation* (Lincoln, NE: University of Nebraska Press, 1972).

Tusa, Ann and John Tusa, *The Berlin Blockade* (London: Coronet, 1989).

Trunk, Isaiah, *Jewish Responses to Nazi Persecution: Collective and Individual Behaviour in Extremis* (New York: Stein and Day, 1979).

UNRRA, *UNRRA: Organisation, Aims, Progress. Instructions and Procedure* (Washington, DC: UNRRA, 1945).

UNRRA European Regional Office. Division of Operational Analysis, *U.N.R.R.A.: Displaced Persons Operation in Europe and the Middle East* (London: UNRRA European Regional Office, 1946).

Vinen, Richard, *The Unfree French: Life Under the Occupation* (London: Allen Lane, 2006).

Wyman, Mark, *DPs: Europe's Displaced Persons, 1945-1951* (Ithaca, NY: Cornell University Press, 1989).

Young, James E., *Writing and Rewriting the Holocaust, Narrative and Consequences of Interpretation* (Bloomington, IN: Indiana University Press, 1988).

Zuckerman, Yitzak and Barbara Harshaw, *A Surplus of Memory: Chronicle of the Warsaw Ghetto Uprising* (Berkeley, CA: University of California Press, 1993).

Contemporary/war-time Accounts

Hyman, Abraham, 'The Undefeated' (Jerusalem: Gefen, 1953).

Murphy, Henry B., 'Flight and Resettlement' (Switzerland: UNESCO history, 1955).

Articles and Chapters from Books

Abolson, Peter, 'The Exodus Affair: Hamburg 1947', *Journal of Holocaust Education*, 6, 3 (Winter 1997), pp.65-79.

Baker, Zachary M. (ed.), 'Jewish Displaced Persons Periodicals – From the Collections of the YIVO Institute' (New York: YIVO, 1990).

Bauer, Yehuda, 'The Kristallnacht s Turning Point: Jewish Reactions to Nazi Policies', in Michael Marrus (ed.), *The Nazi Holocaust, Volume 2. The Origins of the Holocaust* (London: Meckler, 1989).

Bauer, Yehuda, 'The DP Legacy', in Menachem Z. Rosensaft (ed.), *Life Reborn, Jewish Displaced Persons 1945-1951. Conference Proceedings* (Washington DC: United States Holocaust Memorial Museum, 2001).

Bloch, Sam E., 'A Holocaust Survivor's Perspective', in Menachem Z. Rosensaft (ed.), *Life Reborn, Jewish Displaced Persons 1945-1951. Conference Proceedings* (Washington DC: United States Holocaust Memorial Museum, 2001).

Dinnerstein, Leonard, 'The United States and the Displaced Persons'. Taken from *She'erit Hapletah, 1944-1948 Rehabilitation and Political Struggle. Proceedings of the Sixth Yad Vashem International Conference* (Jerusalem: Yad Vashem, 1985.)

Dvorjetski, Mark, 'Adjustment of Detainees to Camp and Ghetto Life'. In *Yad Vashem Studies V* (Jerusalem: Yad Vashem, 1963).

Grossman, Kurt Richard and Abraham S. Hyman, 'The Jewish DP Problem: its Origin, Scope, and Liquidation' (New York: Institute of Jewish Affairs, 1951).

Hilberg, Raul, 'The Judenrat: Conscious or Unconscious Tool', in *Patterns of Jewish Leadership in Nazi Europe 1933-1945. Proceedings of the Third Yad Vashem International Historical Conference – April 1977* (Jerusalem: Yad Vashem, 1979).

Johnson, Daniel, 'What Viktor Klemperer Saw', *Commentary*, 109, 6 (2000), pp.44-50.

Keynan, Irit, 'The Yishuv's Mission to the Displaced Persons Camps in Germany: The Initial Steps August 1945-May 1946'. Taken from *She'erit Hapletah, 1944-1948 Rehabilitation and Political Struggle. Proceedings of the Sixth Yad Vashem International Conference* (Jerusalem: Yad Vashem, 1985).

Kulka, O.D., 'The Reichsvereinigung of the Jews in Germany – Problems of continuity in the Organisation and Leadership of German Jewry under the National Socialist Regime'. In *Patterns of Jewish Leadership in Nazi Europe 1933-1945. Proceedings of the Third Yad Vashem International Historical Conference – April 1977* (Jerusalem: Yad Vashem, 1979), pp.45-59.

Lavsky, Hagit, 'A Community of Survivors: Bergen-Belsen as a Jewish Centre after 1945', in J. Reilly, D. Cesarani, T. Kushner and C. Richmond (eds), *Belsen in History and Memory* (London: Frank Cass, 1997).

Michlin-Coren, Joanna, 'Battling Against the Odds: Culture, Education and the Jewish Intelligentsia in the Warsaw Ghetto, 1940-1942', *East European Jewish Affairs*, Vol.2, No.27 (1997).

Morris, Benny, 'Responses of the Jewish Daily Press in Palestine to the Accession of Hitler, 1933', *Yad Vashem Studies*, 27 (1999).

Reilly, Joanne, 'Belsen Displaced Persons' Camp: British State Responses', in *Belsen: the Liberation of a Concentration Camp* (London: Routledge, 1998).

Reilly, Joanne, 'British Policy', in Menachem Z. Rosensaft and Irving Greenberg (eds), *Life Reborn: Jewish Displaced Persons 1945-1951: Conference Proceedings, Washington, DC. January 14-17 2000* (Washington, DC: United States Holocaust Memorial Museum, 2000).

Rethmeier, Andreas, '"Nürnberger Rassengesetze" und Entrechtung der Juden Zivilrecht' ('The Nuremberg Race Laws and the Deprivation f Jewish Civil Rights'), in *Rechthistorische Reihe* 126 (Frankfurt am Main: Peter Lang, 1995).

Roseman, Mark, 'Surviving Memory: Truth and Inaccuracy in Holocaust Testimony', *The Journal of Holocaust Education*, Vol.1, No.8 (1999).

Simon, Ernst, 'Jewish Adult Education in Nazi Germany as Spiritual Resistance', in *Leo Baeck Yearbook 1*(London: Leo Baeck Institute, 1956).

Trunk, I., *Patterns of Jewish Leadership in Nazi Europe 1933-1945*. Proceedings of the Third Yad Vashem International Historical Conference - April 1977 (Jerusalem: Yad Vashem, 1979).

Index

Abraham, Max, 17-18, 18-19
After Daybreak - The Liberation of Belsen, 1945 (Shephard), x
Ahlem DP centre, 71, 124
Akivisson, Vladimir, 25
Aliyah Bet, 118
Allied Control Council, occupation zones under, 62
Allied Occupational Forces, 64
American Jewish Congress, 3
American ORT Federation, 25
American Relief Organisation, 3
American zone of occupation, defeated Germany, 75, 77, 87-8, 101
Anglo-American Committee of inquiry, 117
Anielewicz, Mordecai, 36
Anschluss, 8
anti-Jewish legislation, Nazi Germany, 7, 9, 30, 36
antisemitism, 6, 7, 67
Appleboim, Yizhak, 47
artisanship, 3
'Artisanship Programme' (ORT), 12
Auschwitz death camp: deportations to, 52, 57; gas chamber at, 34, 35; liberation of, by Soviets, 58; Simon family killed at, 20; women and children at, 51
Austria: annexing by Hitler, 8; DPs in, 123-4; 'New Palestine', area of refugee housing known as, 67; ORT schools in, 105-6, 126; post-war rehabilitation work in, 106

Baeck, Rabbi Leo, 4, 5, 9
Bakst, Nikolai, 1
Balfour Declaration 1917, 116

Barkai, Avraham, 8
Baruchi, Y., 98
Bauer, Yehuda, 117-18
Bavarian People's Party, Germany, 6
Bedzin, ghetto revolts and military actions, 36
Beham, Jehuda, 129
Behrend (civil engineer), 15
Belsen concentration camp: conditions, 60; conversion into DP camp, 71; establishment of, 60; exchanging of prisoners at, 60; as fully functioning camp, 60-1; liberation of, 59, 60, 61; types of camp, 62; unburied corpses found at, 61, 62; women's camp in, 60
Belsen Displaced Persons (DP) camp, xi; conditions, 70, 71-2; Congress of Jewish survivors, British zone (1945), 72, 73-4; conversion from concentration camp, 71; division into four areas, 71; education and training at, 70, 92, 94; as exclusively Jewish centre, 68; Höhne Camp, renaming as, 73; Jewish DPs in, 96
Belsen ORT, 75, 94, 98
Belzec, gas chamber at, 34-5, 57, 58
Ben Gurion, David, 119
Bentwich, N., 97
Bergen-Belsen concentration camp *see* Belsen concentration camp
Berlin: East and West, division into, 62; ORT conferences at, 3, 4; ORT school in *see* Berlin ORT school; World ORT Union headquarters in, 4
Berlin ORT school, x; and British ORT, 14, 15; opening of, 13; United Kingdom, move to, 15-19
Blaustein, Jacob, 27

INDEX

Bloom, Solomon F., 1, 2
Bloomberg, Simon, 98
Blumenfeld, Kurt, 4
Board of Deputies of British Jews, London, 80
boycott of Jewish shops, 7
Bramson, Leon: death of, 24; as executive board chairman, 24; and Oleiski, 46; pre-war years, 3, 4, 10
Branton, Harry, 104, 105, 106
Brest, Jews murdered in, 33
Britain see United Kingdom
British ORT, and Berlin school, 14, 15
British zone of occupation, defeated Germany, 72, 73-4, 87-8
Brodnitz, Justizrat, 4
Buchenwald concentration camp, liberation, 59
Buhler, Josef, 34
Bulgaria, ORT in, 28
Bundists, 33, 36
By the Skill of Their Hands (Rader), viii

Canada, and Jewish DPs, 121
Cantoni, Raffaele, 108, 109
Cassin, Mathilda, 108, 109
Central Association of German Citizens of Jewish Faith, 4, 5
Central Committee of Liberated Jews: achievements, 73; and DPs/DP camps, 89, 93, 94, 98; formation, 72; and UNRRA, 128; in US zone, 99
Centralverein deutscher Staatsbürger jüdischer Glaubens (Central Association of German Citizens of Jewish Faith), 4, 5
Chelmno, death camp at, 33
Churchill, Winston, 116
civil servants, Jewish: compulsory retirement of, 7
Civil Service Law, 1933, 7
Cohen, Leonard, 97
Cohn, David, 17
Cold War, 63
concentration camps: at Dachau, 7, 53; destruction by Nazis, 58; evidence left behind, 58; first, creation of, 7; Kovno Ghetto as, 51, 52; liberation of, 57-85; at Stuffhof, 45, 53; truth, uncovering of, 58; see also death camps
Congress of Jewish survivors, British zone (1945), 73-4
Conservative People's Party, Germany, 6
Cracow, ghetto revolts and military actions, 36
Craftsmen's Guilds, 12
Czechoslovakia, downfall of, 11
Czerniakow, Adam, 32
Czestochowa, ghetto revolts and military actions, 36

Dachau concentration camp, 7, 45, 53; liberation, 59
Dawidowicz, Lucy, 8, 37
death camps: at Auschwitz see Auschwitz death camp; at Belzec, 34-5; at Chelmno, 33; at Majdanek, 34, 35; at Sobibor, 34, 35; at Treblinka, 34, 35; see also concentration camps
dehumanisation of Jews, 35
Democratic Party, Germany, 6
deportations: in 1942, 36; to Auschwitz, 52, 57; to Belzec, 34-5, 57; fear of, 36; to Majdanek, 57; ORT identification card, as protection against, 42; to Sobibor, 57; to Treblinka, 36, 37, 41, 43, 57
Deutsch, Otto, 91
diaries, memoirs distinguished, xii-xiii
Dinnerstein, Leonard, x, 120
displaced persons see DPs (displaced persons)
Displaced Persons Commission, 122
DPs (displaced persons): accommodation availability, 67-8; ages of, 88; British policies towards, x, xi, 66-7; and Canada, 121; country of origin, no wish to return to, 66; experiences in camps, 68-9; freedom, lack of, 72; JCRA, help from, 82; Jews and non-Jews, separation, 68, 81; 'preferential' treatment, avoiding, 67; repatriation goal, 65-6; self-help groups, 72; special treatment, idea of, 67; US policies towards, xi, x
DPs (displaced persons) camps: ages of DPs, 88; clothing shortages, 69; conditions, 69; end of, 115-30; food shortages, 69, 87, 88, 89; and local German community, 86; ORT and mature period of work (1946-48), 86-111; World ORT Union's mission, 74; zones of occupation see zones of occupation, DP camps
DPs: Europe's Displaced Persons, 1945-1951 (Wyman), ix
The Drowned and the Saved (Levi), 58
Dutch, Otto, 98

Eastern Europe: ORT schools in, 13, 28
Edwards, Paul B., 101
Eichmann, Adolf, 13-14
Einsatzgruppen, slaughter of Jews by, 33, 45
Elkes, Joel, 45-6, 46
Emden, ORT school in, 91, 124
Emergency Conference for World ORT Union Affairs, 1942, 25
Enabling Law, 1933, 7
Estonia, labour camps in, 51
European Friends of ORT, 29
Evian Conference on Refugees, World ORT Union delegation, 10
Evian-les-Bains, Conference on Refugees - 1938, 10
Exodus (ship), 118

Federal Republic of Germany, establishment, 63-4
Federation of Associations in Poland for the

Care of Orphans, 37
Feldafing Displaced Persons (DP) camp: as exclusively Jewish centre, 68
Feldman, Iser, 47
Feldman, Yerachmiel, 47
First World War: and ORT's work, 2
Föhrenwald Displaced Persons (DP) camp: as exclusively Jewish centre, 68; German authorities, handed over to, 126; and non-Jewish DPs, 81
food smuggling, 31, 35, 41-2
Fortunoff, Edmund M., 59
Frajman, Norman, 121
France: German-Jewish refugees in, 9-10; Germany, zone of occupation in, 81; ORT activities, 25; World ORT Union move to, 23, 25, 26
Frank, Hans, 30, 34
Frankfurt, Professor, 5
Friedman, Herbert, 118
Friedman, Paul, 64
Fuksman, Zelda, xii, 100-1, 133
Futter, Hans, 16, 17

gassings/gas chambers, 33, 34
genocide, 35; *see also* death camps; Nazism
Gerber, B., 49
German Democratic Republic, establishment, 64
German Völkisch League for Defence and Defiance, 6
Germany: Democratic Republic, establishment, 64; DPs in, 123-4; Federal Republic of, establishment, 63-4; military zones of occupation, division into, 62; Munich, ORT office in, 127-8; Nazism *see* Nazism; ORT activities, 4, 5, 9-10, 123; Poland, invasion of, 30; political parties, 6; Soviet Union, invasion of in 1941, 44; Weimar Republic, 6; World ORT Union, work in, 76-7; *see also* Berlin; Berlin ORT school; zones of occupation, defeated Germany divided into
Gestapo, 9
ghettos: creation of, 30-1; in Poland, 31-2, 35; revolts at, 36; starvation in, 31, 41-2; work programmes in, x; 'working Jews', separation from 'surplus Jews', 34
Gilbert, Martin, 48
Glassgold, A.C., 77, 78
Glatz, Rifka Muscovitz, 120
Glyn-Hughes, Brigadier H.L., 61
Goldman, Sussia, 77
Goldstein, Bernard, 42
Gotz, Elly, xii, 47, 48, 53, 102-3, 134
Gourman, Rachel, 40, 42, 43-4, 53
Graetz, William, 2-3, 4, 15; as chairman, 5
Greenberg, Jeshie, 44
Greenman, M., 94
Grinberg, Zalman, 90-1
Grodno, Jews murdered in, 33

Grossman, Vladimir, 74, 77, 80, 82
Grzybowska Street, Jewish Council of Warsaw Ghetto housed in, 37
Guild Laws, changing of in 1935, 12
Gunzburg, Baron Horace de, 1
Gunzburg, Baron Pierre de, 25

Haas, Adolf, 61
Haber, William, 82, 121, 127
Hagana (Jewish defence force in Palestine), 117
Halpern, Alexander, 25
Hanover DP centres, training provision, 71
Harrison, Earl G., 75, 116
Harrison Report 1945, 73, 75-6, 81, 84n
'Harvest Festival', 1943, 35
Hebrew Immigrant Aid Society (HIAS), 65
Heiborn, F., 19
Heiborn, Regierungsrat, 15
Heller, Joseph, 14
Henriques, Rose, 123
Herbst, Harold, 59
Heydrich, Reinhard, 30, 34
Heymont, Major Irving, 78, 79, 81; on Oleiski, 80
HIAS (Hebrew Immigrant Aid Society), 65
Hilberg, Raul, 37-8
Himmler, Heinrich, 60
Hirsch, Otto, 9
The History of ORT: A Jewish Movement for Social Change (Shapiro), viii, ix
Hitler, Adolf: Austria, annexing of, 8; as Chancellor, 6, 7; as Fuhrer, 7
Höhne Camp, renaming of Belsen DP camp as, 73
Holocaust survivors: and creation of Israel, xi; rehabilitation of *see* rehabilitation of Holocaust survivors
housing, for refugees/DPs, 67-8
Hungary: ORT in, 28

immigration authorities, on World ORT Union, 121
International ORT Union, 3
International Refugee Organization (IRO), 65, 124
internment camps, workshops in, 25, 26
Irgun Zvai Leumi, 117
IRO (International Refugee Organization), 65, 124
Israel: creation of, xi, 111, 122, 123, 128; declaration of state of, 119, 123; emigration to, 129; ORT activities, 129-30
Italy: ORT courses in, 126-7; rehabilitation in, 106-8

Jacobius, Henry, 19
Jaffe, Shlomo, 129
James, Henry, 17, 19
Jashunsky, Joseph, 40, 43, 44

INDEX

JCRA (Jewish Committee for Relief Abroad), 80, 82
JDC (Joint Distribution Committee), 3, 65
Jewish Committee for Relief Abroad (JCRA), 80, 82
Jewish Conference on Immediate Relief in Europe, 80
Jewish Councils: ghettos ran by, 31, 34, 35; identification cards issued by, 34; Kovno Ghetto, 48; pre-war organisations included within, 39; Rumkowski, Lodz Council led by, 32-3; Warsaw Ghetto, 37
Jewish Mutual Aid Society, 37
Joint Distribution Committee, Jewish, 3, 65
JSS (Jewish Self-Help Society), 39
Judenrat (Jewish Council), ghettos run by *see* Jewish Councils

Katzenelsohn, L., 1
Kenchington, A.G., 96
Kingsley, J. Donald, 126
Kitchener Refugee camp, Sandwich, 17-18
Klementinowsky, 13
Klemperer, Victor, 7
Kolben, Ernst, 8
Königseder, Angelika, viii; on Belsen ORT, 94; on DPs, 68-9; on Israel, 122; on Landsberg school, 80; on Mack, 97; on post-liberation trauma, 69-70; publications by, ix-x
Köpen, Commandant, 48, 49
Korczak, Dr, 42
Kovno: as Lithuania's largest city, 44; mass executions of Jews at, 46; and ORT, 2, 9; Soviet forces fleeing from, 45
Kovno Ghetto, vii, x; as concentration camp, 51, 52; Jews, employment of, 45; liquidation of, 53; order for establishment of, 45; Vocational School in, 47-52; and Warsaw Ghetto, 44; workshops, 44, 79
Kramer, Edith, 59
Kramer, Josef, 61

La Guardia, Fiorello, 65
Landsberg Displaced Persons (DP) camp: as case study, xi; as exclusively Jewish centre, 68, 78; first ORT school launched at, vii, viii, 77, 80; make-up of population, 77-8; and Oleiski, 79; ordeals, 81; ORT staff, nurture of pupils, 103; reputation, 81; success of ORT school, 80, 102
Latvia, ORT in, 12
Lavsky, Hagit, x, 72; on Belsen ORT, 92; on British policies towards Jewish DPs, 67; on DPs/DP camps, 66, 71, 88, 89, 93; on liberation of Belsen, 59, 61
Law for the Restoration of a Professional Civil Service, 1933, 7
Leeds, ORT in, 18
Lehman, Herbert, 65
Lester, Mark J., 98

Levey, Colonel J.H., 16, 18-19
Levi, Primo, 58
Levine, Murray, 25
Levy, Y., 101
Lewent, Abraham, 41
liberation of camps, 57-85; Auschwitz, 58; Buchenwald, 59; Dachau, 59; Mauthausen, 59; negative effects on survivors, 69-70; Ravensbruck, 58; by Soviets, 58, 59; Stutthof, 58; suicide following, 59; by United Kingdom, 59; by United States, 59
Lippmann, Henry, 16
Lithuania: agricultural and horticultural training programmes, 28; Jewish community of, 11-12; Kovno as largest city, 44; ORT, 9, 11, 28; Soviet Union occupation, 44; *see also* Kovno
Lodz, as ghetto, 31
Lohamei Herut Israel, 117
Löwenthal, Löre, 7
Luria, Wolf, 49
Lvovitch, David, 3-4; agreement with JDC, 77; in Austria, 104; conference organised by, 127; as executive board vice-chairman, 24; Germany, ORT work in, 76-7; on vocational schools, 74; 'Work Done in the Western Hemisphere and Certain Other Countries', address, 65

Mack, Josef, 97
Maegalith, A., 104
Majdanek, murders at, 34, 35, 57; hiding of evidence, 58
malnutrition, 32
Mankowitz, Zeev, 93
Marguilies, Sylvia, 105, 106
Mariampol, refugee training programme in, 11
Marley, Lord, 16
Marshall, George C., 63
Marshall Plan, 63
Mauthausen concentration camp: liberation, 59
Megged, Aharon, 93, 109, 110
Meisner, Meyer, 44
memoirs, diaries distinguished, xii-xiii
Messac, Harry S., 99
Mosad le-Aliyah Bet, 118
Moses, Siegfried, 9
Munich Agreement, 1938, 11

National Socialist German Workers' Party (NSDAP), 6
Nazism: concentration camps, destruction, 58; and dehumanisation of Jews, 35; and German Jews, 8-9; ghettos, creation of, 30-1; persecution of Jews, British view on reasons for, 66-7; and Polish Jews, 30; rise of, 6, 7; *see also* SS (Schutz Staffel)
Neudstadt DP camp, 87, 124
Northeim DP centre, training provision, 71
NSDAP (National Socialist German Workers' Party), 6

Nuremberg Laws, 8, 9

Oleiski, Jacob, vii, 28, 51-2; on DP camps, 79-80; Heymont on, 80; on Munich ORT office, 127-8; positions held by, in Lithuania, 46; Vocational School established by, 46, 47-52
Oneg Shabbat cultural organisation, 32
'Operation Barbarossa', 33
'Operation Westard Ho', 121
Oranienburg concentration camp, 7
Organisation to Save the Children (OSE), 16
ORT: 'Artisanship Programme', 12; in Austria, 105-6; in Belsen DP camp, 70; in Bulgaria, 28; conferences, 3, 4; Congress of 1946, 25; Eastern Europe, schools in, 13, 28; as educational and vocational charity, 2; establishment of, 1; expansion of, 1-2, 3, 4; first ORT school, Landsberg, vii, viii; and First World War, 2; fundraising activities, 3; in Germany, 9, 13, 14, 15; in Hungary, 28; identification card, as protection against deportation, 42; in Israel, 129-30; and Jewish Councils, 39; in Latvia, 12; in Leeds, 18; in Lithuania, 9, 11, 28; Munich Central Supply Department, 97-8; pre-war years, 1-20; psychological needs, addressing, 2; role, inside DP camps, x; in Romania, 28; Second World War, work during, 23-53; and Warsaw Ghetto, 37, 38, 40, 41, 42, 43, 53; Zionists on, 5; *see also* World ORT Union
ORT Economic Review, 53, 57, 80, 102
The ORT Idea, 124-5
OSE (*Organisation Secour aux Enfants*), 16

Pale of Settlement, 1, 2
Palestine: Hagana (Jewish defence force), 117; White Paper on future of, 1939, 116
Panzer Training School barracks, 76
Passover, at Kovno Ghetto school, 49-50, 51
Petrograd, ORT courses in, 2
Piazza Torre village, Italy, 109
Pilzer, Joe, 78
Piotrkow, first ghetto in, 31
pogroms, 14, 33
poison gas, 33
Poland: German invasion, 1939, 30; ghettos in, 31-2, 35; Polish Jews, and Second World War, 29-30
Poliakov, Samuel, 1
post-liberation trauma, 69-70
Potsdam Conference, 1945, 62
pre-war years, 1-20
'The Problem of Vocational Adaptation of the Refugees' (memorandum), 10-11

Rader, Jack, 19, 26, 90; on Lvovitch, 104; publications by, viii, ix; on Warsaw Ghetto, 44
Raphaelson, Lou, 16

Ratner, Shimon, 47
Ravensbruck concentration camp, liberation of, 58
Rebuilding Jewish American Life (American ORT), 91, 115
Rechenberg, M., 29
rehabilitation of Holocaust survivors: process of rehabilitation, significance, 64; and World ORT Union, 82
Reichstag Fire, 1933, 7
Reichsvereinigung, 9
Reichsvertretung der Juden in Deutschland (The National Representation of the Jews in Germany), 8, 9
Reilly, Joanne, x; on Belsen DP camp, 71-2, 72, 73, 74; on British policy towards Jewish DPs, 67; on divided Germany, 63; on Palestine, 116; on repatriation policy, 66; on UNRRA, 65; on US policy, 121
'Relief Through Work', slogan, 2
Repeal of Citizenship, law on (1933), 7
'Rescue Through Work' policy, x, xi, 38, 45
'reservation' for Jews, Lublin, 30
resistance, Jewish, 35, 36-7
Rickford, Major C.C.K., 72-3
Ringelblum, Emmanuel, 32, 44
Roman Catholic Centre Party, Germany, 6
Romania: Jewish artisans in, 12; trade schools in, 28
Roosevelt, President Franklin D., 10
Rosenberg, Rabbi, 81
Rosensaft, Hadassa, 94
Rosensaft, Josef, 72, 98
Rumkowski, Chaim, 32-3
Rupert, Professor, 15
Russia: World ORT Union origins in, 29
Russian Jewry, 2
Russian ORT, and ORT Union, 3

Sachsenhausen concentration camp, liberation of, 58
Sarner, Nitza, 109, 110-11
Scharf, Norah, 9-10, 13, 14
Schiff, Vera, 70
Sciesopoli, 111
Second Congress of Liberated Jews, 97
Second World War: devastation caused by, 62; end of, 57; ORT's work during, 23-53; outbreak of, in September 1939, 23; and Polish Jews, 29-30
Seigwarden, ORT school in, 91
Selvino village, 109-10, 111
SHAEF (Supreme Headquarters of the Allied Expeditionary Forces), 65
Shanghai city, refugees in, 28-9
Shapiro, Leon, 26, 28, 41; on DPs/DP camps, 126; on Israel, 122-3; on Italy, 126-7; publications by, viii, ix
Shapiro, Nachman, 46
She'erith Hapleitah, 93

Shephard, Ben: publications by, x
Simon, Werner, 13, 15-16, 16, 20
Sobibor, gas chamber at, 34, 35, 57, 58
Social Democratic Party, Germany, 6
Society for the Promotion of Agriculture (TOPOROL), 43
Sofia, Bulgaria: Jewish Trade School taken over by ORT, 1940, 28
Solomon, Colonel, 89
Soviet Union, former: German invasion, 1941, 44; Lithuania, occupation of, 44
special treatment, idea of, 67
Srole, Leo, 86, 87
SS (Schutz Staffel), 30, 33; at Kovno Ghetto, 51, 52; power of, 7
Stahl, Heinrich, 14
starvation: in ghettos, 31, 41-2
Steinberg, Samuel, 104
Stern Gang, 117
Stuttgart ORT school, 99-100
Stutthof concentration camp: deportations to, 45, 53; liberation of, 58
Sudeten and Czech Jews, 11, 12
suicide, following liberation, 59
Supreme Headquarters of the Allied Expeditionary Forces (SHAEF), 65
Syngalowski, Aaron, 24, 74, 126, 128; conference organised by, 127

Tannenzapf, William, 134
Taylor, Myron C., 10
Taylor, R.I.G., 59-60
Ten Years of Jewish Reconstructive Work (Goldman), 77
Theresienstadt: liberation of, 58-9; Simon deported to, 20
Third Reich: rise of, 6
TOPOROL (Society for the Promotion of Agriculture), 43
Tory, Avraham, 48, 49-50
Transferstelle (transfer agency), 32
Treblinka: deportations to, 36, 37, 41, 43, 57; gas chamber at, 34, 35, 58
Truman, President Harry S., 75, 76, 116, 119, 122
Trunk, Isaiah, 38, 39, 43

United Kingdom: Berlin school transferred to, 15-19; Board of Deputies of British Jews, London, 80; British zone of occupation, activities in, 72, 73; on DPs, 66-7; latent anti-semitism of British policy, alleged, 67; Leeds, ORT school in, 18
United Nations Relief and Rehabilitation Administration *see* UNRRA (United Nations Relief and Rehabilitation Administration)
United States: American Relief Organisation, 3; Anglo-American Committee of inquiry, 117; Committee on Foreign Affairs, 80th US Congress, 125; Displaced Persons Act 1948, 123; DPs in, 121; immigration quotas, relaxing, 124; *Rebuilding Jewish American Life* (American ORT), 91, 115; *see also* American zone of occupation, defeated Germany; Truman, President Harry S.
UNRRA (United Nations Relief and Rehabilitation Administration): and Central Committee of Liberated Jews, 128; displaced persons, responsibility for handed over to, 64; goal, 64-5, 65; on housing provision, 68; infectious diseases, prevention of, 69; IRO, taken over by, 65; role, 65
'Unzer Stime' (Belsen newspaper), 74

Varrichione, L., 107
Vear, Ambrose, 70
Vienna School for Radio Mechanics, 106
Vienna Trade School for Dental Mechanics, 106
Vilna, Jews murdered in, 33
violence against Jews, 7
Vrandenburg, H., 91

Waiting for Hope - Jewish Displaced Persons in Post-World War II Germany (Königseder and Wetzel), ix-x
Walinksy, L.J., 104
Ward, Major General Lowell, 65
Warsaw: as Europe's largest Jewish community, 36, 43; ghetto at *see* Warsaw Ghetto; Jewish orphanage in, 42; Jewish Vocational School, shutting down of, 38; JSS (Jewish Self-Help Society) in, 39; prior to Second World War, 36
Warsaw Ghetto, x; courses on offer at, 42, 43; food smuggling, 31, 41-2; and Kovno Ghetto, 44; and ORT, 37, 38, 40, 41, 42, 43, 53; revolts at, 36; starvation in, 41-2; Treblinka deportations started from, 41; when formed, 31
Warsawski, Eduard, 43
The War Against the Jews 1933-45 (Dawidowicz), 8
Wartheland region, first ghetto in, 31
Weimar Republic, 6
Weingreen, Jack, 92, 95
Western Europe, role of World ORT Union in, 4
Wetzel, Juliane, viii; on Belsen ORT, 94; on DPs, 68-9; on Israel, 122; on Landsberg school, 80; on Mack, 97; on post-liberation trauma, 69-70; publications by, ix-x
Wiener (civil engineer), 15
Wilno, ORT courses in, 2
Wischnitzer, Mark, 23, 27, 38-9; on French ORT programmes, 26
Wlodzimierz Wolynski, 39
The Work of ORT in Europe: January-May 31, 1946, 81-2
World ORT Convention: Central Board elected by, 24
World ORT Union: in 1930s, 6, 23; and

American zone of occupation, 77; appreciation of work, 125; and British zone of occupation, 70; Central Administration, 4, 5; Central Board, 128; communication with national ORT branches, 25; conferences, 4, 10, 24, 25, 129; direction of work, 3; documentation production, 96; DP camps, viii, xi, xii, 74-5, 90; expansion of, 4, 13, 28; France, move to, 23, 25, 26; future of, 10; German Jews, support from, 5; Germany, work in, 76-7; goal, 65; headquarters, 4, 23, 26; immigration authorities on, 121; in Italy, 107; membership, 5; origins, 29; and ORT graduates, xii; and post-war years, viii, 57, 89, 132, 133; and pre-war years, 29; propaganda, 5; rehabilitation of Holocaust survivors, 82; reports, 12-13, 15, 101, 104-5, 107, 108, 111, 124; support for, 3; US zone of occupation, work in, 101; vocational training, work in, 11; wartime activities, 27-8, 29; Western Europe, role in, 4;   see also ORT
The World Union and the American ORT Federation: A Study Made under the Auspices of the Budget Research Committee (Wischnitzer), 23

Wyman, Mark: on accommodation 67-8; on DPs/DP camps, 69, 86, 102, 122, 124, 125, 130; on Israel, 120; on post-liberation conditions, 64; publications by, ix

Yalta Conference, 1945, 62

Ze'iri, Moshe, 108, 109-10, 111
Zentnerschwer, Professor, 44
Zimm, Alan, 60
Zionism: and Oleiski, 51; on ORT, 5; and Warsaw Ghetto, 36
zones of occupation, defeated Germany divided into: Allied Control Council, under, 62; American zone *see* American zone of occupation, defeated Germany; British *see* British zone of occupation, defeated Germany; French, 81; pregnancies, increase in British and American zones, 87
Zweifuss, M.R., 44
Zyklon B gas, 34